D1593695

The Sanctified South

The Sanctified South

JOHN LAKIN BRASHER AND THE HOLINESS MOVEMENT

J. Lawrence Brasher

University of Illinois Press

URBANA AND CHICAGO

Publication of this book was supported in part by a grant from Catawba College.

This book is printed on acid-free paper.

Library of Congress Cataloging-in-Publication Data
Brasher, John Lawrence, 1947–
   The sanctified South : John Lakin Brasher and the Holiness
Movement / J. Lawrence Brasher.
      p.   cm.
   Includes bibliographical references and index.
   ISBN 0-252-02050-2 (alk. paper)
   1. Brasher, John Lakin, 1868–1971. 2. Methodist Church (U.S.)—
Southern States—Clergy—Biography. 3. Methodist Church—Southern
States—Clergy—Biography. 4. Holiness churches—Southern States—
Clergy—Biography. 5. Southern States—Church history—19th
century. 6. Southern States—Church history—20th century.
I. Title
BX8495.B754B73   1994
287'.6'092—dc20
   [B]   93-13604
                                                                              CIP

A two-hour cassette containing examples of John Lakin Brasher's extemporaneous
storytelling and preaching is available separately from the University of Illinois
Press: ISBN 0-252-02114-2. Combined book and cassette: ISBN 0-252-02116-9.

For Louise

Contents

Preface

On his birthday in 1969, John Lakin Brasher watched with mingled curiosity and displeasure the first landing of a man on the moon. The same day he recalled his jubilation over the winner of the Grant-Greeley campaign in 1872. His remarkable memory could leap back even farther through the recollections of predecessors he had known. He told tales related to him by folk who had seen the close of the eighteenth century—witnesses of the Battle of New Orleans and the removal of the Cherokees.

Brasher liked to describe his work as a preacher as a call to "stand between the living and the dead to speak the word of God." His self-location between the living and the dead lends itself to a double interpretation: one broadly cultural, the other religious. In his great old age, with his acute memory and descriptive narrative gifts, Brasher was a link to a bygone southern culture that for most living souls was apprehensible only in history texts. For him, it was a tangible memory. He lived between the old culture and the new—because of the lasting influence of the old one, he was reluctant to embrace the new one fully. He delighted in describing old ways, captivating much younger listeners who knew little but the present. He was what folklorists call a "tradition-bearer." The phrase "between the living and the dead," part of a traditional nineteenth-century plain-folk prayer often recited by Brasher, served as a common southern holiness rubric applied to preaching and preachers. The religious meaning of the words thus refers not to a role primarily of Brasher's advanced years, but to one he filled for eighty years, that of a preacher of the Word that divides between the living and the dead.

Brasher was to the minds of many the premier preacher of the southern holiness movement. He was a figure of central importance in the spread of holiness religion throughout the South after the turn of the century and an acclaimed evangelist in the wider American ho-

liness movement. Disciplined and reflective, throughout his life he eval-
uated and responded to the culture of his time in a voluminous correspondence with family and colleagues across the nation. In his prime,
it was not unusual for him to write fifteen letters in a day. He saved
the replies. At his death, he left a legacy of twenty-five thousand letters and documents.

He was the only holiness leader of his generation to preserve such
a sizable collection of personal papers. Moreover, since he lived a full
generation beyond most of his peers—until tape recorders became
available to the general public—friends and relatives over a period of
twenty years captured his storytelling and preaching on over ninety
sound recordings. No such large collection of live performance exists
of any other evangelist from Brasher's circle. These unique written and
oral sources offer an exciting opportunity—a chance to study an intimately documented life history and an oral tradition of preaching and
storytelling that was a major part of that life. Throughout my research,
I have been reminded continually of the possibilities and perils of such
extensive resources. Time and again, I have recalled Brasher's words
spoken at the funeral of his best friend: "There is so much to say, since
the material is so abundant, and since the life is so rich of which we
speak."[1]

Pervasive stereotypes in both the popular and academic minds
burden perceptions of holiness religion. The familiar epithet "holy roll-
er" evokes a cluster of images—poverty, social alienation, ignorance,
coarseness, emotional frenzy, psychological imbalance, perverse doctrines, sectarian asceticism, and southern isolation. Liston Pope's classic study of religion in a southern mill town accurately depicted the
perennial poverty, lack of education, and marginal status of holiness
groups there.[2] Readers often have taken Pope's description of those
particular holiness groups as universally applicable. Wilbur J. Cash fur-
thered stereotypes when he styled southern holiness "general hyste-
ria" and "orgiastic religion."[3] In the popular arena, Erskine Caldwell's
autobiography reinvigorated common notions of holiness as "uninhibited religious exhibitionism" of "impoverished and unenlightened
southerners . . . imprisoned there."[4] Such stereotypes are reason enough
to explore Brasher's life, which represented others in a widespread and
diverse evangelical movement.

The underlying aim of this study is to examine the particular time
and place in which Brasher lived and to determine how that world shaped
his person and preaching. What complex of influences led him to identify with the holiness movement when and where he did? How did his
southern heritage and the holiness movement inform his preaching?

What did he preach? How did he preach it? Why was it important to him and to his audience? How did preacher and storyteller combine? This book is a study in biography, social history, folklore, and rhetoric. My research analyzes the dynamics of holiness religious experience and explores the rituals, theology, institutions, politics, and social makeup of the holiness movement in the South. I have attempted to describe the shape and power of holiness piety, paying attention to the context of holiness preaching as well as to the form and content of the message. I hope this inquiry may begin to fill a gap in the history of southern evangelical religion, for there are no other published, critical biographical-institutional studies of the early southern holiness movement. Chapters 1 through 5 interpret Brasher's life up through his initial involvement in the holiness cause. Chapters 6 through 8 present his preaching and his audience. The extraordinary course of Brasher's evangelistic career and his countless personal and institutional connections after his sanctification—in the North as well as the South—deserve specific and extended treatment. That story, sketched below, I hope will fill another book.

Born in the north Alabama uplands during Reconstruction, Brasher grew up in an intensely Unionist, Republican family whose members were leaders in politics and in the reorganized (northern) Methodist Episcopal Church. After serving ten years as a pastor of Methodist Episcopal churches in north Alabama and Tennessee, he graduated as valedictorian from U. S. Grant University School of Theology at Chattanooga in 1899. In 1900 in Birmingham, he identified with the holiness movement and thereafter traveled 700,000 miles to preach in over 650 holiness camp meetings throughout the United States.

He served as president of two schools—John H. Snead Seminary, a Methodist Episcopal secondary school in Alabama, and Central Holiness University (later, John Fletcher College) in Iowa. His acclaim in the North also gained him the presidency of the Iowa Holiness Association and a brief pastorate at the Detroit Holiness Tabernacle. His phenomenal and diverse itinerancy took him to primitive, rural brush-arbor meetings and to such middle-class resorts as Ocean Grove, New Jersey, where he shared the preaching platform with William Jennings Bryan. None of his accomplishments would have been possible had it not been for the unceasing support of his wife, Minnie Eunice Moore Brasher, who while Brasher traveled raised their ten children. That story, too, remains to be told, and is documented by four decades of devoted correspondence. Brasher preached with vigor through his one-hundred-second year.

An examination of Brasher's preaching probes the very heart of the holiness phenomenon, for preaching was the power of the movement. Camp-meeting sermons were the primary catalyst of religious experience as well as the medium through which most holiness folk learned their theology—from oral rather than printed sources. Hearing Brasher's extemporaneous, unedited preaching provides insights that printed sermons cannot.

Much of my investigation depends upon oral sources, but Brasher's narratives are nicely checked and balanced by a hundred years of letters and documents. Aware of the limitations of memory, I have attempted wherever possible to document recollections with contemporary accounts. But by their nature, stories convey more than facts about historical events: They provide a precious dimension often elusive in printed or manuscript sources—the self-conception and ethos of the people who tell them.

As Brasher's grandson and a member of an extended family who reveres his memory, I have found the task of maintaining a critical-historical stance a constant challenge. I believe Brasher himself would welcome a critical appraisal. Because he loved the holiness of the Spirit, he was both keenly aware of and forgiving of the foibles of human nature. Sometimes embarrassed by the reverence shown him in old age, he in typical fashion responded with a story: "There was a woman whose husband's funeral was in process. They were saying some wonderful things about him, and she said to her little boy, 'Johnny, slip over there and see if that's your pa in the coffin.'"[5] Thanks to Brasher's interest in the preservation of history, the documents remain for future scholars to sift and ponder.

The help of many made my research possible. I am grateful to all those who over the years made sound recordings of Brasher. I am indebted to the staff of the Manuscript Department of Perkins Library, Duke University, especially to Robert Byrd, who expedited the processing of Brasher's papers. The libraries of Duke Divinity School and the University of North Carolina at Chapel Hill, and the United Methodist Archives at Drew University also have served me well. The Department of Folklore at the University of North Carolina provided materials and funds to copy the sound recordings that were loaned to me by many people. A grant from the Center for Studies in the Wesleyan Tradition at Duke Divinity School enabled the transcribing of the sound recordings. Catawba College provided a summer research grant to assist in the final preparation of this book.

The learning, methods, and kindness of my professors have sustained me in my research and teaching. In my undergraduate years, Anne Firor Scott taught me the excitement and necessity of interdisciplinary research. In divinity school, Sydney Ahlstrom encouraged me to explore regional religion and to take seriously vernacular cultural traditions.

The idea for this book came from a luncheon conversation with Daniel W. Patterson, when I was a graduate student in his course Folklore in the South. I am ever grateful for his steadfast interest, helpful criticisms, and friendship. I owe special thanks to Stuart C. Henry, who directed my dissertation and encouraged its revision into this book. His generous spirit allowed me free range in choosing a subject of research. He was a diligent critic at all stages of my writing. I will long remember his wit and wisdom shared over lunch and his own remarkable repertoire of southern tales. Few graduate students are privileged to have such a gracious and skilled adviser.

Other friends have contributed to my research in important ways. I thank Stanley Ingersol, then a fellow graduate student, for many conversations and insights about the holiness tradition. Bishop W. Kenneth Goodson's colorful reminiscences of John Lakin Brasher lightened the burden of graduate work. L. C. Scarborough and Jerry Cotten of Photographic Services at the University of North Carolina produced superb copies of family photographs. William Broom gave unstintingly of his time and expertise in computers. My typists, Dorothy B. King, Ellen W. Howell, Michael Pocinki, Delores Imblum, and Melanie Bookout, have been excellent and long-suffering. I was fortunate to have Carol Bolton Betts as my copy editor. Her astute and graceful work consistently improved the text.

I owe much to my family: to my extended family, who preserved John Lakin's papers and donated them to Duke University; to my sister, Ellen Marie Brasher Harris, who from Brasher's description and scale floor plan drew his boyhood home, and who transcribed the music of his oratory; to my parents, Julius Logan and Lois Watters Brasher, whose financial assistance made the journey less arduous and whose liberal spirit allowed me to write with freedom about my grandfather. The completion of this book I owe primarily to the love and support of my wife, Louise.

Note on the Transcriptions

Many of the transcriptions of sound recordings in this book, especially in chapters 7 and 8, employ devices that attempt to reflect some of the oral qualities of the stories and sermons. By observing the directions below, readers may approximate the original delivery (either silently or aloud) and thereby "hear" the narratives.

New line: brief pause (often to establish rhythm).

Indented line: read without pause as a continuation of the preceding line.

Hyphenation between letters of word: prolonged articulation.

Punctuation: receives no value in time.

Standard type: ordinary volume.

Standard capital type: emphatic voice, increased volume.

Bold capital type: greatly increased volume.

Brackets: kinesic action or audience response.[1]

Chronology of John Lakin Brasher

1868	Born, Clear Creek, Etowah County, Alabama.
1879	Mother dies.
1881	First conversion experience.
1885–87	Works for room, board, and clothing on farm of Robert Battles, Gallant, Alabama.
1886	Second conversion experience.
	Joins Clear Creek Methodist Episcopal Church.
1887	Father dies.
	Works with African-American railroad gang building L & I Railroad, Gadsden, Alabama.
1888	Farms at Gallant, Alabama.
1889–91	Works at Elliot Car Works, Gadsden, Alabama, making wheels for railroad cars.
1889	Licensed to preach, Crawford's Cove, Saint Clair County, Alabama.
1890	Marries Minnie Eunice Moore of Gallant, Alabama.
1891	Farms at Gallant, Alabama.
1892	Admitted on trial to Alabama Conference, Methodist Episcopal Church.
1893	Ordained deacon by Bishop Isaac W. Joyce.
1893–96	Pastor, Methodist Episcopal Church, Wedowee, Alabama.
1896	Ordained elder by Bishop John Fletcher Hurst.
	Pastor, Methodist Episcopal Church, Edwardsville, Alabama.
1899	Graduates, Valedictorian, U. S. Grant University School of Theology, Chattanooga, Tennessee.
1899–1902	Pastor, Simpson Methodist Episcopal Church, Birmingham, Alabama.
1900	Sanctified, Salvation Army Hall, Birmingham, Alabama.
	Called to traveling evangelism, Hartselle Camp Meeting, Hartselle, Alabama.

1902	Appointed Conference Evangelist of the Alabama Conference, Methodist Episcopal Church.
1903–39	Elected Secretary of the Alabama Conference, Methodist Episcopal Church.
1904–5	Teacher, Pentecostal Mission and Bible School, Birmingham, Alabama.
1905	Pastor, Methodist Episcopal Church, Boaz, Alabama.
1906–11	President, John H. Snead Seminary, Boaz, Alabama.
1910	Delegate, Men's National Missionary Congress of the U.S.A., Chicago, Illinois.
1912	Delegate to General Conference of the Methodist Episcopal Church.
1916	Delegate to General Conference of the Methodist Episcopal Church.
	Granted Doctor of Divinity degree, Taylor University, Upland, Indiana.
1917–26	President, Central Holiness University/John Fletcher College, Oskaloosa, Iowa.
1920	Delegate to General Conference of the Methodist Episcopal Church.
1920–22	President, Iowa Holiness Association.
1927	Pastor, Detroit Holiness Tabernacle.
1927–29	Pastor, St. Paul's Methodist Episcopal Church, Boaz, Alabama.
1929–31	Editor, *The Way of Faith,* Columbia, South Carolina.
1930	Granted Doctor of Divinity degree, John Fletcher College, Oskaloosa, Iowa.
1936	Delegate to General Conference of the Methodist Episcopal Church.
1939	Delegate to the Uniting Conference of the Methodist Church.
1940	Establishes Brasher Springs Camp Meeting, Gallant, Alabama.
1943–44	Teacher, God's Bible School, Cincinnati, Ohio.
1950	Teacher, God's Bible School, Cincinnati, Ohio.
1959	Minnie Eunice Moore Brasher dies, Gadsden, Alabama.
1971	John Lakin Brasher dies, Attalla, Alabama.

The Sanctified South

1

Fathers and Mothers
Looking Down

FAMILY TRADITIONS

I have been a Methodist a hundred and fifty years.
—JOHN L. BRASHER, 20 JULY 1968

On a sultry Alabama August afternoon at Hartselle Camp Meeting, John L. Brasher rhythmically exhorted his audience to hold fast to tradition:

> Remember, your FATHers and MOTHers and
> GRANDfathers and GRANDmothers that
> PRAYED here and
> LOVED here and
> SHOUTED here and
> WENT from here to heaven
> are looking down on you folks to see
> if you're going to CARRY ON.[1]

As a child, Brasher often heard tales of "the old soldier," his great-grandfather James from North Carolina, who drilled under Baron von Steuben and "pressed Lord Cornwallis to his ships at Yorktown."[2] However, an equally celebrated—and only slightly less hoary—family tradition was a lineage of Methodist preachers.

Although their lore by the time of Brasher's boyhood probably reached back no farther than the Revolution, the Brashers had lived in Virginia and Maryland in the seventeenth century, and by 1750

Thomas Brasher, the father of "the old soldier," had carved out a homestead in the North Carolina Piedmont near the present village of Snow Camp, Alamance County. Shortly after the war, Thomas's soldier son James migrated with his family first to South Carolina and Georgia and finally, about 1815, in old age, to Yellow Leaf Creek, Shelby County, Alabama. Some of his accompanying relatives patented rich bottomland along the Coosa River and eventually owned many slaves, but James, setting the future pattern for his line, "stopped among the hills."[3]

His son, James, Jr., born 1787, Brasher's grandfather, was a Methodist preacher in Alabama at least as early as the 1820s, his family having converted to Methodism in South Carolina probably by the end of the eighteenth century.[4] A colleague, who in proper southern colloquial respect called James "Uncle Jimmy Brasher," remembered that in old age he lived very humbly, but as a preacher, he "read Greek from the Gospel of John and frequently said from the pulpit, 'If you believe my word, the original says. . . .'" An "able" preacher, he was reportedly very emotional.[5]

Brasher's father, John Jackson Brasher, born in 1820 in Shelby County, no doubt as a youth attended the annual Methodist camp meetings at nearby Harpersville in the 1820s and 1830s. There, "in a grove of great old aboriginal oaks, a vast board arbor was erected under which a thousand people often gathered to hear the gospel. . . . The services were often protracted through the whole night, making the midnight air vocal with shouts and cries of penitence."[6] Converted and called to preach when he was twenty, John Jackson enlisted as a colporteur for the American Tract Society, preaching and distributing tracts and Testaments among the hill folk.[7]

An abolitionist opposed to the division of the Methodist Church in 1844, John Jackson nevertheless served occasionally as a preacher in the Methodist Episcopal Church, South, but as a Republican and representative of Blount County at the Alabama Secession Convention in 1861, "Jack" Brasher voted against the Ordinance of Secession and refused to sign it.[8] At the close of the Civil War, he organized his own Methodist Church independent of the Southern church. He became a charter member of the reorganized conference of the (northern) Methodist Episcopal Church when it returned to Alabama in 1867.[9]

A "resourceful man," he was literally a jack-of-all-trades.[10] He not only served as presiding elder in the reorganized Alabama Conference but also at various times was employed as a blacksmith, carpenter, carriage maker, millwright and miller, postmaster, justice of the peace, and county superintendent of schools.[11] He allegedly sought appointment as Reconstruction sheriff of Blount County and in his spare time taught

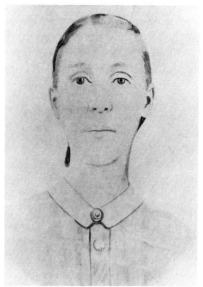

The Reverend John Jackson Brasher (1820–87), father of John Lakin Brasher. Brasher Papers.

Milly Caroline Hafley Brasher (1829–79), mother of John Lakin Brasher. Brasher Papers.

The "big house," birthplace of John Lakin Brasher. Livestock drovers called it a "hog hotel." The earliest portion was the log pen at right; later it was augmented by two log pens with shed rooms (to the left), connected by an enclosed "dog trot." The house was razed ca. 1900. Drawn from Brasher's description and scale floor plan. Brasher Papers.

singing schools and wrote poetry.[12] His wife, Milly Caroline, had been born in East Tennessee and was the daughter of a German immigrant, Cornelius Hafley, a breeder of "blooded racehorses" and a lover of horse racing. The Hafleys had freed their few slaves before they moved to Alabama in the 1840s and were ardent Unionists.[13]

Seven miles west of Attalla, amidst the encircling hills of Greasy Cove, stood a great log house grey with age. Designed as an overnight rest for antebellum livestock drovers, the seventy-four-foot-long "big house" (known earlier to the drovers as a "hog hotel") was graced on the south side with a fifty-foot "piazza" where John Jackson Brasher and his fellow preachers often paced back and forth debating theology and politics.[14] In the big house on 20 July 1868, three years after the Civil War, John Lakin Brasher was born, the eighth and last child of a family "neither rich nor very poor" but part of the southern middle-class majority of self-sufficient farmers that has come to be known as the plain folk.[15]

Situated in the ridge and valley country, a transitional region between the lowland and upland South, the Brashers were influenced by both the customs of the mountaineers to the north and west and the culture of the plantations and burgeoning cities to the south and east.[16] Their farm lay at the entrance to what Frank Owsley has called the "inner frontier." Most of the vast Sand Mountain plateau, three miles to the west, was homesteaded during Brasher's boyhood.[17]

His widely descriptive accounts of his youth indicate that economic extremes in his community were uncommon. There are tales of a nearby family who lived in a corncrib and of "quality folks" such as William Pinkney Shahan, who owned "a large plantation" and a mill, but these people were exceptions to the majority of thrifty tenant and small landowning farmers.[18] Some neighbors were beginning to suffer the captivity of the postwar cotton-credit system—Brasher recalled a local saying that some land was "tied up so tight with mortgages it was hard for the crops to grow"—but the Brashers owned their 240-acre farm free and clear, raising only a small amount of cotton, enough for spinning and weaving.[19] Fields of corn and sorghum, a vegetable garden with a winter turnip patch, peach and apple orchards, cattle for milk, horses for fieldwork, and a few hogs met the family's needs. They were content with "cornbread through the week and biscuits on Sunday morning."[20] It was an "event" for Johnny, living in relative geographic isolation, "to see a wagon a day pass the house." "We didn't know that we were poor," he recalled, "we saw no contrast."[21] It was not until his late teens that he viewed Colonel Robert B. Kyle's "palatial" county-seat residence and afterward never passed it without looking lingeringly at it.[22]

Colonel Robert B. Kyle's "palatial" home in Gadsden, Alabama, ca. 1875. Scarborough Photo Shop, Gadsden.

"Notorious" Uncle Sam Dillard (1830-1909), who "drank and fought and fooled with women and beat his wife." Brasher Papers.

Although in most respects typical of their community, the Brashers nevertheless were conscious of a moral and social distance between themselves and many of their neighbors. The family's strict morality, including prohibition of alcohol, dancing, and card playing, wrought a lasting effect upon Brasher and upon his later holiness ethic. His father pressed a puritanical ethos upon the family. As a young man he had struggled to rise above the amorality of the Shelby County frontier, as lawless as any stereotype of the later trans-Mississippi "wild West." The libertinism and violence of the Old Southwest through the 1840s is well documented.[23] E. B. Teague, in his recollections of the community of John Jackson Brasher's youth, reported weekly drunken brawls, fistfights and gouging practiced as a sport ("where large men were not permitted to impose on smaller ones"), shootings, and stabbings especially among gamblers.[24] Leaving home at sixteen, John Jackson not only fled a cruel stepmother but also left behind kinfolk who delighted in brawling and who on one occasion were indicted for a riot.[25]

His self-elevation exemplified the pattern described by Dickson Bruce in his study of plain-folk religion, whereby people for whom "frontier hedonism" was not attractive sought stability and respectability through religion.[26] The ministry also offered significant status to plain-folk individuals in an essentially closed system where planters held political and economic power.[27]

After the war, Brasher's father—referring indiscriminately to Democrats, former Secessionists, Southern Methodists, and immorality in general—complained of "the rabble" in his community upon whom he "looked down with pitty [sic] mingled with contempt."[28] Again, the problem was that some of these folk were his relatives. The notorious Sam Dillard, for instance, "drank, and fought, and fooled with women and beat his wife." "But the Dillards," John Lakin carefully reminded his own children, "were kin to us only because Uncle Sam married my mother's sister."[29] Brasher's mother, like all of her sisters, played the fiddle, but for fear of scorn because of its association with dancing, she never would play it in her own home.[30] Brasher's account of a cousin's wedding shows the tension bred of a puritanical ethic stamped upon him at an early age: "I went to my cousin's wedding one night. I was a little fellow and awful afraid of the dark. And after supper they gathered in the front room and tuned up the fiddle and began to dance the old cotillions. I was afraid to stay in that house. I was afraid to go home by myself. So I went away out in the shade of that old oak tree, as far as the lights streamed out of the house. I was afraid that house would sink."[31]

This pervasive puritanical element, however, by no means cast a pall over all of Brasher's youth. What Bruce posited as a sharp dichotomy between the daily life of the "unsaved" plain folk and that of those "enjoying religion" was probably not at all so clear cut.[32] The Brashers' religion neither attempted nor intended to supplant all of the frontier ethic. John Lakin's parents told tales about the Dillards that on the one hand condemned their wicked behavior but on the other delighted in "Uncle Sam's" wit and his unerring ability to spot hypocritical religion. The Brashers happily engaged in shooting matches, tests of strength, and jumping contests, and were quick to defend their safety or honor (even in the pulpit) with fists or guns.[33]

When Brasher was ten-and-a-half, his mother died, and the relative stability of his childhood began to dissolve. John Jackson remarried within a year, but his new wife, instead of encouraging his ministry, urged him to stay at home and "lay up something against the days of age." Following her wishes, he constructed a gristmill, which proved unprofitable and encumbered the farm with a mortgage.[34] Within several years, Brasher's stepmother died and his brothers and sister all married. The big house was closed up and young Johnny was left to shift for himself. Hungry and threadbare, for two years he did not enter a church because of lack of decent clothes: "I would slip up to the old church after the singing was all over and the preacher commenced, and sit down on the steps and listen to his sermon until they were going to have the benediction. Then I'd disappear in the woods." "My whole life," he recalled, "was wrecked and blighted."[35]

The traumatic dissolution of Brasher's childhood world implanted in him a lasting desire to recover the stability and traditions he once had known. A heritage of preachers, an isolated, hill-country upbringing where customs and time-honored beliefs changed little, and a puritanical moral code "lived on him" by his parents shaped Brasher's call to preach, his later reactions to urban life and changing theologies, and part of his holiness ethic.[36] Yet, other, larger social and institutional circumstances both intensified his desire for stability and made it difficult to achieve.

2

"In Poverty and Obloquy"

THE POSTWAR RETURN OF THE
METHODIST EPISCOPAL CHURCH

My father organized a church which was as welcome in the South
as a wet dog in a lady's dressing room.
—JOHN L. BRASHER, 1954

In October 1868, Bishop Davis Wasgatt Clark, D.D., overseer of
the postwar return of the Methodist Episcopal Church to Georgia and
Alabama, presided over the first regular session of the reorganized Alabama Conference and baptized the three-month-old son of charter
member John J. Brasher and his wife, Caroline. Convened at Murphree's Valley, near Blountsville, in a countryside thrown open for settlement just fifteen years before, the conference met in a one-room
log house that served triple duty as session room, sanctuary, and sleep-
ing quarters.[1] Holding the baby in her lap, Caroline had traveled across
the mountains—twenty-five miles in an ox wagon—that the child might
be baptized by the bishop from Cincinnati. Among the onlookers at
the ceremony was the secretary of the conference, Arad S. Lakin, whose
ruddy countenance may have disguised a blush as he heard the parents name the child "John Lakin Brasher." The name and the circumstances of the baptism presaged a life whose course would be guided
by an undeviating loyalty to the institution of the Methodist Episcopal
Church.

Lakin, a missionary from Ohio, earlier had marched as chaplain
with Sherman through Georgia.[2] Declared by Bishop Gilbert Haven
to be "the head of our church work in the South," Lakin had been sent

Bishop Davis Wasgatt Clark (1812–71), overseer of the postwar return of the Methodist Episcopal Church to the Deep South. Brasher Papers.

A woodcut from the Tuscaloosa *Independent Monitor,* 1 September 1868. Arad S. Lakin holds the carpetbag marked "Ohio." State of Alabama Department of Archives and History.

by Bishop Clark in 1865 to rebuild a constituency for the Methodist Episcopal Church in Alabama.[3] As a Yankee emissary of the northern church, he not surprisingly was regarded by most southerners with suspicion if not contempt. One Alabama politician, who appeared before a congressional investigation in 1871, in less than a page of withering stenographic testimony branded Lakin "a humbug," "a liar," "a slanderer," "a hell of an old rascal," "an old heathen Chinee," and "an old ruffian."[4] But Brasher's portrayal of Lakin displayed his own and his family's dissenting opinion: "Why anyone would hate him for doing what Jesus would have done is a wonder to angels. This truly great man left on my soul an impress of his . . . loyalty and missionary spirit . . . and gave a life full of devotion to the Negro people."[5] The two viewpoints typify the sharp religious and political tensions that permeated Brasher's childhood and youth in postwar north Alabama.

Even the most objective accounts of the return of the Methodist Episcopal Church after the war to territory held since 1846 by the Methodist Episcopal Church, South, refer to the reentry of the northern church as a "southern occupation" or a "denominational invasion."[6] Military imagery is apt. Legislation of the General Conference of the northern church in 1864 authorized its bishops to extend their jurisdiction to the South. The year before, an edict from the War Department had granted Bishop Edward Ames of the northern church the right and the protection of federal troops to take possession of Methodist Episcopal, South, churches where "loyal ministers . . . did not officiate."[7] At the close of hostilities, northern church leaders openly expressed hope of displacing the white Methodism of the South and further pledged themselves to the tasks of converting and educating the freedmen and of inculcating loyalty among all southerners to the federal government. Religious and political motives of the return were often indistinguishable. Bishop Clark avowed that "the best reconstruction [was] the extension of the M. E. Church. Wherever it was planted there the cause of . . . good government [was] planted also."[8] In January 1866, Clark met in Atlanta with seven disaffected ministers of the Southern church to reorganize the Methodist Episcopal Church in Georgia and Alabama.[9]

Southern prejudice against the return of the northern branch of Methodism was likewise rooted in sectarianism and politics. The Southern church was incensed by "the invasion of its territory, the loss of members and pastors, and the 'unchristian designs' on its property."[10] Northern missionaries were despised for allegedly cultivating distrust of southern whites among blacks, for influencing the freedmen to support the Republican party, and most of all for their personal aid to and occasional office holding in the Reconstruction governments.[11]

The activities of John Jackson Brasher's colleague Arad S. Lakin epitomized all that the majority of southerners resented in the return of the northern Methodists. Active in the formation of Loyal League cells among the freedmen, Lakin kept a diary of alleged postwar outrages committed against blacks and former Unionists, a million copies of which were printed and distributed by the Republicans for the 1868 election.[12] In the same year, Lakin sought and received appointment as Reconstruction president of the University of Alabama, but he was frightened away from office by the intervention of the Ku Klux Klan.

Just a month before John Lakin Brasher's baptism, the Tuscaloosa *Independent Monitor* reported about the mob that had intimidated Lakin. An accompanying woodcut became perhaps the most famous political cartoon of the Reconstruction era. Lakin and an associate were depicted as hanged by ropes from a tree. A mule with the initials "K.K.K." on its side was pictured as walking out from under Lakin, who held a carpetbag marked "Ohio."[13]

Northern leaders of the Methodist Episcopal Church, such as Bishop Haven, publicized Lakin as a symbol of those "representatives of the true church" whose loyalty and courage served as a witness among unreconstructed southerners—renegades who would "ravage, tear, and slay against their brethren but for the strong arm of Grant," and who "write and speak detestable sentiments against [those] who are loyal to the flag . . . freedom, humanity, and Christ." According to Haven, Lakin had been "run out of more than one county by the Ku Klux and plotted against as often as Paul . . . and as unsuccessfully."[14] At the congressional investigation of the Klan in 1871, Lakin helped fuel the Republican campaign by describing north Alabama as in "a perfect reign of terror."[15] In some places it was.

In a report detailing the 1873 Annual Conference of the Methodist Episcopal Church in Alabama, Bishop Haven in a concluding phrase summarized the state of his church there: "in poverty and obloquy, knit together in love."[16] The fact that the conference of necessity met in a tent and not in a "temple of stateliest structure" typical of the same church in the North graphically illustrated the relative poverty and the different social position of the church in the South.[17] Lakin himself testified that his church benefited primarily the "loyal men" of Alabama who were "not among the leading men of the country" but came instead from "the middle classes, the working classes, poor men who had no interest in maintaining slavery."[18] Bishop Mallalieu likewise described his constituency as "for the most part . . . very poor and needing help as much if not more than the settlers of the West."[19] Five years after the conference in a tent, Bishop Wiley presided over the Alabama Conference and reported it as typical of the Methodist Episcopal white membership throughout the lower South: "I held the Conference in a little log church in the woods. Windows it had none save holes cut through to let in the light. The nearest house was three-quarters of a mile distant, where the principal man of our Church and that section lived. The pigs made their bed under the floor of the house, and the chickens roosted all around. And this leading man eked out an existence from a miserable farm of forty-five acres. He could neither read nor write, and he was glad that his little boy could do both for him."[20]

Numerically strongest in the northern, upland areas of Alabama where Unionist sentiment had flamed brightest, the white congregations of the Methodist Episcopal Church remained throughout their existence but scattered islands in the wide sea of the Methodist Episcopal Church, South.[21] The Alabama Methodist Episcopal Conference in 1876 reported 4,788 white members against the approximately 60,000 white constituents of the Methodist Episcopal Church, South. By 1900, the ratio had not changed significantly. The Southern church in Alabama boasted well over 100,000 white members, while the Methodist Episcopal congregations claimed only 9,000. The latter's consciousness of minority status was heightened by a Southern Baptist constituency comparable to that of the Southern Methodists as well as large Presbyterian and Church of Christ elements, all in harmony with the southern political majority.

Standard histories that emphasize the return of the Methodist Episcopal Church as northern "occupation" have obscured the fact that the reorganized church did meet the legitimate needs of a Unionist white minority whose members considered themselves "southern Americans with blood as proud and hot as ever burned in the breast of a brave people."[22] The "nickname" that these proud southerners despised most was that of "Northern Methodist."[23] Brasher's argument for the return of the church presents his family's position: "If the Southern delegates [in 1844] were justified in the formation of a separate organization in order the more perfectly to serve their people, so were our fathers upon the same principle justified in the reorganization of the Methodist Episcopal Church in this territory, that they might more perfectly serve an important and respectable minority, to whom the ministry of the Southern Church was not, nor at that time could be, acceptable."[24]

Brasher's father, an outspoken Republican leader of the "respectable minority," became an abolitionist and a defender of the Union at an early age. In 1844, he was rejected by his annual conference in Alabama for signing a remonstrance against the division of the church into northern and southern bodies.[25] After the war, his support of the return of the "old church" to Alabama was rooted not only in political and institutional loyalties but also in a desire to restore traditional Methodist practices. John Jackson Brasher's letter regarding the return exhibits his resolve and creativity in maintaining his dissenting convictions after the separation of 1844:

> After the war, I determined to sever my connection with the Church South, unless they struck from their discipline the word "South." The cause of the separation had been removed, and consequently there was no further necessity for this distinction. But my wish in this, as in 1844, was not regarded, and I determined, as did two others, to form a separate organization, to be known as the "United Methodist Church." We sought to revive the Methodism of the fathers, to go back to the old landmarks, particularly in relation to class meetings, which had fallen into disuse in the Southern Church. We had the regular conferences and organization of the old Church, with all of the characteristics of Methodism except the episcopacy. Rev. A. B. Watson was elected President for four years, while we were waiting the development of events, when, happily, the Methodist Episcopal Church came to our relief. The number of communicants with us was something over three hundred and fifty, with five ministers, namely, A. B. Watson, Walter B. Drennon, John C. Self, Joseph Beasley, and the writer. One of the tests of membership among us was loyalty to the Government of the United States.[26]

During the war, Brasher and his family were persecuted for their Unionist sentiments.[27] The ending of the war did little to heal the bitterness between local Confederate and Unionist sympathies, and Brasher's new advocacy of the Methodist Episcopal Church stirred old resentments among his neighbors who had supported the southern cause. His home county of Blount, the territory advertised by Lakin as enduring "a perfect reign of terror," lynched its federally appointed sheriff, whose office Brasher wisely had chosen not to accept.[28] Brasher's outspoken Republican sentiments led to threats against his life and to rowdiness among his congregation while he was preaching. He began to carry his pistol when in the pulpit.[29] According to legend, his patience failed him during one meeting, and he shot the back of a bench between two young toughs who deliberately sang off-key and shouted "amen" at inappropriate points in his sermon. Shortly afterward, Brasher's gristmill was burned.[30] He declared bankruptcy, moved to an adjoining county for safety, and accepted a Republican appointment as county superintendent of schools.[31]

Mistreatment and occasional assassinations of Methodist Episco-

An early-nineteenth-century camp meeting. Frontispiece engraved by John Wesley Paradise (1809–62) from *A Collection of Hymns and Spiritual Songs Generally Sung at Camp and Prayer Meetings,* compiled by Peter D. Myers (New York: Collins and Brother, 1847). The Reverend James William Brasher (b. 1787) presented this hymnal to his son, the Reverend John Jackson Brasher, who desired to "revive the Methodism of the fathers." Library of John Lakin Brasher.

pal preachers continued—and fed fears and rumors—into the 1870s. The 1871 Alabama Conference lamented "outrages resulting in the death, torture, and intimidation of ministers and members" by "disguised bands of desperadoes called 'Ku-Klux-Klan.'" The murder of the Reverend Americus Trammel and the "brutal beating" of the Reverend Isaac Dorman were reported.[32] The anxiety of Methodist Episcopal preachers in north Alabama appears in a letter of John Jackson Brasher to a fellow minister, John W. Talley: "This is the third time I have written you since you were at my house. It is very currently reported you and brother Watson had both been assassinated. Your failing to reach your quarterly meeting . . . and brother Watson failing to meet his appointment . . . helped confirm reports which gave us considerable uneasiness."[33]

It was during this turbulent period of the reorganized church, the time of "personal hazards," that John Lakin Brasher became aware of his family's position in the Methodist Episcopal Church.[34] The loyalties of his parents, forged in their struggle against persecution and prejudice, quickly became fixed in him as well. Stories told at the evening hearthside of indignities suffered for the Union and the return of the "old church" provided the context through which he understood the antipathies that plagued his family.[35] "They called us

N-O-R-T-H-E-R-N Methodists," he recalled. "They hated us worse than they did the devil."[36]

"Even when a wee child," Brasher remembered, "I could sense the tragedies and hardships through which Father and Mother were passing."[37] Fear for his father's life was a constant companion of his childhood:

> Traveling large circuits . . . for weeks he would be away. And to his absence was added the anxiety for his safety, for his life was often threatened and some of his comrades in the gospel had been hanged and beaten terribly. . . . Mother never could be certain that he would come home alive, indeed, not certain that she should ever be permitted to look upon his dead body.[38]

> I don't remember Mother ever getting a letter from him. We just knew that sometime he'd come back, if he didn't get killed.[39]

The disturbing sound at night of Ku Klux whistles outside the log house was a reminder to Johnny of the rancor harbored by some neighbors toward his family and church.[40] But his father's pluck served as antidote for Johnny's fears:

> One time Pa was over at Gadsden, and he bought him a nice double-barreled shotgun. "Well," [the storekeeper] said, "whatcha gonna do, Parson?" "Well, the boys have been waiting on some folks lately around, and I didn't know what they might decide to come to see me." And he bought some buckshot and some waterproof caps. "I guess I just well load it. I might see a turkey on the way home." They saw what a shot he put in there. And not long after that he was at a log-rolling where they were cleaning up new ground, and one of the neighbor-boys said, "Parson, if you hear any Ku-Klux whistles, don't worry, they're not after you."[41]

From childhood, Brasher's loyalty to the Methodist Episcopal Church was sealed by a tradition of his family's persecution and sacrifices endured on its behalf. This particular church, reborn "in poverty and obloquy," was his own genesis, a part of his very being. Referring to the reorganizing of the Alabama Conference in 1867, he unashamedly proclaimed: "I was born nine months from the adjournment of that first session. As Napoleon was made a soldier by his mother having lived in the fields of battle, so I was pre-empted for a preacher, being bred in the holy hour of heroic Christian devotion to a great cause."[42]

Devotion to the Methodist Episcopal Church played a leading role in Brasher's later identification with the holiness movement, an element that had origin and greatest influence in the northern branch of the church. When Brasher entered the holiness cause, he believed a revival of holiness would cure the languishing condition of his church in Alabama as it stood embattled in its fourth decade against the increasing majority of the Methodist Episcopal Church, South. Brasher's adoption of holiness emphases was in part a means of coping with the minority position of his church in the South. Accustomed to prejudice against his religious affiliation, Brasher was well prepared to cope with, at times to take advantage of, the opposition he met throughout his career—ironically, often from his own church—because of his espousal of holiness beliefs. Brasher's conviction that his holiness tenets represented a restoration of original Methodist doctrines followed his family's tradition of seeking "to revive the Methodism of the fathers, to go back to the old landmarks."

3

"Pre-empted for a Preacher"

THE CALL

> My mother, they said, when I was laid by her pillow, said, "This is
> my preacher."
> —JOHN L. BRASHER, 20 JULY 1968

Call Narratives and Convention

In the midst of a sermon, Brasher reminded his listeners: "I think it was foreordained before the foundation of the world that I should preach."[1] His assurance of having been prenatally "pre-empted for a preacher" notwithstanding, Brasher's call to preach began to take shape early through a complex of familial and community influences and innate gifts that prepared him, as he later gratefully acknowledged, for a "labor exactly suited to [his] personality and selfhood."[2]

Brasher confessed that as a boy he "almost worshipped" his father, whose preaching he would rather hear than anyone else's, and whose moral and educational elevation above the community gave Johnny a sense of pride and a consciousness of being set apart.[3] Reading his father's library and learning the art of storytelling from family and circuit riders who spent the night at the big house nurtured Johnny in intellectual and oral skills. Of equal if not more influence than home was the effect of worship at the nearby meetinghouse. There occurred the primary religious rituals of the community, sanctifying the circumscribed routine of Johnny's rural boyhood with eternal meanings. There, through the agency of the preached word, the conversion of the soul—that fundamental event of life—frequently and demonstratively took place.

These and other influences formed Brasher's sense of calling. His own accounts of his call to preach were couched in the conventions of the spiritual autobiographies of contemporary and earlier evangelical preachers. Brasher's need—conscious or not—to conform in some degree to the conventions of the call of other preachers paralleled his concerns in his quest for conversion and sanctification. The important bearing of convention upon his spiritual journey from conversion through sanctification will be treated in chapter 5.

The long Anglo-American tradition of spiritual autobiography as a model for conversion has been thoroughly documented.[4] The conclusions of such studies also apply to what appear to be common conventions in the call narratives of many evangelical and holiness preachers. Seventeenth-century New England Puritans developed a detailed morphology of conversion that delineated a pattern of experiences whereby the faithful were known to receive grace. Seekers after conversion who could claim such experiences assured themselves and their community that they were truly Elect. The portrayal of one's life was thus shaped according to the ideals of a group.[5] Attention to the form of piety thereafter remained an important element of American evangelical Christianity.

The experiences that Brasher cited as fixed points in the pattern of his call not only reveal his quest for self-understanding, they also bear remarkable congruence to the signs and movings of the Spirit that appear in the spiritual autobiographies of his colleagues. His call narratives, which appear frequently—in his written autobiography, editorials, correspondence, and oral sermons and reminiscences—functioned, as do all such conventions, to assure himself and his particular community of the validity of his summons to preach.

Brasher's conviction that he was foreordained to preach rested on such biblical precedents as God's word to Jeremiah: "Before I formed thee in the belly I knew thee, and before thou camest forth out of the womb I sanctified thee."[6] Other biblical models for such predictions or dedications before or at the time of birth may be found in the birth narratives of Samson, Samuel, John the Baptist, and Jesus.[7]

From its founding, American Methodism had modeled its own definition of the call to preach upon these scriptural precedents. The father of American Methodism, Francis Asbury, had a mother with a vision before his birth "that he would become a great religious leader." The heroic circuit rider James Finley had a grandmother who "dedicated him to God" when he was "a wee child."[8] O. P. Fitzgerald, a nineteenth-century Southern Methodist bishop, related that a petition that he might preach was a part of "the prayer at [his] baptism at two days old."[9]

Such claims of predestination were common among Brasher's peers. Bishop Fitzgerald began the account of his call with the statement, "It must have been foreordained that I was to be a preacher." He could have been speaking for Brasher when he added, "A sort of presentiment that it was to be so had been with me from my early boyhood."[10] Brasher substantiated the preordination of his calling not only by citing the providential timing of his conception but also by including in every account the formulaic narrative of his mother's precognition at his birth: "I was a natural born preacher, because they told me that when they laid me beside Mother's pillow she said, 'This is my preacher.' They didn't tell me that until after I was preaching."[11]

Closer still to Brasher's story were the claims of his holiness evangelist colleagues. W. B. Godbey, a friend of Brasher and one of the earliest holiness leaders in the South, wrote that when he was born his mother "gave [him] to the Lord for a preacher and had heard from heaven that [he] was to . . . preach the gospel." The most interesting parallel to Brasher's narrative was the story told by Henry Clay Morrison, who was often perceived by others to be in rivalry with Brasher on shared camp-meeting preaching platforms: "After I had been in the ministry many years, I met a woman whose mother had lived near neighbor to my mother, and she told me that . . . when my mother went to church the first time after I was born . . . she . . . came home . . . and said, 'Today I gave my little H. C. to God to preach the gospel, and I believe . . . when I am dead and gone this baby boy, grown into manhood, will preach Jesus.'"[12]

Autobiographies frequently reported that childhood presentiments of preaching included practice-preaching to animals or playmates—a sure sign of future vocation. Brasher told of his delight as a little boy in preaching to the chickens and sometimes holding their "funerals."[13] The black preacher Rubin Lacy, as a child of seven in Mississippi, sermonized to the birds and the trees. W. B. Godbey exhorted his playmates from a fence-corner pulpit, and they "became serious, attentive, and got convicted."[14]

In addition to practice-preaching, Brasher reported a direct manifestation of the Spirit to him as a child, which he later interpreted as part of his call: "I was a little tiny boy. There was nobody on the place but me. I remember all of a sudden a warmness of heart. I didn't know what it meant. And then I began to talk, language that I hadn't heard of in the world. I spent three-quarters of an hour, nearly, just speaking as if I were speaking to an audience. Never did it before. Never did it since. I think the Lord was sealing me then for the speaking ministry."[15] Through this narrative, Brasher emphasized that his call was truly of the Spirit and not a response to mere human expectations. Hence, also, his and Morrison's disclaimers that they did not know of their mothers' prophecies at their birth until well after they had answered a more direct call of God.

Brasher's narrative of a numinous experience in childhood, not found commonly in other spiritual autobiographies, reflected his holiness emphasis on the critical importance of the indwelling of the Spirit for effective preaching. One other holiness account of a childhood "sealing" of the Spirit was that of W. B. Godbey, who recalled that as he preached to his playmates, he "got happy and heard the call from heaven which never did leave."[16] Brasher also reported that shortly before he was licensed to preach he experienced "divine illumination of the Word," and that he "walked many a mile . . . pouring out the preaching to the woods."[17]

A final experience that put to rest any possible doubts Brasher harbored about his call came in a dream—the revenant of his recently deceased father: "I more and more felt I ought to join the conference my father helped organize," he later recalled.[18] "That summer and fall [1891] I gave more attention to the call of God in the larger field of ministry. I had good offers for farming in 1892, but when wavering in the balance as to my life's work I had a remarkable dream. My father, it seemed, came to me in my dream and, like Paul to Timothy, exhorted me to 'make full proof of my ministry.' I hesitated no longer and decided to make application for admission on trial in the Alabama Conference M. E. Church."[19] A vocational call through a dream, often occurring during a time of indecision, appears as one of the more frequent conventions of preachers' autobiographies. Donald Byrne, in his study of Methodist folklore, cites nine similar accounts that appeared in the narratives of Methodist itinerants, including those of the eighteenth-century evangelist George Whitefield, the renowned nineteenth-century editor-preacher Nathan Bangs, and the holiness bishop William Taylor.[20] Byrne maintains that these dreams which Methodist itinerants "considered significant . . . were those that reinforced convictions they already held."[21] Brasher's dream, following the recent death of his father and reanimating his loyalty to the church his father had organized, supports Byrne's premise.

At the Big House

Brasher always related these remarkable signs when describing his call, but other reminiscences of his childhood reveal a daily context that equally shaped his decision to become a preacher. His home

John Lakin Brasher at the time he was
licensed to preach, 1889. Brasher
Papers.

life nourished an incipient sense of calling, of being set apart. The last
by five years of eight children, he was physically "the runt of the family," a "feeble little thing" who his parents feared "might not live to the
teens." His mother, who a decade earlier within two months had lost
her first four children to diphtheria, and his pious grandmother, who
every Sunday read from Baxter's *Saints' Rest,* considered him "a sickly
little child" and restricted and pampered him. His older brothers and
sister, jealous of the favors he received, delighted in teasing him, often magnifying his childish mistakes to his great misery.[22]

With no close siblings, Brasher spent much time to himself
"dreaming of what lay beyond the hills" and yearning for his father,
who was away on the circuit.[23] However, his solitary days were enlivened by evening visits of traveling preachers, whose arrival made him
"glad to the depths of [his] soul."[24] His parents' home was "the place
for preachers to stop"—men "of note and intelligence."[25] Taught to
show respect by addressing all preachers as "Uncle," Johnny had no
trouble recognizing their status, but he invited the derision of his brothers and sister when he announced, "I am going to make [*sic*] a Methodist preacher so I can get to eat fried chicken."[26]

For a boy who wondered what lay beyond the ridges and who
pondered the fate of friends who "went West and were never heard
from again," the life of the traveling preachers held great fascination.[27]
Circuit riders were his primary link to the world beyond the cove and
offered Johnny "a liberal education."[28] A. S. Lakin, from the faraway

North, an associate of bishops and national politicians, told of his testimony before congressional committees. A favorite itinerant, T. R.
Parker, originally from Georgia, reportedly had been offered the presidency of Emory College at Oxford.[29] One can sense the allure of their
wider world for Brasher from his recollection years later: "I well remember the first time I went to town and saw a painted house, how
my heart beat pit-a-pat, and how the man who kept the store seemed
so impossibly beyond me."[30]

At the Meetinghouse

The itinerants preached to the folk of Greasy Cove at Clear Creek
meetinghouse, the social and spiritual center of the community.[31] It was
a plain log structure, just over the shoulder of a hill to the west of the
big house. Johnny attended weekly services there where the spoken
word was the centerpiece of a ritual that created both a hunger for
conversion and an expectation of a visible response to the inward assurance of sins forgiven. Such rituals assumed greatest power during
the "protracted meetings" held between "laying-by and fodder-pulling
time" (between 20 July and the last of August).[32] Daily services were
held in the morning and "at early candlelight," the latter possessing a
peculiar solemnity with "subdued light and the serious people who
waited for the word that made sinners feel uncomfortable."[33] These
meetings, Brasher recalled, transformed the dim log church into "a
place of glory."[34]

Worship was structured by "unvarying customs" that had evolved
in the rural South to highlight the sermon as the key to religious experience.[35] A ritual was observed, "regular patterns of behavior invested
with symbolic significance and efficacy."[36] The customary form of the
"early candlelight" service included two preliminary "grove meetings"—
one for men and one for women—held simultaneously "an hour by
sun." The primary task of these meetings was to pray for the preacher
and his message, but there were sometimes anticipatory conversions
in the grove. When the "two sides" later assembled at the meetinghouse, an atmosphere had been created that made it "easy for the
preacher to preach and to bring conviction upon the sinner."[37] The
preacher also had prayed by himself in the woods before the commencement of the service. Entering the church, he first knelt in prayer
before the pulpit. Then he selected a hymn and began singing with the
few older members already at their seats. This was the signal for all to
come inside. Men and women entered through separate doors and sat
on opposite sides of the church, allegedly in order that sinners might

feel freer to go to the mourners' bench, a railing or bench in front of the pulpit where they knelt to seek forgiveness, than if they sat with members of the opposite sex.[38]

A further symbolic segregation was observed beyond that of male and female. All Christians, souls who had received the new birth, took seats exclusively in the front of the room, behind and to either side of the pulpit, in a restricted space known as the "amen corners" or the "devout corners." The remainder of the congregation filled the benches in front of the pulpit in an area sometimes nicknamed the "stiff-knee corners." These worshippers who sat facing the preacher and the pious constituted "the world of sinners and other folks," "stiff-kneed" because most did not kneel during prayers as all "amen-corner" folk did. Such a division between saints and sinners was rigorously maintained and, on occasion, led to disputes over the state of grace (choice of seat) of a particular individual. "They had times about it," Brasher noted.[39]

After all had found their proper places and had sung a hymn or two, one of the Christians at the front would offer a prayer, concluding with a ritual petition for the preacher: "Oh Lord, bless this man as he stands between the living and the dead to proclaim the Word of God." The stage was set for the sacred drama of conviction and conversion, for souls to pass from death to life through the agency of the words of the preacher. For sinners, the mourners' bench in front of the pulpit, dividing the "devout" from the "other folks," served as a literal and symbolic threshold leading from worldly distinctions and the death of sin into equality and *communitas* with the saints alive in the Spirit.[40]

The preacher, who spoke from the "pulpit stand" (called "the sweat box" by Brasher's father), stood between the sinners and the saved, his words and person providing a vehicle for the Spirit and linking earth and heaven.[41] His message of "anointed, illuminated speech" brought supernatural power to convert sinners and bless saints.[42] Songs urged seekers to join in the foretaste of the other world, and the meetinghouse became a place of glory:

> Come, soul, and find thy rest,
> No longer be distressed,
> Come to the Savior's breast,
> Oh, don't stay away.
>
> Prayers are ascending now,
> Angels are bending now,

Both worlds are blending now,
Oh, don't stay away.[43]

Visible conversions, the longed-for result of such praying, preaching, and singing, were often dramatic. Assurance of salvation, the "touchstone" of southern religion, was perceived as primarily connected to the convert's emotions. Deep-felt struggles, weeping, and rejoicing normally accompanied the new birth.[44] "In those days," Brasher asserted, "there were no 'still-born Christians.' They passed from death unto life, and knowing it, they clearly proclaimed it."[45] The plain folk, moreover, viewed the work of the Spirit mostly "in terms of irregular and extraordinary occurrences"—instantaneous intervention that took place primarily at conversion when emotions were sensitized.[46] The conversion of one of Brasher's older brothers demonstrated the expected pattern in a sensational manner: "My elder brother, James, was prostrated under conviction at an afternoon service, and became helpless physically, and was carried from the church to our house by friends and laid upon the bed where he lay entirely motionless without sound or sign for some hours. About eight or nine o'clock that night while friends stood around him and were singing some good old hymn, he came to with a shout and sprang from the bed with joy and old-time rejoicing."[47] At conversion, it was believed, the presence of the Spirit could be measured as well as felt. When a convert "got religion," the implication was of quantity as well as quality. Brasher's belief in the quantitative nature of the Spirit's intervention at conversion appeared in his tale of a black preacher and a seeker:

> A colored man was seeking salvation and his pastor was giving counsel and help. After a little prayer, he arose and said, "I got it." His pastor said, "No, you didn't. Git down there and pray." He rose a second time and professed, but his pastor said, "No, you got nothin'. Git down there and pray." Now, the man got down to business, confessed his sins, and cried for mercy and forgiveness, and arose with joy to tell that he had been blessed. The preacher said, "Yes, you got it." The man said, "How'd you know I didn't get it awhile ago?" "'Cause," said the preacher, "I knowed the Lord could not come that close and bless you and not bless me too." In those days . . . the people nearby got the overflow. If the seeker gets something from the Lord, those that stand by get the extra in their own hearts.[48]

The degree to which the religion of Brasher's youth found focus in the event of conversion cannot be overstated. Brasher loved to quote his father's words that portrayed the moment of conversion as the be-all-and-end-all of religion: "He used to say when he lived in this territory and there were so many folks backslid every Christmas, the only way to get them to heaven was to take a dollar-and-a-half shotgun, and when they got blessed in August, shoot 'em. Get 'em to heaven. You'd never get 'em any other way. When I was a boy, lots of young folks got converted in the summer, but they lost it in the dance in the winter."[49]

The burden of speaking the words of life to sinners belonged primarily to the preacher. Some hardened transgressors regrettably never relinquished their places in the "stiff-knee corners," but those whose hearts were melted by "anointed speech" were assured of new temporal and eternal location. Indeed, preachers looked forward to greeting their particular converts in heaven.[50] The solemnity and celebrity of the preacher's task captured Brasher while he was yet a child, and his mature understanding of his role as a preacher departed at one point only from the traditions of his southern plain-folk heritage: As a holiness evangelist, he insisted that a preacher must be sanctified as well as converted in order effectively to lead souls from death to life.[51]

4

Popular Perfectionism

THE HOLINESS MOVEMENT

It's unthinkable a holy God, sitting in a holy heaven, surrounded by
holy angels . . . would require less than holiness.
—JOHN L. BRASHER, 15 JULY 1962

In an hour-long sermon delivered in the open air before an immense crowd on his hundredth birthday, Brasher claimed the privilege
of having preached John Wesley's doctrine of sanctification longer and
later in life than anyone in history.[1] Brasher's proclamation of perfect
love, while according in spirit and in many respects in substance with
Wesley's doctrine, owed certain emphases to the nineteenth-century
American holiness movement. A complex movement that began taking form before the Civil War, it eventually counted members among
a number of denominational, social, and racial groups. Most holiness
adherents cited Wesley as authority but taught variations of his original doctrine of Christian perfection.

John Wesley, founder of the Methodists, declared it the task of
his followers "to spread scriptural holiness over the land."[2] His doctrine of holiness, which he variously styled as "sanctification," "Christian perfection," or "perfect love," rested upon his perception of a God
who acts in the lives of his fallen creatures to restore them to harmony with him. This interaction of God's gracious activity and human response reaches its climax in sanctification, the goal of the mature Christian life.

In Wesley's conception of salvation, God's saving love first encounters men and women, marred by original sin, through "preventing

grace," which as the "beginning of deliverance from a . . . heart . . . insensible of God" brings initial awareness of having sinned. The work of salvation continues in "convincing grace," whereby one is led to increased self-knowledge and repentance. Subsequently, by faith alone (not works), one may receive the pardoning gift of justification, through which one is "saved from the guilt of sin and restored to the favor of God." Concurrent with justification, in "regeneration" or "the new birth," sanctification begins, whereby through imparted grace one is "saved [or 'cleansed'] from the power and root of sin and restored to the image of God."[3]

Wesley described sanctification as a lifelong process of daily cooperation with God's grace in which the believer grows in love of God and neighbor, trust in the sufficiency of the grace of Christ, and joy in the presence of the Holy Spirit.[4] As holiness of heart and life gradually increases, there can come a moment when "in an instant, the heart is cleansed from all sin, and filled with pure love to God and man."[5] This decisive experience of "entire sanctification," like justification, comes solely as a gift of God, at his appointed time, by faith alone. Even after this moment, one continues to the end of earthly life to mature in love for God toward the ultimate hope of conformity with the mind of Christ. Thus Wesley's doctrine of Christian perfection claimed both process and consummation: "All experience as well as scripture show [*sic*] this salvation to be both instantaneous and gradual."[6] Entire sanctification, Wesley argued, never denotes sinless perfection; rather, it signifies the believer's purity of Christian intention.[7]

At the organization of the Methodist Church in America in 1784, the new denomination adopted Wesley's vision of spreading scriptural holiness over the land as its central purpose and continued vigorously to proclaim the distinctive doctrine at least through the first decade of the nineteenth century.[8] Methodist historiography, since the publication in 1956 of John L. Peters's *Christian Perfection and American Methodism,* has maintained that the preaching and experience of sanctification suffered neglect in the ensuing three decades as a result of the church's concentration upon winning converts on the raw frontier. Recent studies, however, show that there may never have been such a pronounced hiatus in the preaching of the doctrine.[9]

What is certain is that interest in the doctrine of perfect love dramatically increased and crossed denominational bounds through the efforts of Phoebe Worrell Palmer (1807–74), a Methodist laywoman. Her leadership after 1839 of the New York Tuesday Meeting for the Promotion of Holiness, her international preaching tours, her books and support of the periodical *Guide to Holiness,* and her close association with noted religious leaders won a newly receptive and broader audience for the doctrine—not, however, through careful revival of Wesley's emphasis but rather through her modifications of it.

Although the changes wrought by Palmer characterized the subsequent holiness movement, the motivations behind her well-known modifications have received little notice.[10] She revealed them in her first and most popular book, *The Way of Holiness* (1843). Palmer's doctrine of holiness, derived from experience, resolved her own vexing spiritual dilemma arising from an inability to meet the religious conventions of her peers.

The pervasive revivalism of her time saw both conversion and sanctification essentially as emotional events in the Christian pilgrimage. Palmer unfortunately could not witness to such "luminous" experiences in her own quest for salvation. Writing in the third person, she confessed: "Though for many happy years she was enabled to testify . . . that she had passed from death unto life, yet the precise time when that change took place, she could never state."[11] For years troubled by what sounded like "irresistible" moments of assurance described by others, Palmer finally concluded that her "former perplexities in experience had too frequently arisen from a proneness to follow the traditions of men, instead of the oracles of God."[12] She therefore fashioned a "shorter way" to holiness, not dependent upon the vagaries of emotion.

Developed as a "simple" method by which to receive sanctification, Palmer's theology of Christian perfection deemphasized Wesley's view of holiness as a lifelong goal to be pursued and instead stressed holiness as a present obligation available here and now.[13] Entire sanctification, Palmer asserted, could be obtained immediately by any seeker who had met the requirements revealed in the words of the Scriptures. Thus after a complete consecration of all of one's powers at the altar or mourners' bench, the Christian seeker, free from intimidation and emotion, could, through faith in the promises of the word of God alone, claim sanctification: "*Faith is taking God at his word,* relying unwaveringly upon his truth." Palmer, accordingly, said that "she was enabled by the help of the Spirit to resolve that she *would take God at his word,* whatever her emotions might be."[14]

Employing as proof-text Matthew 23:19 ("You blind men! For which is greater, the gift or the altar that sanctifieth the gift?"), Palmer reasoned that when one had consecrated one's life to God, "actually laying all upon the altar," the offering was thereby made holy as "the altar sanctifieth the gift."[15] No other assurance of sanctification than this covenant was necessary. The traditional Wesleyan emphasis on the direct witness of the Spirit as an inward persuasion or conviction was discarded by Palmer as too closely tied to the emotions. Instead, the witness of the Spirit was identified with the Scriptures themselves.[16]

The immediacy and certainty of the "simpler way," reflecting the American penchant for efficiency and results, attracted a remarkably wide group of followers from the Protestant spectrum at midcentury. Palmer's Tuesday Meetings, which soon spread to other cities, were frequented by Methodist notables such as bishops Edmund Janes, Leonidas Hamline, Jesse Peck, and Matthew Simpson, the New York editor Nathan Bangs, and Stephen Olin, president of Wesleyan College. Admirers from other denominations included the Congregationalists Asa Mahan, president of Oberlin College, and Thomas C. Upham, a professor at Bowdoin College; the Baptist evangelist A. B. Earle of Boston; Hannah Whitall Smith, a Friend from Philadelphia, later the author of *The Christian's Secret of a Happy Life* (1875); and Charles Cullis, a Boston Episcopal physician.[17]

Though not directly associated with Palmer, the preeminent midcentury Congregational revivalist Charles G. Finney and the Presbyterian William E. Boardman, author of *The Higher Christian Life* (1858), popularized Reformed versions of the doctrine. The British Methodist William Arthur's *The Tongue of Fire* (1856), a best-selling treatise on the power of the Holy Spirit in the Christian life, was adopted and adapted by the American holiness movement as descriptive in particular of the work of sanctification.[18]

The pervasive perfectionist impulse in American Protestantism immediately prior to the Civil War has been recognized rightly as "a kind of evangelical transcendentalism" and has even been called "as widespread a popular quest for the beatific vision as the world had known."[19] One writer has noted, "The ethical ideals to which Emerson and Henry David Thoreau aspired on a highly sophisticated level plain men of the time sought at a Methodist mourners' bench or class meeting."[20] Eager desire for entire sanctification was part and parcel of the optimism, idealism, and moral striving endemic to midcentury America. The pre–Civil War holiness tide crested in the great revival of 1858, which began in New York City and quickly encompassed most of the urban Northeast.[21] By the eve of the war, however, American proponents of holiness had wrought further changes in the doctrine of perfect love originally espoused by Wesley and the early Methodists.

Donald W. Dayton, in his study of American holiness theology, has delineated several emphases characteristic of Christian perfectionism at midcentury that departed from the earlier Methodist doctrine of sanctification. The changes included (1) a transition from primarily

Christocentric language and thought to Pneumatocentric terminology and concepts; (2) a shift to a "dispensational" view of sacred history in which the post-Pentecost age belongs to the Holy Spirit; (3) a focus upon the Book of Acts as the scriptural validation for the doctrine of sanctification; (4) a related emphasis on the power and gifts of the Holy Spirit, including prophecy; (5) deemphasis of Christian perfection as a process or lifelong goal in favor of sanctification as an immediate event or "second blessing"; and (6) renewed interest in assurance and the evidence of having received the "Pentecostal Baptism" (synonymous with entire sanctification).[22]

After the war, the dominant emphasis on entire sanctification as a distinct "second blessing" went hand in hand with holiness leaders' revival of the camp meeting, soon the distinguishing institution of the holiness movement. Promoted as interdenominational, the first great "national" camp meeting devoted to the special work of holiness convened at Vineland, New Jersey, in 1867. Organized by Methodist ministers William B. Osborn of New Jersey, John S. Inskip of New York City, and their colleagues from New York and Philadelphia, the successful first camp, thronged mostly by Methodists, gave birth to the National Camp Meeting Association for the Promotion of Holiness. The association became the heart of the postwar holiness movement, conducted as many as eight national camp meetings each year throughout the country, and soon gained the support of new state and local holiness associations.[23] These meetings institutionalized the growing popular interest in powerful manifestations of the Holy Spirit at conversion and especially in the experience of the "second blessing," while at the same time employing traditional practices of an earlier rural revivalism.

Promoted and attended primarily by city clergy and their flocks, the first holiness camps were to an important degree a reaction against the increasing gentrification of the church, the new learning of the universities, and urban-industrial social change. The camps embodied a nostalgia to reinstate the "evangelicalism of the countryside."[24] The secretary of the national association, George Hughes, in his history of the national camps, entitled *Days of Power in the Forest Temple* (1873), proclaimed the "primitive simplicity and power" of the holiness meetings as antidote for besetting ills of urban Methodism: the neglect of emphasis on religious experience; preoccupation with worldly amusements; "opulent," "ambitious" styles of architecture—especially Gothic, "worthy only of the dark ages . . . with darkened auditoriums at war with every instinct of Methodist life"; "ritualistic" worship with music of "operatic style"; and a ministry lacking "spiritual power" offering only "doctrinal indefiniteness" and "glittering generalities."[25]

COME TO THE GREAT
CAMP MEETING
RIVERSIDE PARK
RIVERSIDE, ILL.

REV. THOMAS C. HENDERSON
Columbus, Ohio

June 30 to July 9, 1911
FIRST SERVICE JUNE 30
7:00 P. M.

REV. J. L. BRASHER, Praz, Ala.

CONDUCTED BY THE
ILLINOIS STATE HOLI-
NESS ASSOCIATION

HENRY C. MAITLAND, Wilmore, Ky.

Children's Meeting conducted by Mrs. Addie Favorite, Chicago

LOCATION
This camp is located at Riverside Park, Riverside, Ill., about a fifty-minute ride from the Loop District. The grounds are being improved and a large tabernacle will be pitched to protect from storm and damp weather.

HOW TO REACH THE GROUNDS
From Englewood, South Chicago and all Southern Localities—North on any street car or Illinois Central R. R. to Twenty-second street; west to end of line. Transfer to La Grange Electric, thence to Riverside Park.

From North Side Localities—South to Ogden avenue car line; west on Twenty-second street; La Grange electric to Riverside Park.

From Loop District—Douglas Park branch Metropolitan Elevated to end of line; transfer to La Grange electric to Riverside Park. It is always safe to ask for a transfer.

From Points of C. B. & Q. Railroad—Get off at La Grange, instead of Riverside; take electric to Riverside Park.

South Side friends may be glad to learn that there will be no change of cars on the Twenty-second street line at the Pennsylvania R. R. viaduct. as last summer, and also that ALL La Grange cars now run via Twenty-second street every twenty minutes.

BOARDING
The boarding tent this year is to be under the direct management of the Association, who have engaged Rev. William J. Bone and wife to take charge. This couple has had large experience along this line and complete satisfaction is guaranteed. For further information address Rev. William J. Bone, 2145 Lexington street, Chicago, Ill. Phone Seeley 6828.

LODGING
The Association has purchased seventy-five new cots, plenty of bedding and good accommodations may be secured for 25 cents per night. Mrs. C. L. Felmlee, 240 Englewood avenue, has charge of this department and it would greatly accommodate the Association, as well as assure yourself of a good place if you would write her at the above address at as early a date as possible.

A broadside advertising one of Brasher's northern meetings. Brasher Papers.

Predominantly northern, urban, and educated, early holiness leaders included powerful Methodist ecclesiastics who wholeheartedly endorsed the first efforts of the National Camp Meeting Association. In
1872, six of the eight new bishops elected at the Northern General
Conference advocated or were favorable to the holiness reawakening.[26]
First aimed primarily at established Methodist membership, the holiness message soon was carried through urban missions to the un-
churched poor.[27] In the postwar South, although an occasional native
voice spoke for Christian perfection, northerners most often sparked
the beginnings of the holiness movement, initially through special meetings usually conducted in large city churches.[28]

The South

A fellow over in Texas said, "I'm going to stamp this craze out if
it takes me five years!" And he stamped until he had a hundred and
fifty holiness camp meetings blazing in Texas. I've been over there
[Waco, Texas, 1904], and they came up in those old prairie
schooners. . . . And they sat down on the front [rows] and said,
"Feed us, we're hungry." And we poured it into them three hours
a day, and they said to come back next day—gluttons for more.
—JOHN L. BRASHER, AUGUST 1950

In 1846 at the first General Conference of the Methodist Episcopal Church, South, the bishops reminded the new church that "its
true original vocation" was "to spread scriptural holiness."[29] From 1846
to 1870, however, when once again the bishops urged (perhaps in imi-
tation of northern developments) "a powerful revival of scriptural holiness," the doctrine of Christian perfection in Southern Methodist theory and practice was largely absent.[30] Antebellum southern theologians
had concentrated on the defense of slavery and had found holiness links
to abolitionism repugnant.[31] The Civil War temporarily disrupted whatever holiness literature had been flowing from outside to the South;
but even after the war, the holiness movement in the South flowered
later than in the North.[32]

The immediate postwar holiness movement, which in the North
promoted an "old-fashioned," waning revivalism and to a large extent
defined itself in reaction to religious and social change, found itself in
the South without a cause. The South remained "a land of piety and
tradition," a religion-culture where frontier-style revivalism had never
been abandoned, where urbanization, new mores, and new theologies
arrived late.[33] When holiness did spread throughout the changing South
in the final two decades of the century, the preaching of a decisive sec-

Campers at the Waco, Texas, camp meeting, 1904. According to Brasher, "They came up in those old prairie schooners." Brasher Papers.

The James Metcalf family on their way to Hollow Rock Camp Meeting, Toronto, Ohio, ca. 1910. Brasher Papers.

ond blessing found warm acceptance among a people who continued to perceive conversion and most religious experience in terms of supernatural intervention. In fact, many elements of holiness religion—or rather the elements that became identified with the holiness movement—were already in place in the traditions of plain-folk revivalism that continued unabated in the upland South. After the Civil War, it was primarily the articulated holiness theological formulations—not the worship practices, belief systems, and religious traditions—that flowed north to south.[34] Rural southern outposts of holiness established by northerners as early as the 1870s were soon joined by numerous city missions that met the needs of former country folk living and working in the new urban industrial centers.[35]

By the 1870s, the holiness movement claimed scattered adherents below the Mason-Dixon line, but in almost all cases initial interest in holiness theology in the South came through individuals, periodicals, or institutions from beyond its borders. Less a respecter of region than the established religious bodies, the holiness impulse played a part in the early postwar reintegration of the South into the national culture.[36]

Despite some apprehension, the northern-based National Camp Meeting Association ventured to hold its last national camp for 1872 in Knoxville, Tennessee. The successful camp returned for another season the following year. A national meeting, again in the South, convened at Augusta, Georgia, in 1885, in the church served by a future Methodist bishop, Warren A. Candler.[37]

John S. Inskip and his coworkers of the national association introduced the holiness message in special evangelistic tours of the South, none more gratifying or well received than his extended visit to Charleston, Savannah, and Richmond in 1880. Inskip's revival at Trinity Church, Charleston, continued for five weeks, during which he elucidated the doctrine of holiness as found in "the Bible, Methodism, and the Methodist hymnal."[38] Rejoicing in the fraternal spirit of the meeting, Inskip reported: "We so far nowhere have known anything of the cold and repulsive feeling alleged to prevail toward northern men. It is the perfectly natural result of the character of our work and mission. We are invited by our southern brethren to come among them and aid them in awakening an interest in the great work of holiness."[39] William Wightman, an aged Southern Methodist bishop and Charleston native, responded, "In the memory of no living man was there ever witnessed in the Methodist Churches of Charleston a religious movement comparable to this."[40] Inskip and others clearly hoped that the holiness revival might serve as a unifying force to heal the division between the two Methodisms.

In Tennessee, under the editorship of the Reverend William Baker, the first holiness periodical issued in the South came from the press in 1871. Appearing initially as *The Home Altar,* the journal in 1875 moved to Spartanburg, South Carolina, and revealed indebtedness to Phoebe Palmer's theology by a new name: *The Way of Holiness.* Baker, a Methodist Episcopal minister and publisher from the North, had come south first to McMinnville, Tennessee, immediately after the war. As editor of the "only Republican paper in the mountain district of Middle Tennessee," he promoted the Methodist Episcopal Church and aided speculators in the sale of cheap lands to other immigrants from the North.[41] His *Way of Holiness,* which encouraged "old-time Methodist usages," depended heavily on excerpts from northern holiness journals and authors, but it answered an inquisitive correspondence that by 1876 arrived from subscribers in every southern state.[42]

Even in the Deep South, the first holiness revivals admitted to northern provenance. In Georgia, the influential Georgia Holiness Association was organized in 1883 at Gainesville in the home of the Reverend A. J. Jarrell, soon elected president. Jarrell had found sanctification in 1876 while attending the national camp meeting at Ocean Grove, New Jersey.[43] At Flovilla, Georgia, the opening session of Indian Springs Camp Meeting, later one of the grandest in the South, met in 1890 in tents donated by the Illinois Holiness Association.[44] The Texas holiness movement likewise was sparked from the North by the sermons in 1877 of Hardin Wallace, a Methodist Episcopal preacher from Illinois. The following year, meetings held by W. B. Colt, a Free Methodist also from Illinois, issued in the formation of the Texas Holiness Association.[45]

At the close of the century, southern holiness again received impetus from the North as the Methodist Episcopal Church sought to establish new congregations and attract converts through emphasizing sanctification. Holiness evangelists such as Samuel Ashton Keen and E. S. Dunham of Ohio, and Thomas Harrison of Boston, preached at the request of bishops to Methodist Episcopal annual conferences in the South. The northern Methodists also sponsored southern urban holiness missions, some of which became established Methodist Episcopal congregations.[46] At the same time, J. O. McClurkan, a Tennessean who was a Cumberland Presbyterian sanctified in California, established the independent Nashville Pentecostal Mission, modeled after the New York City missions of A. B. Simpson's Christian and Mission-

John Lakin Brasher at the "preacher's cabin," White Cross Camp Meeting, Blount County, Alabama, 1905. Brasher Papers.

The "Evangelists' Lodge" at the camp meeting at Eaton Rapids, Michigan, ca. 1910. Brasher Papers.

ary Alliance. Early workers at the mission traveled to New York City for their training.[47]

Popularity of the holiness movement within the Methodist Episcopal Church, South, peaked in the mid-1880s. Holiness strength was particularly evident in the North Georgia Conference, where the Georgia Holiness Association later helped elect Warren A. Candler bishop.[48] When in 1892 the national association listed the names of 304 traveling holiness evangelists, there appeared among them some native southerners.[49]

Concurrently, however, developments within the southern holiness movement were leading toward its alienation from the Southern Methodist Church. A controversy arose over both polity and doctrine. The increasing independence of the predominantly Methodist, but autonomous, regional holiness associations and a growing number of "unauthorized and unregulated" holiness evangelists threatened episcopal authority.[50] Radical innovations in the doctrine of sanctification, especially in Texas, also alarmed denominational leaders. Fanatical notions were taught, such as sinless perfection and a "third blessing" of "the fire" following sanctification.[51] Moreover, by 1890, the majority of the holiness movement in the South was outspokenly premillennialist, while the official emphasis of Southern Methodism, as in the North, remained postmillennialist.[52]

Questions of denominational authority came to a head as early as 1883, when the first "come-outers," members of the Southwestern Holiness Association in Missouri, broke ties with the Methodist Episcopal Church, South, and joined the newly formed Church of God, the first of many sects to spring from holiness ranks.[53] In 1893, Atticus Haygood, a Georgia bishop, incensed holiness evangelists when he refused to reappoint the noted evangelist Sam Jones as "agent" for the Decatur Orphans' Home, a position that had facilitated his traveling evangelism.[54]

Haygood earlier had voiced alarm over doctrinal aberrations among "the herds of imitators of noted evangelists in small towns, villages, and country places."[55] Southern Methodist seminaries likewise began to challenge holiness doctrine in 1884 when Wilbur F. Tillett, a theologian at Vanderbilt University, condemned "second-blessing" teachings as "semi-pelagian."[56] Four years after Tillett's attack, a Southern Methodist preacher, J. M. Boland, published *The Problem of Methodism,* which boldly criticized Wesley's own teaching on sanctification and argued that the experience of conversion contains both pardon and entire sanctification.[57]

Meanwhile, Southern Methodist orthodoxy looked with increasing dismay upon the recent, dynamic wedding of the second blessing and premillennialism, a combination that not only gave doctrinal offense to the church but that also seemed to give the holiness movement extraordinary new power. By the 1890s, the major holiness leaders in the South and the folk to whom they preached espoused a premillennial view of the End Time. They expected Christ to return before the millennium to take up his saints from the earth in a dramatic event called the "rapture." Rejecting premillennialism as a "pernicious and whimsical heresy," the church held to its postmillennial tradition, which expected Christ to return in judgment after the millennium, a period hastened by earthly spiritual and social progress.[58]

Explanations for the popularity of premillennialism in the South often cite postwar social conditions there as inhibiting the more "optimistic" postmillennial vision that survived in the victorious and progressive North.[59] In fact, however, southern premillennialists cited as evidence of the failed postmillennial vision the growing squalor of northern cities.[60] Premillennialist doctrine, moreover, was first disseminated in the South by northern exponents.[61] Its southern success probably was less a result of peculiar socioeconomic conditions than of the championing of the doctrine by a few charismatic leaders. Prediction of an apocalyptic intervention of the Son of God appealed especially to the supernaturalism in the tradition of southern common folk, still credulous of remarkable providences and extraordinary manifestations of the Spirit.[62]

Linked to premillennialism, sanctification quickly acquired new meaning as the required initiation preparing believers to meet the coming Lord. In the cleansing, sometimes ecstatic, moment of the second blessing, the sanctified proleptically experienced the glory of the awaited Second Coming.[63] The evangelist W. B. Godbey urged sanctification as "the wedding garment" necessary for the "marriage supper of the Lamb": "Are you robed, ready, watching, and waiting? If not, settle it quickly. Radically and eternally plunge beneath the crimson flood that washes whiter than snow, and then rise to walk in heaven's own light above the world and sin, with heart made pure, garments white, and Christ enthroned within."[64]

Enacting a millennial role, sanctified southerners joyfully proclaimed the holiness revival as the first stirrings of the worldwide spiritual outpouring prophesied to occur immediately before the rapture.[65] The holiness movement, Godbey declared, was "the last call of the Gospel age" to "give the church power and glory such as she had never known."[66] In the closing days of the century, J. O. McClurkan saw "the mighty revival of holiness which swept [the South]" as the central

A couple relax at their camp-meeting tent, Sulphur Springs, Arkansas, 1909. Brasher Papers.

manifestation of a group of latter-day truths. He and his friends also believed that the age would conclude "with the most marvelous displays of divine grace and glory."[67]

A turning point in the church's growing controversy over holiness came at the Southern Methodist General Conference of 1894. The bishops acerbically rejected proposals to create a separate office of evangelist: "We do not want an order of pastors to keep up a routine or a higher, freer, bolder order of prophets to bring down fire from heaven. The offering of the regular army is more important than any guerrilla warfare, however brilliant." The same address reaffirmed the church's commitment to "holiness of heart and life" but condemned devotees of the "holiness party" with their "associations, meetings, and preachers . . . in so far as they claim a monopoly of the experience, practice, and advocacy of holiness, and separate themselves from the body of ministers and disciples."[68]

These official statements shocked sanctified Methodists, many of whom proceeded to "come out" of the Southern church to form a score of independent holiness denominations in the ensuing decade. The bitterness on both sides caused by the church's so-called "war of extermination" occasioned further skirmishes such as the highly publicized

Pickett-Smith debate in August 1896 at Terrell, Texas. L. L. Pickett, a fiery premillennialist evangelist, defended second-blessing doctrine; M. A. Smith, a Southern Methodist pastor, denounced it. The exchange only further widened the breach between holiness folk and the Southern Methodist church.[69]

At the turn of the century, holiness people in the South chose one of three paths. Many remained as "loyalists" within the diffident, sometimes hostile, Methodist Episcopal Church, South. Others joined one of the several new independent holiness sects. A few defected to the Methodist Episcopal Church, which was more favorable to holiness than its southern sibling and actively sought members from among the "come-outers." Holiness, which earlier had been a hope of unity between the two Methodisms, was now viewed by the Southern church as an unwelcome "party," and, accordingly, by the northern church as a source of potential strength in the South.

5

"The Seal of the Covenant"

THE BLESSING IN BIRMINGHAM

At last my heart outran my head.
—JOHN L. BRASHER, 23 JULY 1968

My old sermons weren't worth a nickel.
—JOHN L. BRASHER, 1954

The Quest for Assurance

On the Wednesday after Easter 1900, the Birmingham *Age-Herald* reported a sudden storm of the previous day that had inundated the city: "Rains were the heaviest for several seasons, the precipitation being over six inches. Every stream outflowed and the waters spread in solid sheets over almost the whole of Jones Valley."[1] By the end of the week, calm had returned to the "Magic City" cleansed by the flood. The paper pronounced the cloudburst an "experience of appalling magnitude."[2] During the tempest, an inner storm had been buffeting Brasher—a turmoil in his nature so intense that he likened it to the battles of Chickamauga and Gettysburg.[3] On Thursday when his private conflict ceased, he "wondered at the cleanness of his heart" and the "new world" of "unfathomed peace that filled his soul."[4] Brasher had received the second blessing. On Sunday, he preached on the Transfiguration.[5]

Unlike the flash flood that surprised the city, the clouds of Brasher's spiritual discontent had been gathering for many years. In the summer of 1899, he with his family had come to Birmingham as an eager, fresh seminary graduate to be pastor of Simpson Methodist Episcopal Church. It was not long, however, before the New South city for John turned into an "awful fire and test-place"—the immediate cause of the crisis in his restless soul.[6] The miseries and vices that accompanied the lingering socioeconomic depression of the city, the jarring cultural pluralism, the acrimonious rivalry of the Southern Methodists, the failure to inspire his own worn-out congregation, and the increasingly precarious health of his wife all combined to cause Brasher to question with new seriousness the sufficiency of his own religious experience.

The underlying cause of Brasher's spiritual malaise, however, lay in the difficulties and uncertainties that since his youth had plagued his personal journey of faith; for his testimony of God's saving work in his life did not meet the norm of religious experience that his southern evangelical upbringing taught him should be his. For years intermittently unsure of his status before God, Brasher in his sanctification finally received a convincing experience of grace—a personal assurance of salvation—which, in words Wesley used to describe his own spiritual pilgrimage, deepened his faith from that of "a servant of God" to the assured "faith of a son."[7]

From childhood, Brasher had accepted the necessity of a conversion that could be measured, felt, and seen. In recalling that there were no "stillborn Christians" in the community of his youth, Brasher affirmed not only the Wesleyan emphasis on assurance but also its more narrow traditional southern interpretation that saving grace was apprehended and evidenced primarily by the emotions.[8] The witness of the Spirit to the new birth was essential: "Do they know God as a pardoning and regenerating Savior and do they have the witness of the Holy Spirit to that fact? Anything short of that is a sidetrack outside the depot of salvation."[9] The normal convert felt the witness: "You can't have God's grace without some emotion."[10] Feelings were an important barometer of the Spirit's activity. Their absence was cause for discouragement. Writing home in the midst of a Kansas revival, Brasher complained: "I doubt if these people were courted. I guess they just said, 'Come on, Jane, and let us marry.' There is about as much response in them as in a stump. They neither know how to laugh or cry. God help me to hold out faithful and get back to people that feel and who can smile and cry."[11]

Brasher often portrayed himself as a person of tender sensibilities who valued the emotional in religion. On one occasion he wrote, "I was born July twentieth in Alabama. I have always had a nonfrozen exposure of soul and heart."[12] In a lecture he once said, "There are two words in the New Testament that I would not have taken out for a gold mine—'Jesus wept.'"[13] As a child listening to sermons, he could not help but cry during poignant stories told by his favorite preachers.[14] Yet it

Hendricks Brasher (1860–1940) "shouted himself hoarse" at revivals. Brasher Papers.

was this very sensitivity that probably made Brasher wary of claiming too easy a familiarity with what he knew was holy, or of identifying shallow emotions with the presence of the Spirit.

Throughout his ministry he remained an ardent opponent of "enthusiasm"—emotion "worked up" by the subject and not a genuine response to the Spirit: "It is the product of the impact of personalities under spiritually emotionalized occasions. It is as unsubstantial as a dream. It has no abiding source."[15] In "The Danger of Yielding to Impressions," an important sermon in his revival repertoire, Brasher also warned that not all inner promptings derive from God; some come perhaps from Satan and others from one's own mind: "Your feelings [can] run you into a swamp if you follow them."[16] Above all, Brasher despised artificial emotion produced for show: "If the cup runs over, that is all right, but I never did like to see anybody tilt it."[17]

Although blessed with a "nonfrozen soul and heart," Brasher at the same time tended to be more intellectual, reflective, and self-contained than most. He valued the ability to "shut himself off with his thoughts," even when in a crowd.[18] Always a diligent student, he inherited from his father a love not only of books but also of order and decorum. He thus could define true spiritual feeling as not simply "passionate" but "deep, intelligent, rational, and well-directed" as well.[19]

His reserve at this point was in marked contrast to the behavior of his older brothers, whose demonstrative religious antics amused, and sometimes embarrassed, him. Hendricks "shouted himself hoarse" at revivals. Jim, who sprang from his bed converted after allegedly being struck insensible by the Spirit for many hours, competed with Hendricks at shouting: "Jim would get down on his knees and get blessed and stay on his knees and holler, just fast little howl-yells. At the altar-call at Clear Creek Presbyterian Church one night, he got shouting in the altar like that and hollered, 'Whoop! Whoop! Whoop!' Here came a little dog up the aisle, just as hard as he could right up to Jim, and said, 'Yoop! Yoop! Yoop! Yoop!'"[20] The difference in religious temperament between John and his brothers had significant educational and cultural parallels. John and his family pursued education and eventually traveled widely. His brothers acquired only rudimentary learning and remained local.

To his chagrin, Brasher's innate reserve sometimes inhibited his warm-hearted qualities. On occasion he was at war with himself. After one of his visits home between summer revivals, he wrote to his family revealing the unhappiness of a divided self: "Oh, will I ever get to be what I am not? Will my old, stiff, hard, iron-willed self ever get out of the way of the tender element of my nature until I won't seem like a cold, unsympathetic iceberg? Will anyone ever know my inside qualities? I would have us all as blithe as birds in a bower, but instead there is the sing of the anvil and the sound of iron."[21] This conflict in his nature was no less present in his early life as he repeatedly sought the assurance of the requisite emotional event signifying his sins forgiven. His persistent, yet never fully resolved, quest for a conventional, plain-folk conversion experience bore striking resemblance to Phoebe Palmer's unfruitful search for a "luminous" moment of grace like that reported by her peers.[22]

Brasher's confession in his autobiography that as a youth he "went into the depth of sin" may be more formulaic than factual.[23] A more credible judgment, perhaps, of his adolescence was offered by a friend of those years who in old age remembered John as "a very religious boy and well raised."[24] Never far from the strict moral influence of his family, Brasher in another account admitted, "I did want to be always good."[25] Yet in spite of his religious heritage and the far more than usual spiritual advantages that surrounded him, young John found the ritual threshold dividing sinners from saints a difficult one to cross.

The first reported episode in his earnest pursuit of conversion occurred at a camp meeting held on the banks of the Warrior River. His father was the preacher: "I was eleven years old. The men came from their prayer meeting and the women from their prayer meeting. And they came rejoicing. Pa was to preach that night, and instead of beginning to preach at once, he sang a solo. And before he was through, the thing went wild. He never preached. Nobody else got to say a word. It was midnight when they dismissed, and all over that tabernacle was a mourners' bench. They had fifty conversions that night. And I wanted to be so bad, but nobody thought I was worth fooling with—just a boy in cotton breeches."[26] Two years later, alarmed by a doomsday prophecy, Johnny found temporary peace through the counsel of his brother: "In the twelfth night of November, 1881, I was to sleep with my oldest brother, but could not get to sleep. He asked what was troubling me. I said, 'You know that woman prophesied that the world would come to an end tonight.' He said, 'Don't you pray to God?' And I said, 'Yes.' He said, 'You don't think the Lord would let anybody go to hell praying to him, do you?' I caught hold of that and rested in sleep. The next morning it seemed we were in a new world. I was so restful and peaceful."[27]

Brasher's experience of peace did not last, however, and he took the path of a seeker again as he became convinced during his teens of "the wickedness of his heart."[28] Desiring conversion with a new intensity, he tried various means to make others aware of his inner plight. He sought in vain to prompt a visiting preacher to inquire after the state of his soul. He deliberately used profanity with his friends, so they might rebuke him and talk to him about religion, but "they would just grin and walk off." Finally, he took a direct approach: "I had to corner a young fellow and take him out in the orchard and ask him, 'Why don't you try to help me get saved?' He was very much surprised."[29]

At eighteen, Brasher found "assurance" at a revival, but the exact nature of the assurance he did not describe:

In August, 1886, we had a revival in our church and I was awakened and convicted of my sins and sought pardon and salvation very earnestly. I prayed in the barn and fence corners, in the woods, and went to the altar as a seeker several times, but got no victory. One afternoon, instead of going into the church, I went to my father's blacksmith shop, and there on my knees told the Lord that from that time on I was going with him, whether I ever had any feeling or not. I got up off my knees and went to church. The service had progressed until they had "called mourners," as they expressed it, and after they had prayed they asked them to stand and all who would pray for them to come around and shake hands with them. I remember I was not moved in any emotion, but since I had made no public profession, I decided that if I was going to be a Christian I ought to take up the duties of a Christian. So I went with the others and shook hands with the seekers and felt better for doing so. I judge I was being reclaimed from the lapse since that November night years before when I had found such peace and rest. Anyway, I became a real Christian and received the assurance that I was a child of God.[30]

His experience departed significantly from the ideal of conversion that he and his community proclaimed. Commenting on his conversion many years later, Brasher remembered, "I was about as still a one as has been around."[31] Variations in his dating of his conversion further indicate Brasher's uncertain claim to a decisive emotional experience of pardoning grace. In some accounts, he cites as his conversion the experience of the night of 12 November 1881; in others, he names the revival of 1886.[32] In his extant sermons and writings composed before his sanctification, Brasher placed little or no emphasis upon heartfelt experiences of grace. In one address, in fact, he argued that early Methodism appealed to the people's "conscience and intellect."[33]

Brasher was candid in admitting that immediately before his sanctification in 1900 he was still earnestly seeking assurance: "I was having a hard time keeping what [experience of grace] I had."[34] When he first saw Salvation Army Commissioner Samuel Logan Brengle, under whose preaching he was sanctified, the quality of religious experience that seemed to surround Brengle like a nimbus immediately convinced Brasher of his own inner need: "I looked at Commissioner Brengle's face, and I couldn't argue with it. There was something in that face that said, 'He knows God in a way you don't. He's got more than you have.'"[35] "My heart was hungry, and my heart beat heavy, and I knew I was on the threshold of danger. And I felt if I didn't get something stronger than I had the devil would get me. I'm so glad that at last my heart outran my head."[36]

Brasher believed that his intellect had thrown up barriers to the Spirit's witness in his heart. He was persuaded that Brengle knew God in a way he did not—at the point of feelings:

My opinions got in the way. I had fixed a doctrinal system. My struggle was giving up my opinions—a system I had built for myself of theological thought.[37]

I knew [holiness] was what God required, but I said, "I would no more touch holiness than the apple of God's eye."[38]

I wasn't against it. I was scared with [*sic*] it.[39]

I saw a few people who advocated holiness, but who seemed unbalanced. Some of them amused me, some repelled me.[40]

Brasher's rescue came through the way to holiness elaborated by Phoebe Palmer, promoted by the holiness movement, and preached by Samuel Logan Brengle. It was a model for religious experience perfectly suited to his peculiar spiritual needs. He had been uncertain of his experience in the past because he had been led to expect an emotional crisis with the bestowal of divine grace. But Brasher's nature disposed him to apprehend revelation through his intellect or through more private, subtle feelings such as "peace" and "restfulness."[41] Brengle proclaimed the distinctive message of the holiness movement that the blessing of sanctification was dependent in no way upon emotions but rather upon a deliberate consecration of the will.[42] In effect, Brasher had followed this pattern at his conversion in 1886 when he had told the Lord that he was going with him, whether he had any feeling or not.[43]

Holiness theology declared that the blessing could be claimed by the seeker at the moment of full consecration, regardless of emotions, but the seeker thus sanctified also was given to expect a subsequent witness of the Spirit in his emotions. This "coming of the Spirit" or "sealing of one's faith" might occur close to the moment of consecration, yet in the experience of many it took place days or weeks afterward, often not in public worship but in private. Palmer and her spiritual progeny did not deny that feelings accompanied the second work; rather they insisted that effective consecration through "naked faith" did not depend upon emotions: "Faith is taking God at his word, relying unwaveringly upon his truth. The nature of the truth believed . . . will necessarily produce corresponding feeling." Palmer believed that in her early seeking, she mistakenly "had been much more solicitous about feeling than faith—requiring feeling, the fruit of faith, previous to having exercised faith."[44]

Following Palmer's way, holiness preachers often warned seekers not to expect ecstasy at the moment of consecration. Such desires could even prevent the blessing. W. B. Godbey, seeming to controvert the southern evangelical penchant for felt experiences of grace, cautioned: "If you are concerned about feelings, of course you can't get sanctified till you put the desire for feeling on God's altar to stay there forever. If God would let you go by feeling, you would plunge headlong into fanaticism and lose your soul. For this reason, perhaps, God in mercy will withhold the feeling you desire till he can learn you to stand by faith."[45] Leonidas Rosser, an early champion of holiness in Virginia Methodism, also spoke encouraging words to those troubled by a lack of feeling: "Indeed, ordinarily, when the blessing is received, it is accompanied by no ecstatic joy. . . . It should be observed here also, that the witness of the Spirit unto sanctification is sometimes delayed after the blessing is imparted; and the only advice we can give in this case, is continue to hold up the faith to the promises that especially refer to the blessing of sanctification, till the witness is bestowed."[46] The holiness emphasis on the role of the will, the certainty of the blessing in response to "naked faith," and the promise of a later witness of the Spirit to one's emotions (often in a private setting) answered the needs of Brasher and other evangelicals who were imbued with an ideal of emotional experiences of assurance, but who were by nature more receptive intellectually to revelation, more reflective than demonstrative in the presence of the holy.[47]

Brasher made his consecration on the afternoon of 19 April 1900 at the "penitent form" (the mourners' bench) in the Birmingham Salvation Army Hall: "When I came to see that this was God's requirement, and it was my absolute duty to meet it, with all my earnestness of soul, I met it."[48] He recalled, "I prayed a while until a strange silence seemed to come into me. I got up and sat down on the altar. Commissioner Brengle came 'round and said, 'What's he done for you, Brother?' I said, 'I don't feel so different, but I've given up all and trust in him.' 'Do you take him for your sanctifier?' And I said, 'Yes.'"[49] Later came the witness of the Spirit: "I had a call to the funeral of a friend in Chattanooga, and took along with me A. M. Hills' great book, *Holiness and Power.* Somewhere between Birmingham and Chattanooga the Spirit came gently, quietly, assurably [*sic*], and with such fullness of peace I had never experienced before, and what sweetness and rest!"[50] Sanctification thus satisfied Brasher's longing for certainty, for an abiding sense of God's grace in his heart. As the days passed after the blessing, he became more fully aware of its enduring meaning in his life: "I wondered that I could be so peaceful and restful so long after the experience. I said, 'Now, Lord, how long does this last?' And he seemed to say, 'I've come to stay.'"[51]

A Familiar Doctrine

Brasher's sanctification in 1900 offered him "a new world," but the holiness message that mediated his experience could not have been more familiar. In fact, Wesley's doctrine of Christian perfection and

John and Minnie Brasher and their
children, Birmingham, 1900, the year of
their sanctification. Brasher Papers.

Commissioner Samuel Logan Brengle
(1860–1936) of the Salvation Army,
under whose preaching in Birmingham
Brasher was sanctified. Brasher Papers.

especially its distinctive form proclaimed by the holiness movement had met Brasher previously at every turn. It touched him in childhood, claimed consideration in his first churches, pervaded all of the Methodist annual conferences he attended, and confronted him in his courses and professors at theological school.

Brasher learned to read by spelling out words in his father's copies of Phoebe Palmer's *Guide to Holiness*.[52] By his teens he had digested the contents of *Binney's Theological Compend*, standard fare of all Methodist preachers, which presented sanctification as a distinct second work of grace attainable in this life.[53] His father, not surprisingly, preached the doctrines "peculiar to the Methodists," as did at least one other of Brasher's favorite circuit riders, the aged James P. McGee, who proclaimed entire sanctification "without hesitation."[54] Another of Brasher's childhood heroes, Arad S. Lakin, also may have advocated holiness. In the 1850s before he came south as a missionary, Lakin reportedly had worked among the indigent in New York's Five Points Mission, founded and promoted through the efforts of Phoebe Palmer.[55] The first distinctively holiness preacher whom Brasher recalled hearing was a traveling woman evangelist who preached in nearby churches and visited his home when he was a teenager.[56] The next was Bishop Isaac W. Joyce, who presided and preached at the Alabama Conference of the Methodist Episcopal Church in 1892, the year Brasher joined the conference as a preacher.[57]

By 1900, some Southern Methodists were referring to the minority northern Methodist Church in their midst as "the holiness church."[58] Earlier hopes of a rapprochement between the two Methodisms through the promotion of holiness had died as southern resentments solidified after Reconstruction. In 1879, the *Texas Christian Advocate* displayed Southern Methodism's increasing tendency to associate holiness with the North: "Nearly every one of the [holiness] people date their awakening to a certain sermon on . . . 'instantaneous sanctification,' preached by some visiting brother, and they profess often to have never heard the truth preached until this angel of peace flew down from the regions of snow to Texas's sunny land and preached the 'know-now-full-salvation.'"[59]

In the 1890s, as the Southern Methodist Church hardened against holiness sympathizers within its ranks, the struggling Methodist Episcopal Church in the South began proclaiming holiness with new vigor—more loudly, in fact, than the same Methodism in the North. This renewed advocacy of holiness in the southern conferences of the Methodist Episcopal Church was one way of coping with their minority position, a strategy that included—in some cases quite openly—a deliberate wooing of disaffected Southern Methodist holiness folk. In 1899, a former Southern Methodist pastor, J. W. Lively of Texas, made a plea to Southern Methodist holiness preachers on behalf of the Methodist Episcopal Church: "Come home, boys, to your Mother. Methodism is the Mother of Holiness. Come home and we will do as they used to do: give you a horse to ride, and a pair of old fashioned saddle bags, with a Bible on one side and a Methodist Hymnbook on the other; and put some money in your pockets, and send you out to preach holiness."[60] A small number of Southern Methodist preachers with holiness leanings did join the northern church. In a few years, however, most of them moved on again into the growing independent holiness sects.[61]

The Alabama Conference of the Methodist Episcopal Church, reorganized the year of the first National Holiness Camp Meeting and true to its northern ties, championed holiness from the beginning.[62] In 1871, the *Minutes* reported that Bishop Levi Scott urged "personal holiness and zeal as the requisites of success in the ministry." A Thanksgiving sermon delivered by Bishop Cyrus D. Foss in 1883 caused "tears of sanctified experience to flow"; while at the centennial celebration the following year, Bishop Walden stressed "the importance of personal experience of regeneration and sanctification."[63] In contrast, the *Minutes* of the Alabama conferences of the Southern Methodists maintained an uninterrupted silence on holiness from 1870 to 1900. Southern Methodism in Alabama may in fact have been a stronghold of antiholiness sentiment. The leading southern antagonist of the holiness movement, the Reverend J. M. Boland, held membership from 1855 to 1889 in the Alabama conferences, where he penned the popular anti-second-blessing polemic, *The Problem of Methodism.*[64]

During the first nine years of Brasher's attendance at the annual conferences, up to the year of his sanctification, every bishop who chaired the sessions either defended or, more often, actively promoted second-blessing holiness.[65] Throughout the 1890s, while the surrounding Southern Methodist Church was alienating its perfectionist partisans, these northern bishops bombarded Brasher and his colleagues with pleas for holiness. Beginning in 1892, when Bishop Joyce prayed that the ordinands be "made holy and perfected in love now," the campaign continued each year through 1900, when Bishop J. N. Fitzgerald expounded sanctification as a "birthright" and exhorted the preachers, "Claim your inheritance as a child of God."[66]

In 1883, bishops Joyce and Bowman brought the Ohio holiness evangelist Samuel Ashton Keen to lead the annual conference at Birmingham in daily morning and afternoon "Pentecostal services."[67] Bishops Ninde, Foss, and Goodsell preached on sanctification at the conferences of 1894, 1897, and 1898, respectively.[68] In 1899, Bishop Willard Mallalieu, devoted member of the National Holiness Association and author of *The Fullness of the Blessing of the Gospel of Christ,* urged holiness upon the preachers of the conference.[69] Candidates for membership in the conference during this period gained admission on condition of having read Arthur's *The Tongue of Fire,* the treatise on the baptism of the Holy Spirit that was added to the ministerial course of study by the general church in 1892.[70]

In spite of the bishop's perfectionist ardor, the end-of-the-century holiness campaign failed to attract many Southern Methodists to the Alabama Methodist Episcopal ranks. One notable catch, however, who soon had influence in Brasher's career, was the Reverend Benjamin W. Huckabee, a Southern Methodist pastor whom Bishop Mallalieu admitted to the Alabama Methodist Episcopal Conference in December 1899. Earlier that year, in the north Alabama town of Hartselle, Huckabee had opened a promising holiness tent meeting, but the local Southern Methodist presiding elder, with "ecclesiastical approval . . . visited from house to house and bade his people 'stay out of this fanaticism.'" The meeting failed, and an embittered Huckabee joined Mallalieu's conference. Undaunted, Huckabee returned to Hartselle with his new credentials and in 1900 organized the Hartselle Camp Meeting. At his invitation, at the initial session in August 1900, Brasher first preached to a holiness camp meeting.[71]

The holiness strategy of the 1890s in the Alabama Conference undoubtedly had a positive, although delayed, effect upon Brasher's attitude toward the second blessing. The episcopal emphasis on the doctrine at least left a legacy of support in the conference for Brasher's evangelistic work after his sanctification. Given his utter loyalty to the church of his fathers and to his conference, however, it is remarkable that Brasher consistently held out against—even vigorously opposed—the extraordinary official holiness emphases present in his first years of attendance. "For years," he said, "I was an opponent of the second work of grace. I don't suppose there was any more pronounced than I was."[72]

In 1893 in his first parish, Brasher received a copy of Boland's *The Problem of Methodism,* which convinced him of the error of viewing sanctification as a second distinct work. He crafted an effective anti-second-blessing sermon entitled "One Work," based on Boland's premise that sanctification also occurs at the moment of justification.[73] Three years later in his second appointment, Brasher attended a revival led by a strong Southern Methodist preacher and was "further mentally fortified" in his position against a second work.[74]

Brasher not only "cleaned up the patch" of holiness partisans through preaching "One Work" in his rural pulpits; in pointed statements he also boldly dissented from the bishops' program at conference sessions.[75] Echoing Boland, Brasher denounced the doctrine of a second work before the Conference Training Institute for pastors in 1894:

Regeneration is an act done in us by which we receive again the image of our God which we lost in the Fall, are washed and made clean in heart and pure in purpose—in other words, sanctified and made ready for the Master's use. For sanctification is nothing more than being made holy. And if God's spirit fails to make us holy in his first work, he might fail in his second or hundredth. It now remains after man has been made holy to go on to perfection, which is the development of Christian character, the christening of all the graces, and which is to be reached by being led by the Spirit and abiding in Christ. This implies a constant growth in grace.[76]

Brasher continued his address with an even sharper denunciation of the practices and institutions of the holiness movement—a passage strikingly similar to the Southern Methodist General Conference pronouncement of the same year:

But when we speak of holiness we do not mean this latter day fanaticism posing as the holiness movement, and inviting men out of the Church to get sanctified. We have no sympathy with such so-called holiness societies. Anything which cannot be had in the Church is not worth having. The Methodist Church has ever been, and I trust will always be, the living champion of the holiness movement throughout the earth! But God deliver us from this cranctimonious [sic], sacrilegious tendency on this question. There is no need of forming squads of men and women to go about over the country without authority from anyone, to call faithful members and ministers up to the mourners' bench to get saved. There is absolutely no apology for it. Anything which can not be accomplished through the regular working force of Methodism is not worth accomplishing. What we are seeking to do is to build up a solid, scriptural holiness of heart and character among all men. Every pastor needs to be his own evangelist, and the pastor who has not got religion enough about him to convince men of the beauty of holiness needs to be outlawed from the Methodist pulpit.[77]

At the 1897 session of conference, Brasher turned his verbal condemnation of traveling evangelists into action. A special committee called to consider authorizing a conference evangelist reported in favor of such an appointment. Brasher presented a minority report opposing the office and moved its adoption as a substitute for the majority report. Brasher's motion won, defeating the appeal for an official evangelist. It was a post he would seek for himself six years later.[78]

Not long after he had squelched the proposal for an evangelist, Brasher left for Chattanooga to attend the School of Theology at U. S. Grant University; as its name indicated, the institution was an agency of the northern church. Nonetheless, he had not escaped from holiness propaganda. The school at the time was acting in concert with the surrounding Methodist Episcopal conferences in boosting the second blessing. Envisioned by the northern church as early as 1872, the school was established in Chattanooga in 1883 as "one central university for the white membership of the Methodist Episcopal Church in the 'Central South.'" The school of theology served seven conferences, employing four northern professors and offering a curriculum similar to those of northern seminaries.[79] (See Appendix A for a list of books read at the school of theology and in the conference course of study.)

At the same time, a similar project for a central university was being promoted by the Southern Methodists, assisted by Cornelius Vanderbilt, in Middle Tennessee. Founded in 1872, Vanderbilt University sought its strength west of the mountains, where southern sentiments prevailed. U. S. Grant University was located in Tennessee's eastern uplands, friendly to the North. After 1884, when a Vanderbilt professor, Wilbur F. Tillett, criticized sanctification as taught by the holiness movement, Vanderbilt gained reputation as a center of anti-holiness thought.[80] Its rival theological school at U. S. Grant eagerly promoted the second blessing.

During the 1890s, the same Methodist Episcopal bishops who preached holiness to their southern conferences filled important offices at the Chattanooga school. Mallalieu and Goodsell served as trustees; Joyce held sway as chancellor. The Reverend George Everett Ackerman and the Reverend George T. Newcomb, both warm exponents of the second blessing, served consecutive terms as dean of the school of theology.[81] Brasher studied Hebrew with Newcomb, a graduate of Garrett Biblical Institute. Ackerman, Brasher's professor of systematic theology, was a graduate of McGill University, had been a classmate of Newcomb at Garrett, and wielded substantial influence in the Alabama Conference as its secretary. At Garrett, both men had studied under William Xavier Ninde, a future bishop and a strong advocate of holiness.[82]

Less than a year after Brasher's graduation, Ackerman published his views on holiness in a book entitled *Love Illumined,* widely advertised by the Methodist Episcopal press. He dedicated his work to Ninde. Newcomb wrote the introduction, which enjoined "all our ministers . . . to present this great central truth of Christianity . . . so earnestly as to mightily lift all their people to higher levels of Christian experience."[83] Ackerman upheld mainline Wesleyan holiness-movement teachings, defining sanctification as a second, "supernatural, instantaneous work of inward cleansing."[84] In 1899, during Brasher's final year at U. S. Grant, Robert G. Pike, a Canadian, assisted Ackerman in teaching systematic theology and delivered a series of lectures on sanctification. Brasher heard ten of his lectures, but after each he would "return to the study hall to attempt to refute it."[85] By chance or providence, Pike and Brasher were thrown together the following year in Birmingham—Pike as superintendent of a holiness mission, Brasher as pastor of Simpson Methodist Episcopal Church.

Immediate Influences

I lived in Birmingham for awhile, and . . . I had a lily in my front yard, and you know what Birmingham is—the soot of it. And they bloomed as spotlessly white, you'd think that they'd grown on a mountaintop drenched with dew. If God can put such a gloss on a flower as that, so nothing dark will adhere to it, he can put such a glory and a shine on you and such a gloss on your soul, that you can walk in the world of darkness and of sin, spotless.
—JOHN L. BRASHER, 7 AUGUST 1966

When, on a May afternoon in 1899, Brasher arrived with his family at Birmingham to take his first appointment after graduation, no one met them at the train station. He and his wife, Minnie, and the two children walked across town to the parsonage and discovered their new home "only partially furnished, with many disagreeable conditions."[86] They found that the church matched the condition of the parsonage, both financially and spiritually.[87] A "scattered, comparatively poor" flock of about eighty members—not the disinherited, but rural newcomers to the city—sustained a total budget of $670—$350 pledged for the pastor's salary. The church was deeply in debt. Sunday mornings saw an average attendance of forty souls—"a small, discouraged group," according to Brasher, "who had held out against great odds."[88] To the young seminary graduate, Simpson Church appeared "nearly dead, with no hope in it at all."[89]

Birmingham itself seemed "almost a ghost town." Business had not yet recovered from the depression of the early 1890s.[90] Compounding the immediate financial plight of the boom town were the underlying social inequalities and dislocation that accompanied its hectic industrialization. Carl Carmer, in *Stars Fell on Alabama,* personified the city: "With an arrogant gesture she builds her most luxurious homes on a mountain of ore yet unmined. . . . She has no traditions. She is the New South. On one side of her rises a mountain of iron. On another a mountain of coal. She lies in the valley between, breathing flame."[91] Incorporated only in 1871, the city by 1900 had attracted a diverse population of roughly 40,000. The very rich, who could sail to Europe for the opera season, lived on "the highlands" overlooking the city; the miners lived in outlying makeshift camps with such names as Beer Mash, Hole-in-the-Wall, and Scratch Ankle.[92] A startling diversity of race, culture, and religion had evolved by 1900. Blacks, rural-born whites, and immigrants—especially southern Europeans—worked the mines and carried on business in town. Sizable Episcopal, Lutheran, Catholic, Greek Orthodox, and Jewish congregations challenged the familiar southern hegemony of Baptists and Methodists.[93]

The rapidly increasing population of the city constantly threatened effective law enforcement. As early as 1885, the *Weekly Iron Age* opined, "Everything that ever got loose that was in the least wild flocked to Birmingham." By the 1890s, the nickname "Bad Birmingham" had settled on the town. A remarkable abundance of saloons abetted the crime rate, which in 1900 was the highest per capita among cities of similar size anywhere in the nation.[94]

The Brashers had come from a quiet, middle-class neighborhood in Chattanooga and had previously served congregations in rural north Alabama county-seat towns. Challenged by the need for ministry in the city, they were at the same time affronted by conspicuous urban vices and unfamiliar mores.[95] Although a nearby ice factory delighted the children and provided frequent excuse for making ice cream, the city prison yard lay directly behind the parsonage. Leona, the oldest daughter, was punished when her mother discovered her on the back porch watching and imitating the uninhibited dancing of black women inmates during their exercise time.[96] Urban iniquity seemed inescapable: A man was murdered on the sidewalk in front of their house; a passerby gave the children a bag of candy that was mostly mothballs; vagrants peered into the windows at night.[97]

John and Minnie's effective "rescue work" among the poor and victimized of the town demonstrated that they felt called to redeem the city, yet in their hearts they did not feel at home. In later years when Brasher held revivals in large cities, he reported that at the end of the day he always thanked God "for deliverance and safety." The noisy shop whistles that punctuated the days in Birmingham were to him "brazen-throated monsters."[98] His image of the spotless lily unblemished by urban soot revealed his belief that one indeed needed a special dispensation of grace to live with integrity amidst the wickedness of the city. Writing home in 1913 of his experience in the St. Louis train station, Brasher's oldest son, Paul, epitomized the reaction of his family and many other transplanted rural evangelicals to the features of urban life: "I got awful lonely there in the great hurrying throngs surrounded by brick walls, hissing, panting engines, clattering feet, buzzing cars, ticket stampers falling, roar and shout and cramped-ness. I got to singing 'The Pearly White City' and was refreshed graciously."[99]

While adjusting to the stresses of urban life, Brasher and his struggling Methodist Episcopal flock also had to cope with the superior numbers, wealth, and political influence of the Southern Methodist Church. In spite of the obvious dominance of the latter, open rivalry prevailed between the two churches. "The pressure," Brasher recalled, "not to say the prejudice, of the Southern Methodist Church was hard to bear. Simpson Methodist Episcopal Church was [originally] called 'First Methodist Church,' but the Southern Church later built a large church and called it 'First Methodist Church.' So the M. E. Church changed its name to honor the great Bishop Matthew Simpson."[100] To Brasher's consternation, the *Birmingham News* persistently referred to his church under the heading of "Northern Methodist." Adding insult to injury, most Methodist newcomers from the North shunned his small church and joined the most prominent Southern Methodist churches of the city.[101]

Amidst these unpropitious circumstances, John poured himself into the work of reviving Simpson Church but made little headway.[102] Discouraged, he began to wonder if the lack of visible fruits of his ministry might be due to a spiritual inadequacy of his own. Daily responsibilities of the pastorate turned into heavy burdens. In his uncertainty, he began to compare his personal religious experience with that of others. One such person was his former theology instructor, Robert G. Pike, who had recently moved to Birmingham to superintend a new downtown holiness mission. "Sometimes," Brasher confessed, "I would say to my wife, 'I am as good as Pike.' She would say, 'I don't believe you are, dear. He reminds me more of what Wesley would be like than you do.'"[103]

In the 8 March 1900 issue of the *Methodist Advocate-Journal,* Brasher read an address by Bishop Charles H. Fowler entitled "The Seal of the Covenant," which, had it been written explicitly to him, could not have spoken more precisely to his situation and self-doubts.[104] It was a jeremiad issued in response to the previous year's net loss of twenty-one thousand members from Methodist Episcopal national ranks. Presenting a ringing appeal for a week of fasting and prayer, Fowler called for a renewal and deepening of the spiritual life of all Methodists. The decrease in membership along with other ecclesiastical ills Fowler traced specifically to the neglect of personal assurance of salvation, to an absence of the witness of the Spirit—the "seal of the covenant" between the penitent and God:

> Methodism was called into being to teach and illustrate the seal of the covenant, the witness of the Spirit, and that to every state of grace: conviction, justification, regeneration, adoption, and sanctification. Methodism began in experience. There are now, unhappily, many Methodists who lack present knowledge of New Testament Salvation. They have slipped a cog in their experience, and, like many old families, who have to date back to some buried ancestor to find their virtue and title to their nobility, have to date back to some dead experience to find their assurance and title to spiritual nobility. . . . In our case it is simply lack of spiritual power, of personal experience, lack of the witness of the Spirit, lack of the seal of the covenant, that makes the difficulties so prominent.[105]

After citing the demise of camp meetings, the denial of supernaturalism, and the inroads of higher criticism as symptoms of the "slipped cog in experience," Fowler, in a final climax, warned, "We must not be found dead on the highway, with a card pinned onto our bodies bearing the fingermarks of Satan, saying: 'This man quenched the fire on the altars of Wesley and Asbury.'"[106]

Fowler's appeal stirred Brasher to his depths. The speech was liberally salted with military imagery: "The lost ground is paved with the dead. . . . We are born of heroes . . . we must not fail to perpetuate their spirit, duplicate their scars, and match their victories."[107] Such images called forth in Brasher the potent memories and myths of his father's heroic defense of the Union and his sacrifices in reorganizing the church in hostile territory. "My sector of the church shall not retreat," Brasher vowed.[108] More important, the appeal touched his inner need and focused his desire for a deeper, more definite witness of the Spirit to empower his life. Brasher began to pray and fast, and thereby unknowingly set his course toward his sanctification.

While John was fasting and praying, his wife, Minnie, lay seriously ill. Believing herself near death, Minnie prayed for forgiveness and for "dying grace" to prepare for heaven. In the depth of her sickness, she experienced a spiritual blessing, which, in her words, brought a holy "calm" to her soul and "a sweet sense of cleanness and readiness." When she unexpectedly recovered, she claimed this experience as her sanctification and testified to it throughout her life. The blessing that Minnie received increased John's hunger for a similar witness of the Spirit.[109] (See Appendix B.)

These immediate influences—the disconcertments of urban life, a disheartened church, the prejudice of the Southern Methodists, the intensified desire for assurance, Fowler's appeal, and his wife's experience—hastened Brasher's spiritual crisis, which came to resolution in his sanctification. Urged by Robert G. Pike to seek the second blessing, convinced by the intelligent preaching and counsel of Samuel Logan Brengle, and "established in the doctrine" through the preaching of the Indiana evangelist C. W. Ruth, John entered "the Canaan of rest, peace, and power."[110] (See Appendix B.)

"The Importance and Results of That Crisis"

A few weeks after his sanctification, Brasher sent news of his "spiritual transfiguration" to the *Methodist Advocate-Journal,* exclaiming that his "whole being" was "on fire for God."[111] His ministry, especially his pastoral visitation, took on new zest: "Before, it had been a task that had to be done," he confessed, "but after I got this experience, it was a joy to go see my folks. It wasn't a duty. It was a pleasure . . . to tell them of the great things the Lord could do for them."[112] Brasher had moved from the faith of a servant to the assured faith of a son. His testimony of the definite work of grace in his heart and the subsequent witness of the Spirit enabled him to speak with new authority about the supernatural. Shortly after his experience, Simpson Church held the most fruitful revival since its founding.[113]

Brasher's sanctification revivified and consummated the plain-folk evangelical supernaturalism of the community of his youth. In his early preaching and in theological school, he had departed from that tradition, accenting instead divine immanence and personal redemption as process.[114] As a result of his sanctification experience, however, Brasher reaffirmed his earlier ideal of a God who intervenes decisively at a particular moment, transforming the spiritually dead into life. His new testimony in every way fulfilled the ideal that in his youth he had sought with less clear success: "I thank God that in April, 1900, on the sixteenth day, in the afternoon about five o'clock, in Birmingham, Alabama, in the Salvation Army Hall . . . I consecrated my all to

Rescue workers, street preachers, and students at J. O. McClurkan's Pentecostal Mission and Bible School in the former Thomson Hotel, Birmingham, 1904. The Brashers lived there 1904–5. John (standing, tenth from left) taught Bible, and Minnie (seated, third from left) conducted street preaching. Brasher Papers.

God, and the Holy Ghost in answer to my faith took the blood of Jesus and applied it to my heart and by his mighty baptism sanctified me wholly, set me on fire for lost souls, and started me going for God, and I have never yet run down."[115]

For Brasher, identification with holiness meant a return to the "doctrines and experiences . . . which made our fathers' hearts flame."[116] His reappropriation of the familiar language and rituals of rural evangelicalism satisfied a need for certainty and stability amidst the ambiguities of urban culture and the liberal trends in theology of the larger Methodist Church. Loyalty to old patterns nevertheless did help Brasher and others like him to adapt successfully to the new challenges of urban life. John and Minnie's most effective ministries in Birmingham, including "rescue work," began after their sanctification.[117]

In October 1902, Brasher announced to his congregation that God was summoning him to the larger field of traveling evangelism.[118] It was, he asserted, a call "fully as clear to me as my call to preach." The vocation was confirmed by the fruits of his ministry since his sanctification.[119] In three years, the church had witnessed 200 souls converted, reclaimed, or sanctified, along with a heartening increase in attendance and payment of all debts.[120] Beyond the several "altar services" each week at Simpson, Brasher also had been assisting other pastors in revivals and preaching at several camp meetings.[121] Surprised by the results of his labors, he "studied carefully where the Lord seemed to pour out his Spirit in greatest power and where [he] received greatest help in preaching."[122] In the "busy and happy year" of 1902, Brasher saw about 300 people converted, reclaimed, or sanctified—50 in his church, the remainder "elsewhere."[123] The logic of his call to a wider evangelism lay in statistics: "Where I had spoken to tens, I now spoke to hundreds. Where a few souls a year were saved, hundreds were."[124]

With Bishop Fowler's plea for two million new converts still fresh in mind, Brasher decided that holiness evangelism could swell the ranks of his hard-pressed minority Methodist Episcopal Church in Alabama.[125] He perceived his vocation as much a call to rescue his church as a summons to save individual sinners:

> I have a desire that I shall be of most service to God and the church. . . . I have listened to a real Macedonian cry coming to me from all over Alabama . . . while my heart was breaking for the revival of the church. This Conference must have a revival or perish. The preachers need it as badly as anybody else, perhaps worse. The heart of this conference has never been stirred much either on ministerial support or missions. . . . We need an evangelist who is alive to all these questions and on whose heart a holy passion rests to see them prosper.[126]

The memory of his father, which had decisively influenced his call to preach, now compelled him to save the conference: "I cannot desert this field. If I had no religion, the blood of my brave, heroic father flows in my veins, and I cannot be untrue to the glorious past. What has come over us that we shrink from hardships which characterized [our fathers'] lives and were their crowning glory!"[127]

In choosing traveling evangelism, Brasher sought not only to revive traditional doctrines and the "grand old church."[128] He also imitated an earlier style of ministry. His romantic ideal of his new calling was that of the intrepid circuit rider with an urgent message to proclaim, not that of a settled minister with pastoral responsibilities. As an evangelist, Brasher identified with former itinerants on horseback, the memory of whom shaped his ministry and preaching. "I'm an old circuit rider," he declared.[129] But his "circuit," first viewed as the Alabama Conference, expanded until his holiness itinerary took him to 35 states and 650 camp meetings, and required 700,000 miles of travel by rail.[130]

Brasher's identification with holiness led to his adoption of premillennialism, a doctrine that supported his choice of traveling evangelism. Taught in seminary that the new wave of premillennialism sweeping the South was the "rankest heresy," Brasher at first espoused the orthodox Methodist postmillennial view of broad social progress culminating in the return of Christ. In 1896, he wrote: "Reforms wholesome and lasting are being effected and humanity is being lifted higher in the ways of civilization, science, art, literature, and religion. The great forward movements of today are but the car on which shall ride the Son of Man with his millennial escort."[131] Yet, in a radical turnabout after the second blessing, Brasher offered a pessimistic prognosis for the social order and predicted the "any moment" return of Christ to rescue his faithful in rapture from an ill-fated world: "Men and women with vision cry and weep for the lost and because of the woes that are to soon come upon us. . . . There is a hand upon the wall; it is writing the doom of the age. 'Let us be sober and watch unto prayer.' 'He cometh as a thief in the night.'"[132]

Although waiting for imminent apocalypse was new, premillennialism maintained the essence of plain-folk revivalism in its emphasis upon supernatural intervention and in its concern for individual salvation rather than broad social reform. Premillennialism, however, shifted (or expanded) the goal of holiness from fitness for heaven to preparedness to meet the Lord in the rapture. At the turn of the century, Brasher and other southern holiness partisans viewed the burgeoning southern holiness movement as part of the great worldwide revival prophesied for the End Time. The vigor of the movement itself was a sign that the end was near.[133] A sense of eleventh-hour urgency provided impetus and validation for the special work of evangelism.[134]

Bishop Fowler's jeremiad, Brasher's initial lack of success at Simpson Church, and the economic depression in Birmingham may have predisposed Brasher to a shift away from his vision of grand social progress. But immediately after his sanctification he was won to premillennialism through promotional literature and through association with premillennialist holiness evangelists. John and Minnie had acquired a copy of William E. Blackstone's (1841–1935) *Jesus Is Coming* (1878) well before their holiness experiences. The most widely read premillennialist book of the time, Blackstone's work was a compilation of biblical proof-texts allegedly showing how current events were the "signs of Christ's speedy coming."[135] The holiness evangelists C. W. Ruth (1865–1941) of Indiana and J. O. McClurkan (1861–1914) of Nashville were the personal instruments of Brasher's conversion to premillennialism.

Two weeks after his sanctification, Brasher invited Ruth to hold a combined ten-day revival with R. G. Pike's Pentecostal Mission and Simpson Church. An ardent premillennialist, Ruth entertained his audiences with the line that "he wasn't looking for the undertaker, he was looking for the Uppertaker."[136] Brasher later claimed to owe more to Ruth than to any other man in "the establishment of the doctrinal content" of his preaching.[137]

A closer friend was McClurkan, who in 1898 founded the Pentecostal Mission in Nashville. Brasher first met McClurkan in 1901, when he came to Birmingham to establish a branch mission based on the fruits of Brasher's and Pike's recent holiness revival.[138] McClurkan, who believed holiness was one of a cluster of latter-day truths, patterned his missions and premillennialist theology after A. B. Simpson's (1843–1919) New York Christian and Missionary Alliance. The same year that he met Brasher, McClurkan announced in his paper that the origin and purpose of his mission were explained in a small book, *The Eleventh-Hour Laborers* (1898) by Frederick Leonard Chapell (1836–1900), published by Simpson's press.

Chapell argued that the recent proliferation of holiness churches and missions signaled the end of the age.[139] By 1903, Brasher was serving as an agent for McClurkan's premillennialist paper, *Living Water.* McClurkan frequently invited Brasher to preach at his annual conventions, and Brasher preached at his funeral in 1914.[140] Years after McClurkan's death, Brasher acknowledged him as one of "a few great souls who have influenced me more than all the rest."[141] Within several years after his sanctification, Brasher also counted among his close associates W. B. Godbey, H. C. Morrison, Bud Robinson, and Charlie Tillman—all southern holiness evangelists looking for "Christ's speedy coming."[142]

Brasher justified his call to evangelism by citing the crying needs of the conference and his conviction that little time remained in which to harvest souls. However, the proof of his new calling was the homiletical conversion wrought by his sanctification. "My old sermons weren't worth a nickel," Brasher declared.[143] "They would not measure up to the requirements of my new experience."[144] "I had to start new as if I'd never been a preacher."[145] The second blessing precipitated a radical change in the style, content, and purpose of his preaching. "I began to speak in a new tongue," Brasher said.[146]

Grounded in the assurance of his sanctification, he now proclaimed the word with a new tone of authority that marked all of his subsequent preaching. In a sermon sixty years later, he noted the change: "It's been so long since I've preached what I THOUGHT was so, that I don't remember the day. I only preach now what I KNOW is so, and there is no apology nor any hesitation."[147] Authority carried with it a new sense of freedom. Prior to his experience, Brasher had "worried over" his sermons and lost sleep over those that did not measure up to his ideal.[148] Once he was sanctified, his new perspective allowed him to be more relaxed and philosophical. His first attempt at preaching after his sanctification lasted only fifteen minutes. The ideal was an hour or more. Brasher nevertheless went home happy, resting in the knowledge that he "had the blessing, and some day it would come all right."[149]

Beyond authority and freedom, the distinguishing mark of his new preaching was its peculiar power to call forth religious experience. Perceived as immediately directed by the Spirit, a sanctified preacher was considered an unobstructed "channel of [supernatural] power and blessing."[150] Brasher thus claimed "new pleasure in preaching and new and larger results." In his three years at Simpson after the blessing, he reported "not a week without souls converted or sanctified."[151] Before his sanctification, Brasher had preached with little or no emphasis upon religious experience; afterward, in virtually every sermon he urged the necessity of conversion and sanctification upon his hearers.[152]

Holiness preachers believed themselves the special instruments of the Spirit, but the message of redemption was conveyed by the language of men. Brasher's new preaching required a rhetoric through which the Spirit might touch the audience, a speech that elicited definite religious experience. Brasher had no better model than the familiar preaching of his father and the circuit riders of his youth—a rhetoric specifically fashioned to summon those dead in their sins to a decisive new birth. He thus harnessed the power of traditional rhetorical patterns to new ritual settings, institutions, and doctrinal emphases. In preaching style also, Brasher returned to an earlier norm. His "new tongue" was much in debt to an old one.

At Simpson Church, the additional weekly "altar services" that Brasher instituted immediately after his sanctification allowed him to perfect his new preaching. Three months into his new dispensation he wrote that the membership was "growing" and that the people "loved to stay two hours at a service."[153] He was now preaching effectively and for longer than fifteen minutes. Early in August 1900, Brasher accepted the invitation of his friend Benjamin Huckabee to preach at the opening session of the holiness camp recently organized by Huckabee at Hartselle, Alabama. On the last day of the camp, the results of Brasher's preaching confirmed him in his new style of rhetoric and called him to the work of evangelism:[154]

Workers and friends at Hartselle Camp Meeting, Hartselle, Alabama, 1904. Bud Robinson is shown standing, far right, with Brasher next to him. Minnie Brasher appears in the front row, kneeling, second from left. Brasher Papers.

The last Sunday morning was a time never to be forgotten and a climax of all before it. I was a bit sick. Brother Huckabee came to my tent at the west end of the tabernacle and said, "I will need some time to take an offering this morning." I said, "I am not feeling very well. I will make a little talk and you can take your collection." He said, "Brasher, the people are and will be here from all over the county. We want a sermon this morning." Well, I prayed and made what preparation I could, and took for a text Ephesians 5:25–27. I was not conscious of anything but simply [*sic*] speech. The Lord took full possession of every power of mind, body, and spirit. It was a Pentecost of power. The people on the rear seat were as much affected as at the front, and when I opened the altar it was filled and much over in one instantaneous rush. Prejudices of many were swept away, and all acknowledged it was the mighty power of God. One old hard church member said, "I could have sat on a dozen eggs and not broken one of them." It was God's absolute power on the work sealing it as his own.[155]

Brasher's experience of "full salvation" in April 1900 proved to be the central integrating event of his life, imparting personal wholeness and an unwavering sense of purpose to his ministry. Sanctification was both a new departure and a reappropriation of tradition. It sealed his faith with assurance and gave power to minister successfully amidst the needs of Birmingham. It resulted in his adoption of premillennialism and in his call to evangelism. At the same time, his experience led to his reidentification with the supernaturalism, individualism, doctrines, rituals, institutions, and preaching style of his plain-folk religious heritage. In the confidence of his new experience, Brasher set out upon a seventy-year itinerary proclaiming "the importance and results of that crisis."[156]

6

"Their Hands on My Head"

MODELS FOR PREACHING

I can feel the touch of their hands on my head when I was a wee one. And the thrill of those old, fine, dear preachers touches me now and then with great unction.
—JOHN L. BRASHER, 7 AUGUST 1966

Childhood Impressions

Brasher undoubtedly sharpened his preaching skills through homiletics courses at seminary, but in his holiness preaching he was most indebted to the preachers and orators of his youth. The early influence of plain-folk camp-meeting religion in upland Alabama permanently shaped both the content and style of his sermons, despite his marked literacy. Bruce Rosenberg, in his study of the tradition of southern chanted sermons, has investigated the stages through which an aspiring chanting preacher passed to proficiency of style and sufficiency of repertoire. He discovered that his group of self-taught preachers began training in early childhood—sitting in church learning the stories of the Bible, popular preaching themes, illustrations, and, unconsciously, the rhythms of song and speech. He could even trace specific phrases used by mature chanting preachers to sermons they had heard as children.[1]

Samuel Hill, in his book *Southern Churches in Crisis*—and from an entirely different perspective—noted with dismay a tendency of present-day, southern, seminary-educated preachers to revert to their early models. He lamented that the period of professional training did not always prove successful "in extirpating the young minister from popular religious patterns."[2] In his preaching, Brasher did not cast aside knowledge from seminary disciplines of church history, theology, and exegesis; he joined it to a traditional southern preaching style in a rich and effective synthesis. His holiness auditors appreciated his uncommon erudition, and, themselves products of popular or rural folk culture, they responded with glad hearts to the familiar traditional style.

Brasher's extensive written and oral accounts of the preachers of his youth make clear his debt to them. His reminiscences of the preaching of eleven circuit riders he heard as a child indicate his early close attention to both the content and rhetoric of their messages. Brasher specifically cites these itinerants as his models: "As soon as I was able to understand language, I have known and felt their influence."[3] As a child, he regarded A. S. Lakin, T. R. Parker, and his father as his "highest ideal of preachers."[4] His biographical sketch of the circuit rider J. L. Freeman concludes, "Farewell, my father in the gospel of Jesus Christ."[5]

Brasher was not alone among his peers—even those with more than average professional training—in paying respect to the lasting influence of circuit riders, bishops, and evangelists heard during childhood. The Southern Methodist bishop O. P. Fitzgerald vividly recalled the preaching styles of five "old-time revivalists" who during his youth "thrilled and awed" him by "the strange power that attended their preaching."[6] H. C. Morrison spoke of the bishops he heard as a lad, who preached sermons that "people remembered for twenty-five years" and to which he listened "with rapt attention and delight."[7] Beverly Carradine, in a book about his own preaching, devoted fifteen pages to the homiletical gifts and eccentricities of the preachers who "blessed his childhood and youth."[8] J. O. McClurkan's daughter attributed the effectiveness of her father's preaching to "those proven ways which his sponge-like mind had absorbed from his father."[9] Popular holiness evangelists, even bishops, attested to the influence of childhood models on their preaching.

Much of what Brasher absorbed from the preaching of the circuit riders was unconscious. In one account, Brasher recalled that he was "too young to grasp the content" of a particular itinerant's sermons, but he remembered that they held him "in their thrall with a power supernatural."[10] Nevertheless, Brasher's memoirs of preachers whom he heard as a child are remarkably detailed descriptions of their personalities and preaching.

Arad S. Lakin was one such memorable speaker. Lakin was a preacher to the Brasher family for a brief time when they resided at Andrews Institute, DeKalb County, Alabama, when John was four or five years old.[11] Brasher recalled that "only one year" of his childhood "was touched and thrilled by his association," yet his memories of Lakin are numerous and quite specific. Lakin was "about five feet ten inches in stature," "a rotund old gentleman," "weighing . . . about 180 or 190 pounds . . . smooth shaven, ruddy complexion, pleasant countenance." Brasher was captivated by Lakin's "wonderful voice," capable of "eloquent speech" and a "beautiful flow of rhetoric." Gems of his eloquence fixed themselves in Johnny's mind: "One night, I don't know what he was talking about, but this is a quotation from one of his flights: 'We'll dive into the hoary deep and drag up drowned honor by the locks, and pluck bright honor from the pale-faced moon.' . . . It was so striking an expression that I remembered it."[12] In old age, Brasher delighted in imitating the "tone and modulation" of Lakin's voice.

Lakin was gifted with a "round, full, baritone singing voice" and often sang several of his favorite hymns at preaching services and on visits to the Brasher home. Brasher recalled these hymns, including six stanzas of one of Lakin's religious ballads. One of these stanzas reads:

> On Jordan's banks Elijah stood,
> And with his mantle smote the flood,
> And cut the stream in two.
> He and Elisha, hand in hand,
> 'Twixt watery world and solid land,
> Like heroes traveled through.[13]

In other accounts of the preachers of his childhood, Brasher commonly recalled specific Scripture texts; humorous, high-sounding, or unusual quotations; and favorite anecdotes, themes, and doctrines of particular itinerants. He also remembered unique aspects of their style and delivery; remarkable effects of their preaching; and, almost always, the itinerants' physical attributes. These preachers were only some of Brasher's early models. There were other orators in postwar north Alabama.

Southern Folkways

The fondness of the nineteenth-century South for oratory of all kinds is legendary. "One of the most remarkable characteristics of the Southern people before the war," recalled Reuben Davis, a nineteenth-century Mississippi politician, "was their universal enjoyment of public speaking. . . . In consequence of this, the art of fluent speaking was largely cultivated, and a man could hope for little success in public life unless he possessed this faculty in some degree."[14] W. J. Cash, in *The Mind of the South,* stated that rhetoric "early became a passion—and not only a passion but a primary standard of judgment, the *sine qua non* of leadership."[15] In his book *The Oral Tradition in the South,* Waldo Braden argues that the penchant for eloquent oratory continued unabated after the war, when public speech became increasingly ornate, grandiloquent, and frequently employed the myths of the Old South.[16]

A cluster of southern institutions and folkways, according to Braden, nurtured this distinctive oral tradition: hearthside storytelling, flowery passages in school readers, commencement recitations, camp meetings and revivals, the "theater" of the civil courts, and electioneering speeches. So devoted were the people to these pastimes that, "like the Indian fighter, the hunter, and the military hero, the masters of the oral medium became folk heroes."[17]

Braden's list reads like a catalog of the pre-seminary influences upon Brasher's preaching. Brasher's upbringing in a family and community where storytellers were "heroes" endowed him with outstanding ability as a taleteller. Even so, some of his earliest rhetorical models came from the printed page. When he was eight, before he could read, Brasher asked his father to subscribe to *Golden Hours,* a "magazine for boys and girls" published by the Methodist Episcopal Church. It was the year of the American centennial, and the monthly issues were replete with patriotic poems and serialized stories about the exhibition at Philadelphia.[18]

That same year, at the nearby log meetinghouse school, Brasher learned to read in a "blueback spelling book" and began the recitation of passages from McGuffey's readers. Clement Eaton maintained that McGuffey's readers, with their poetry and ceremonial speeches, "inspired young boys to become orators."[19] What was memorized and recited, the student later imitated.[20] Brasher completed all six volumes of the readers and memorized many of their selections, for he and his classmates were required to recite eight times a day:[21] "They gave you a lesson and you had to get it [laughs]. And if you came up and didn't have it, they sent you back to your seat to get it, so that it saved them making grades. They didn't pass him 'til he got it. . . . It was about as awkward a thing as you could think of. Sometimes poor children would come up and try to recite at the table of the professor, and just bawl, and commence crying and bawl, scared to death."[22]

Little wonder that compulsory recitation filled students with trepidation, for the prose and poetry chosen by McGuffey set high standards for provincial scholars. The readers included stirring passages of speeches by Patrick Henry, Henry Lee, Jefferson, Webster, Calhoun, Charles Sumner, and Robert Y. Hayne. Excerpts from such diverse writers as Shakespeare, Franklin, Dickens, Parson Weems, Hawthorne, and Irving were interspersed with the poetry of Milton, Gray, Byron, Poe, Tennyson, and Longfellow. Not to be overlooked were sermon nuggets of Timothy Dwight, Lyman Beecher, and William Ellery Channing.[23] Clearly, in McGuffey's choice of material, eloquence was a primary criterion for acceptance. Like other compilers of similar readers, he "markedly preferred the polished, grand, and ornate style," excerpting for use the very passages "likely to be emotional and figurative."[24]

At the close of the school term, students crowned their work with an evening community "exhibition" at which they declaimed the perorations memorized from their textbooks. If visiting dignitaries were present, they also were invited to deliver addresses. It was on such an occasion that Arad S. Lakin plagiarized Shakespeare in a speech to the credulous crowd at Andrews Institute.[25]

Although Brasher recited his lessons for his teachers during the yearly three months of subscription-school, he was not content to leave his memorization at that. When school was out, he recalled, "I went home with my books and mastered them before I went back again, and started higher up . . . I would mind the cattle and then make speeches. I'd commit beautiful pieces of poetry or prose and then orate it [*sic*] while the cattle grazed."[26] By the time he reached his teens Brasher had read everything in his father's library, which contained about a hundred volumes, among them spiritual autobiographies, theological treatises, devotional works, and books of sermons.[27] Printed sources complemented the primary influence of oral traditions in Brasher's preaching.

Brasher's exposure to polished rhetoric in his reading may have made him a more critical listener to the long sermons of the Methodist and Cumberland Presbyterian preachers of his boyhood. Customarily there was preaching twice on Sunday and often at midweek prayer meeting. The intensive preaching schedule of the summertime "protracted meetings" was similar to that of the camp meetings that Brasher also attended with his father. Besides a substantial company of itinerants at Clear Creek meetinghouse who "heard from heaven before they went into the pulpit," Brasher knew (and probably heard preach) seventeen of the charter members of the reorganized Alabama Conference, only one of whom was not southern born.[28] In oral and written accounts, Brasher presented as models and commented explicitly on the preaching of ten of these charter members and one Methodist Episcopal, South, minister. Of these eleven, all but two were middle-aged or older when Brasher was a child. Their preaching skills had flowered in the antebellum South when "the art of fluent speaking was largely cultivated."[29]

Broad Street, Gadsden, Alabama, 1878, crowded perhaps for county court day. Scarborough Photo Shop, Gadsden.

Although he had no opportunity to visit the county seat of Gadsden, twelve miles away, until he was seventeen, Brasher's recollections of the bustling river town record that along with other outlying visitors, traders, and shoppers, he thereafter frequented the courts as a spectator.[30] Gadsden's bar in the 1880s was reportedly "one of the strongest and most distinguished in the state." Brasher stood in awe of the lawyers who "wore silk or stovepipe hats and were set apart from the common lot."[31] County court days were popular events. Rural folk planned their journeys to market so that they might hear the "wit, repartee, and antics" of the lawyers who "undoubtedly played sometimes as much to the spectators as to the judge and jury."[32] Brasher recalled with admiration that the Gadsden lawyers "were hard to handle," and he listened closely to their different styles: "Hurst and Standifer—common sense and touch; Whitlock—the judicial; Denson—the stormer, the bulldog; Dortch and Disque—dignity, transparence; Martin—the man of honest plea; Cunningham—the astute, the subtle; Dunlap—the quiet, painstaking; Goodline—the alert, the quick."[33]

In his first two church appointments—both in county-seat towns—Brasher attended court specifically to help his preaching. "At Wedowee and Edwardsville," he told a congregation, "I waited on the court, listened to the lawyers, learned the tricks of the business, and got great profit in how to plead your case."[34] He discovered the need for a tightly woven argument, as well as eloquence, to convict sinners when he heard Thomas Heflin, later a senator, make his first speech before the bar at Wedowee: "Handsome as a . . . Greek god, with beautiful rhetoric and fine voice, he seemed to have the case settled. An old lawyer, his opponent, got up and leisurely pulled the young lawyer's speech to pieces."[35]

Brasher also attended the impassioned speeches of the hustings. Frank Owsley claimed that "seldom has the suffrage of the common folk been so courted as in the late ante-bellum South."[36] Political debates, usually combined with eating, drinking, and other festivities, drew throngs of listeners. "No neighborhood was so remote," reported Hamilton W. Pierson, that the people "had not been honored by the visits of aspiring politicians." "The remarkable attention" of the crowds to the candidates and "the visible effects produced by their words" encouraged the speech makers to "draw out all their powers."[37] The same customs prevailed after the war. Brasher's account shows that as a youth he heard such speeches and enjoyed the accompanying amusements:

> Before election day they had "speakin's" at the various "beats," and the candidates put on their best attempts to charm the voters with their eloquence as they showed how they loved and desired to take care of the "peepul." The various candidates usually had a friend with a wagon loaded with lemonade ice cold from the spring—"made in the shade and stirred with a spade," as they proclaimed. And at intervals between the speeches a candidate would "set up a treat" to the crowd. "Here is your good lemonade by Mr. J. who will be your next sheriff or legislator." All the crowd would run to the wagon and drink it all up. Then after another speech, another would treat from another wagon and the same crowd would all run over to that wagon and drink THAT tank dry.[38]

In addition to the influence of these rituals and folkways Brasher found pattern for his preaching in the oral tradition of the pulpit princes of the Methodist Church—its bishops. In the nineteenth century, Methodist bishops were revered as preeminent exemplars in the pulpit. H. C. Morrison reported that "people would travel a long distance to hear a bishop preach, and it was common for preachers and laymen . . . to entertain themselves talking about the bishops, their fine qualities, their great sermons." After Bishop Marvin had expounded on "The Church the Bride of Christ" at a Kentucky conference, "for twenty-five years preachers and people talked about that sermon, the impressions that were made, the thrill of joy they received."[39]

Brasher was no less adulatory about the bishops of his early ministry: "Those old bishops came with a load, and their introductory remarks were equal to the finest [sermons] the bishops get off now in opening the conference."[40] The more lengthy and emotional the sermon, the more highly it was esteemed—almost relished. Sixty years afterward, Brasher vividly recalled hearing Bishop Joyce: He would "preach until the people would just lean toward him, and tears poured down his cheeks and off his chin, until the crowd was stirred to the depths. I've heard those great old preachers preach and found myself thinking, after about twenty or thirty minutes, 'Oh, I hope he won't quit in less than an hour and a half.'"[41] As late as 1920, a Tennessee layman, W. R. Murphy, wrote glowingly that Bishop Bristol "preached Methodist doctrine first to last" to the Holston Conference for one hour and thirty-five minutes. By the twenties, however, audience taste—or endurance—had changed. Murphy lamented, "I complimented his sermon to several of the official members, and all I could get out of them was that he is long-winded."[42] In contrast to the sentiments of Bristol's Tennessee audience, Brasher in 1962 regretted that his bishops no longer had "time to build those great sermons like they used to have."[43] Methodist bishops held such high rank among Brasher's preaching models that for many years he maintained a list of all bishops he had heard preach or make special addresses.

The platform power of other popular orators and evangelists who toured the South also marked Brasher. While in seminary at Chattanooga, he heard a large number of "notable men," of whom he "reckoned none more important" than Sam Jones and Thomas Harrison.[44] Jones, preaching at the city auditorium, "poured out holy wrath against sin and intemperance and the liquor business."[45] Harrison, a Methodist Episcopal holiness evangelist from New England, held forth in First Methodist Episcopal Church and carried on athletic pulpit antics that presaged those of Billy Sunday.[46] Also at Chattanooga, Brasher heard William Jennings Bryan deliver a righteous denunciation of Mark Hanna the year after Bryan was defeated by McKinley.[47] Brasher reserved highest praise for the oratory of General William Booth of the Salvation Army, whom Brasher heard in Birmingham: "I had the rare privilege of hearing General Booth in three great messages in one day. I have never gotten over it. He was the greatest master of sentences and words that marched and burned of any speaker I have ever heard."[48]

Preachers Remembered

The remainder of this chapter draws almost exclusively upon Brasher's memory of the preachers and preaching of his youth. Little attempt is made to document these recollections, because "facts" are less important here than what Brasher chose to remember. His selective, idealized descriptions reveal what his early plain-folk community valued and embody the norms that informed his own holiness preaching.

The person and message of the preacher were inseparable. Brasher's recollections match the tone of nineteenth-century biographies, which often viewed circuit riders as muscular champions willing to endure any hardship and ready to do physical as well as spiritual battle to advance the gospel.[49] In Brasher's repertoire, tales of "a hardier bunch" of progenitors served as a standard against which to compare the soft church and society of later years: "Those were days when men didn't think they had to ride around the block to get a spool of thread. Days when men were men and not Pygmies. Also days when men had convictions."[50] His tale of a sawing accident at nearby Shahan's mill displays Brasher's ideal of frontier fortitude:

> [They had] an old-fashioned, up and down saw. One of the men was running it one day and he fell across the log and the saw cut him, liked to have cut him in two, and the bowels dropped out. And they put a man on a horse and ran into Attalla, nearest doctor. And the doctor came in a hurry, and by that time the bowels had swollen a good deal. They washed it off, you know, hot water and soap, and he was having trouble getting them back in, they'd swollen so. And he's lying there watching them without any [anesthetic], says, "Take a knife and cut the hole bigger. Ain't that what you're here for, to get 'em in?" And he lived. Sewed him back up. Him awatchin' 'im! People were people then! My goodness, what these folks go to hospitals for now, they'd hardly have stopped working for.[51]

Preachers were no less hardy. Circuit riders "used their saddles for pillow" and sought only lost souls, not "a fine suit-case full of clothes and a parsonage with two bathrooms."[52] Brasher boasted that his father often walked twenty miles to a preaching appointment and home again the same day.[53]

Brasher's narratives dwell on itinerants' lack of shelter or willing hosts for overnight lodging, and on the jealousies and jesting of folk who believed that traveling preachers had it easy compared to their own toil. One of his tales nicely combines the two themes:

'Twas a very common occasion for folks to stop there in the road and say, "Hello, could we get to stay all night with you?" And Pa's answer generally was, "If you can put up with our fare, you're welcome." He knew how hard it was for him to get to stay all night places. Well, he and old Uncle Bob Battles, and old Uncle Jenkins, and some other old fella went to Clay County once, thinking of taking a colony of us down there and taking up some land. They went to see about it.

And old Uncle Bob was always teasing about preachers having "brown-faced coffee and hump-back biscuits and fried chicken." So they all went on horseback, and late in the evening they came to a stream down there that was out of banks, and nobody around there to stay with. "Brother Brasher," he said, "well, what in the world'll we do?" "Why, we'll go right up there in the piney woods and build us a fire and have some hump-back biscuits and brown-faced coffee and fried chicken" [laughs]. He was putting it back on him, you know.

So they went up there in the woods and made them a fire and didn't have ANY supper AT ALL, slept all night and by that time the stream had gone down 'til they could ford it next morning. He never teased him anymore about hump-back biscuits and fried chicken after he'd tested it out.[54]

The true sustenance of Brasher's childhood models was preaching the gospel. Accompanying perils and privations were incidental. Another story, which apparently circulated widely, summed up his ideal of the circuit riders' passionate commitment to their task:

Jimmie Axley of Tennessee was of the old variety. A land owner who loved the old saint gave him forty acres of land and built him a good log cabin on it. Old Jimmie kept it one year and brought the deed back to the man and said, "Brother B., there was one song I used to sing that I enjoyed very much. I can't sing it anymore, so I am giving you back your land. I thank you for your good intentions." "What song is it, Uncle Jimmie?" Uncle Jimmie began to sing, "No foot of land do I possess, No cottage in this wilderness. I seek a house not made with hands, Way over in the glory land." Mounting his horse, he rode away in search of the lost sheep in the wilderness.[55]

In some of Brasher's preacher tales, the focus shifts from approval of a circuit rider's unflinching resolve to preach to simple admiration for brawn. Brasher's repertoire contained stories of Methodist Episcopal preachers in Alabama who allegedly braved lynch mobs to meet their appointments. His account of Christopher Columbus Burson, a circuit rider who in appearance "resembled General Sherman," emphasized that he was always ready to fight: "Once ruffians passed his house and used insulting language. Without waiting to dress, he ran out of the door in his night clothes and chased them quite a distance, but they whipped up their horses and fled." On one occasion, Burson came to his circuit's yearly meeting with a black eye.[56] The same simple delight in sinew appears in one of Brasher's stories about his father: "A fellow said at the door of the church, 'I'm gonna whip you.' Pa said, 'No, you won't.' 'Why?' 'These brethren won't let you.' 'I'll get you out and whip you.' 'No, you won't.' 'Why?' 'I won't let you.'"[57]

Good looks were as valuable as grit. A preacher as well as a lawyer could be deemed "handsome as a Greek god." After describing the nineteenth-century Southern Methodist bishop George Foster Pierce, his biographer wrote that "men loved to look upon and listen to a man whom they knew to be as consistent as he was beautiful."[58] Brasher no less ashamedly cataloged the itinerants' beauties, paying particular attention to shape of head, facial features, and physique.[59] Bishop Isaac W. Joyce stood "five feet ten inches in height with a fine head above broad shoulders, smooth-shaven face, and hair which fell in curls about his ears."[60] Sam Jones, also the conventional five feet ten, was "well formed, graceful, and easy like a prince in his carriage," and had a "well-shaped head, large enough to properly crown his body."[61] The "old master preacher in eloquence" of Brasher's boyhood stood more than six feet tall and weighed over two hundred pounds. J. L. Freeman was "truly a magnificent specimen of manhood. . . . His tall, magnificent form, his dignified but not stiff carriage, his handsome face, capable of expressing any emotion, his tender deep blue eyes all conspired to make him a marked man in any presence. . . . His approach to the communion table was with such reverence and in such form that his very appearance was more impressive than the whole service performed by other gifted men."[62]

Although Brasher painted heroic portraits of his early preaching models, he also reported their foibles and eccentricities. The faithful have always known that the treasure of the gospel is carried in earthen vessels, and the peculiarities of some itinerants were legendary. The venerable James P. McGee was "never known to laugh" and was "buried by request in pure white linen." He believed in immortality for animals and "treated his horse as kindly as a human being, never allowing anyone but himself to either feed or water him."[63] "Harmless and devout" James E. McCain weighed 290 pounds and possessed a

notorious voice "of corresponding volume," which "in a church was almost deafening." He mercifully prefaced his pulpit shouting spells with
the ritual warning, "I am about to get blessed."[64] Old brother Lemuel
Bowers's voice was not as loud as McCain's, but his listeners dubbed
him "the old saw mill" because in his sermon delivery "he got going at
such speed."[65]

None of these quirks, however, marred the effectiveness of these
gospel messengers. It was the call of God, not flawed human traits, that
validated ministry. Brasher was fond of quoting his father's statement
that "the one thing that proved to him that a man was called to preach
was that he could preach."[66]

Brasher's ideal image of the preacher—heroic as it was—also
prized tenderheartedness. Sam Jones, when not "hurling bombshells"
from the pulpit, was "the 'great heart' to the needy or broken"; his final
act of mercy the night before he died was to give up his berth on a
Pullman to a sick man.[67] Brasher's father, who "was never scared in his
life," was "the fondest man of children; babies would go right to him."[68]
Brasher once expressed gratitude that the circuit riders had not passed
from the stage before he "caught a glimpse of the compassionate God
in their faces and felt His warmth in their handclasps."[69]

Preaching Remembered

Not everyone was a "master preacher." Brasher was quick to af-
firm that the word of God could be transmitted through poor homiletics and unlikely mouthpieces. Sam Jones loaned Brasher a favorite
maxim when he insisted, "If you fail to preach, you can give your testimony in spite of the devil."[70] Only an exceptional sermon could have
included all the homiletical ideals with which Brasher credited his early
models. Some preaching stressed the need for certain skills by their
absence. For example, old Lemuel Bowers, "had preeminently . . . the
spirit of exhortation."[71] Brasher said, "He couldn't preach. He fooled
you every time he came. He'd come and start his sermon and he'd lay
down a fine proposition, just as fine as any preacher to preach. But he'd
catch fire, out of the pulpit he'd come and mount the front bench and
exhort like the world was coming to an end, and sometimes fill the altar with mourners."[72]

In spite of Bowers's success, Brasher faulted him on failure to
follow through on his opening "proposition." Good preaching was logical. This primary ideal no doubt was underscored by the courtroom
style of the lawyers Brasher had heard. In contrast to Bowers, several
of the circuit riders did exemplify the ideal. Brasher reported that Levi

Aaron Clifton possessed a "strong, logical, rugged intellect, and his preaching was sound and logical and moved people by its direct process of thought rather than by any oratorical passion."[73] Brasher's father delighted in disputation and had "read books until it wouldn't do to debate with him." His passion for dialectic reportedly was greatest in the pulpit: "One of his favorite joys," Brasher recalled, "was to preach on water baptism for two hours, or two and a quarter, and clean up all the immersionists, until he dried every pond and put all the rivers dusty."[74]

Sound preaching was logical and always scriptural. In Brasher's recollections, he often identified itinerants by their favorite biblical texts for sermons. J. L. Freeman immortalized himself through "that great quartette of texts which he used to deal with the subject of the Resurrection." And who could ever forget his "great sermon on Jacob's ladder . . . and the rungs by which we climb to God?"[75] T. R. Parker's sermon on the text "My heart is fixed, O God, my heart is fixed!" was so famous that the verse was judged to be an epitome of his life and was carved on his tombstone.[76]

Logic and Scripture were joined in the preaching of doctrine, a third component of an ideal sermon. In late-nineteenth-century Alabama when Methodist itinerants battled not only for souls but also for converts amidst competing Baptists, Presbyterians, and Campbellites, clear doctrinal arguments often meant the difference between victory and defeat. A veteran of many such skirmishes, the aged circuit rider James P. McGee showed "more than ordinary preaching ability . . . to preach and maintain Methodist doctrines."[77] Brasher's father controverted the Calvinists in his exposition of "knotty texts" on predestination; and after he had "dried up the ponds" of the immersionists, he could taunt the Landmark Baptists with the question, "NOW where is your apostolic succession?"[78]

The higher purpose in preaching doctrine was to strengthen church members in their faith and to persuade seekers and skeptics into the fold of Christ. Effective doctrinal preaching was not merely didactic but could be soul stirring. The sermons of J. L. Freeman reportedly reached their "greatest ranges and heights" when he rang clear on the doctrines of the person of Christ, the Cross, the Atonement, and the Resurrection. Doctrine preached by Freeman took on the tone of intense drama.

The doctrines that Freeman and his colleagues preached "lived" because they were applied to the experiences of listeners. Doctrine not only explained the cosmic "plan of salvation" but also informed everyday life. Freeman, Brasher noted, "was rich as a practical preacher."

Practical preaching illuminated doctrine, relating it to experience through anecdote, graphic imagery, and occasional humor. A Confederate veteran, Freeman had been "profoundly impressed by particular battlefield incidents," which he recounted in his sermons with telling effect upon Reconstruction audiences. These anecdotes, Brasher remembered, "enabled him to open and walk into the hearts of men."[79] Many of his stories had been polished by frequent repetition. His listeners did not complain. Brasher recalled: "I've heard him tell some stories over and over, and I'd say to myself, 'Old fellow, I'll not cry this time. I'm determined I won't.' But before he was through, my face was all drawn up in a pucker. Couldn't escape him."[80]

Doctrine came alive when preaching employed graphic imagery to portray some great theme. Brasher cited T. R. Parker's sermons for their "profound imagery," but once again J. L. Freeman took the laurels for dramatic, pictorial gifts. "On one occasion," Brasher related, "I heard him preach on the Resurrection until it seemed I could see the ground tremble where the saints were getting up."[81]

Humor joined imagery and anecdote in relating doctrine to life. With sermons often two hours long, even the most "profound imagery" and poignant stories required periodic humor to refresh a congregation. The earthy humor of Sam Jones, "incisive and sometimes devastating," remains legendary in the South, while the pointed, "consecrated wit" of his fellow evangelist, Thomas Harrison, was cited by a listener as "one of the chief sources of his power."[82] Even the unexcitable itinerant Levi Clifton, whose logical preaching was devoid of any "oratorical passion," relied on humor in his sermons. True to character, he possessed "the power to make people laugh without manifesting the spirit of mirth himself."[83] J. L. Freeman allegedly could recite as many funny incidents as Peter Cartwright.[84]

The persuasive potential of all preaching, though, depended upon delivery. James McCain's "deafening" voice notwithstanding, some itinerants were providentially endowed with voices unusually able to enthrall their listeners. When Brasher attended his first camp meeting, his father's "trumpet voice"—still acclaimed in local folklore—so awakened the gathering audience that before he could begin his sermon, "the whole tabernacle became a mourner's bench."[85] J. L. Freeman's voice, "as flexible as the wind," was "perfectly adapted to his personality—rich, clear, full, and capable of rare modifications, easily expressive of every emotion."[86]

Striking physical features, freely expressed emotions, and sometimes cultivated gestures added to the power of natural vocal endowments. Sam Jones's eyes "were so very black and could flash with holy wrath," or would "sparkle as a smile played over his fine features."[87] Bishop Isaac W. Joyce would pause occasionally during his sermons to brush his brow and wipe away some tears.[88] When Joyce's colleague, Bishop Charles H. Fowler, became impassioned, he "would put his left foot forward, incline himself, and come down at the end of his sentence with his fist like a pile driver."[89]

An elusive quality of "presence" crowned ideal sermon delivery. For Brasher, this crucial dimension was the Spirit. This presence manifested itself in various ways. Sam Jones conveyed a sense of assurance: "Self-contained, always master of himself, thus he was master of others."[90] T. R. Parker emanated such "strength, dignity and mental poise" that even strangers were immediately impressed.[91] J. L. Freeman, even in his routine serving of the sacraments, could move his congregation to its depths. Brasher recalled, "I never have seen a man, bishop, or whoever, who could so impressively administer the holy communion. I remember some of the hymns he used to give out . . . and you'd cry when he'd just repeat one single line."[92] On another occasion, Brasher said of Freeman, "Many are yet living who remember how that a few words of introduction or the reading of a line or two of a hymn would often move the whole audience to tears."[93]

Equal in importance to delivery was choice of language. "Eloquence" was the essence of good preaching style. Brasher's paradigm of eloquence was Henry Bascom, the bishop of the Methodist Church, South, but many of the local circuit riders Brasher described came close to the ideal.[94]

Arad Lakin, who quoted Shakespeare, was "eloquent of speech" and had a "beautiful flow of rhetoric." Brasher's father was "eloquent in speech" even on "small occasions."[95] T. R. Parker, famous for his sermon "My Heart Is Fixed," was "eloquent in marked degree": "When he began to soar in his eloquence, he seemed to forget the audience was present, and taking a sort of a look slantingly upward, puckering up his fingers as if he were hold of a thread, he then began to climb, and climb, and climb, with a great marvelous climax."[96]

In his descriptions of preaching, Brasher never defined his use of the term "eloquence." But it was more than a convenient, catch-all word of approval. He referred to a particular style of rhetoric. Brasher's recollection of a preacher in the early 1920s partly reveals his definition of eloquence:

There are no great preachers today. Men used to try to BE preachers. Now most of our colleges . . . make light of anything like eloquence and oratory, so that lots of our people . . . can't preach a bit. They get up and talk a little like any businessman can talk. When I think of the great preachers I used to hear, and think of the scarcity of them now, almost the absence of them now, it makes my soul hungry. Some years ago when I lived in Iowa, one night I went down to a little Free Methodist Church in Oskaloosa and heard one of their old bishops. When I went out to the car I was laughing and rejoicing, and I said, "Mama, I thought they were all dead, but here's one of them." That great old preacher—his periods were as rounded, and his language as chosen, and his expression fitted his words. He was an orator. A great message in a little bit of a meeting-house. Now you've got a great big church with stained glass windows and a choir, and a little bit of a preacher.[97]

Eloquence denoted a carefully crafted style of oratory identified by floridity, use of imagery, dramatic rendition, and attention to cadence.

Studies of nineteenth-century Methodist preaching have depicted a universally "plain" style. Henry Bascom's eloquence, they argue, gained reluctant approval among Methodists and was an exception to the rhetoric of the more "common" circuit rider. In view of Brasher's memories of numerous circuit riders, however, these studies seem to have overlooked the popular oratorical tendencies of the South. The pervasive eloquent style in the South was not only the possession of lawyers, politicians, and bishops; it also belonged to a number of the "common" preachers.[98]

Brasher, however, carefully distinguished between sacred and profane eloquence. The candidates of the hustings may have "put on their best attempts to charm the voters with their eloquence," but the task of the circuit riders was of the Spirit. They preached "in deadly earnest about . . . redemption." Sacred oratory supposedly contained no "studied attempt at effect." It was a divine bestowment described as "native."[99] "Our most spiritual bishops," Brasher declared, "have been, as a rule, our most eloquent preachers."[100] Sacred eloquence was the natural outpouring of the preacher's inner spiritual life. Brasher insisted: "Indeed it is well nigh impossible to have the fire of a great experience, and the burden of a great truth, and the vision of a great Christ, and the faith of a great destiny, and the presence of a great Comforter, and not be eloquent according to our personality."[101]

Sacred eloquence therefore could never be acquired solely through learning or study. In fact, "native eloquence" was often spoiled by schools with conventionalized instruction that "brought students down to their one-by-two dimensions."[102] In defense of native elo-

The faculty of John H. Snead Seminary, Boaz, Alabama, 1908. President John L. and Minnie Brasher are seated, center. Brasher Papers.

quence, Brasher repeated Bishop Gilbert Haven's injunction: "If a lion's in a man, don't trim his mane. If the eagle's in a man, don't pluck his feathers."[103]

Although "the beauty of a divine rhetoric" could not be obtained through formal schooling, Brasher nevertheless respected whatever erudition the itinerants had been able to secure and believed that education could enhance a preacher's eloquence.[104] He proudly noted his own father's mastery of "grammar and language" and also that of the preachers T. R. Parker and John Potter.[105] Brasher commented admiringly on Bishop Daniel A. Goodsell's preaching: "For perfectly classical English, I have never heard his equal."[106]

The circuit rider's audience, however, expected sacred eloquence to be democratic both in the requirements of its message and in its appeal to individuals of widely varying social and educational levels. Although the folk of postwar north Alabama, according to Brasher, "would have shaken hands with the king and felt no inferiority complex," they remained in a nearly frontier condition with very little formal education.[107] Eloquence that was unrelated to their experience, unremittingly lofty, or esoteric won neither approval nor souls.

In the early ministry of J. L. Freeman, Judge Sanford took him under his wing and offered advice regarding style: "Do not preach to lawyers or professional men. Select the persons in your audience who are of the least intelligence, who are considered of sound mind, and make your message so simple that they comprehend your meaning. All others will be charmed by the simplicity of your preaching. Use short sentences whose meaning is direct and clear. When you are older, this method will enable you to use longer and more involved sentences with clarity of meaning."[108] Freeman did just that. He became noted for "thoroughly holding the attention of all classes from first to last of the delivery of his discourses."[109]

Brasher's early preacher-heroes supposedly "sought no oratorical effect"—an unspiritual concern—but they did always strive to be "immediately impressive," urging hearers to religious experience. When all was said and done, a sermon was judged by its effect.[110] Brasher's assertion that "it took eloquence to turn fighting, brawny chaps into shouting saints," romantic as it may seem, was anchored in vivid childhood memories. Civil War veterans who had withstood "the fierce fires of bloody battlefields . . . cried aloud for mercy" as they "fell under the preaching" of J. L. Freeman—"preaching like a mountain river, torrential and irresistible."[111] T. R. Parker's sermons—scriptural, profound in imagery, and eloquent—were also effective:

> I remember my dear old friend, Brother Parker, preaching over in the old log meeting house, "My heart is fixed, O God, my heart is fixed." And there was a big burly guy there that claimed to be an infidel, and when Parker opened the altar, he came tumbling down the altar line and didn't kneel, he just fell FLAT on his face. And his wife gave him some theology that ain't in Miley or any of the rest of them. She said, "Oh, William, give up everything. God wants whole hog or none" [laughs]. He understood it better than he would if some of us . . . had told him in theological terms. He knew God wanted that whole hog and he got him. And he made a good church member.[112]

The plain folk recognized sacred eloquence not only by its fruit of conversions but also sometimes by allegedly visible supernatural effects. When the itinerant preacher James McCain lifted his sonorous voice in prayer, he reportedly could change the weather. Legend reports that McCain was preaching outside when "a sudden summer rain cloud came in sight raining heavily. The people became restless. He shouted aloud, 'Stand still! It will not rain here while I preach.' Then he lifted his voice in prayer. The cloud parted as if it had been slit with scissors and passed by on either side without rain, and after passing united again and poured out its floods upon the ground."[113]

The unwelcome preaching of Methodist Episcopal itinerants in Reconstruction Alabama nevertheless sometimes succeeded in melting would-be attackers. T. R. Parker, threatened by a "gang" of the Ku Klux Klan, fearlessly preached to them "with power and eloquence," allegedly winning their "embraces and confessions of wrong."[114] Effective preaching sometimes settled interdenominational conflict. After a sermon delivered by Brasher's father, about thirty Baptist parents reportedly brought their children to be baptized by sprinkling. "He had convinced that many at one shot," Brasher boasted.[115]

In later years, Brasher continually lamented the decline of effective preaching in which eloquence issued in clear, bright conversions. After attending a "preaching crusade" in north Alabama in 1953, he typically commented, "If that was a crusade, it looked more like someone with a weed for arms and a sourwood whistle for a trumpet."[116] It was indeed a far cry from Brasher's description of Bishop Joyce's "mighty" 1892 Alabama Conference sermon, which "flamed and poured forth from his soul . . . until the whole audience was suffused with the presence and power of the Holy Spirit."[117] The quickening presence of the Spirit counted above all else. A sermon might be logical, scriptural, doctrinal, and practical, but only with the Spirit's power could preaching achieve its primary tasks: Under such preaching, "sinners saw their sins and saints saw their inheritance and rejoiced in the hope of the glory of God."[118]

Holiness camp meetings and revivals provided an appropriate stage for Brasher's traditional preaching style. His memories of the preachers and orators of his youth show ideals that were fixed in him well before he joined the holiness movement. These ideals were the origin of his holiness preaching and of the title "the great southern orator," by which he was known among the holiness people.[119]

7

Style with a View to Power

DISCIPLINED ELOQUENCE

> I heard Bob Jones, the celebrated piney woods Alabamian, last
> night in a tabernacle a block square. Small works compared to
> one of our heavy-draft holiness preachers.
> —JOHN L. BRASHER, 2 DECEMBER 1925

> Keep real holiness preachers and workers on your platforms.
> Nothing else can maintain your power and glory.
> —JOHN L. BRASHER, JUNE 1969

Claiming the Power of the Spirit

At the time Brasher entered the holiness movement, holiness folk
universally cited power as the distinguishing mark of their preaching.
Fifty years later, looking back at his own career, Brasher testified: "I
have found that . . . the only power for sustained zeal in soul-winning
and missions is the personal indwelling of the Holy Ghost, sanctifying
the heart and mind. The recovery of this power is the only hope for
the world's evangelization."[1] Combining Wesley's and John Fletcher's
differing emphases upon sanctification, the nineteenth-century Wesleyan holiness movement interpreted the second blessing in terms of
both purity and power. Wesley's concept of "love excluding sin" lay
behind the theme of purity, while Fletcher's additional identification
of sanctification with the experience of the apostles at Pentecost gave
rise to the emphasis on spiritual power.[2] Although Brasher's theology
struck a balance between the two themes, much of the holiness movement after the Civil War had become increasingly enamored with the
idea of power.[3]

Holiness adherents located the scriptural basis for this interpretation in the statement of Jesus that presaged the supernatural experience at Pentecost: "And, behold, I send the promise of the Father upon you: but tarry ye in the city of Jerusalem, until ye be endued with power from on high."[4] In 1876, Lovick Pierce, the senior Southern Methodist champion of holiness, proclaimed: "There is not an ounce of moral force in all the church beyond the few or the many in whom dwells this Holy Ghost power. There is no saving power in the church away from this baptismal presence of the Holy Ghost." Those who lacked this power Pierce called "dead-heads."[5] By the end of the century, the Methodist Episcopal evangelist George W. Wilson could declare: "Holiness is power. It utilizes ability, fertilizes the soul, and energizes the whole man. Holiness is God's power with man, and man's power with God. Without holiness we are weaker than a bruised reed. With it we are like an impregnable and well-garrisoned fort, which will stand unharmed the hottest siege; at the same time raining like a hailstorm red-hot balls from the magazine of the gospel on an armed world against Christ."[6]

Listeners often described Brasher's preaching and its results in terms of power. In 1917, Central Holiness University in Iowa reported: "The meeting under the leadership of Rev. J. L. Brasher of Alabama was most wonderful in numbers saved and demonstrations of divine power. The preaching was remarkable. The last night witnessed demonstrations of power very rarely seen among us; we cannot think at this time of but one unsaved student in our number of 200."[7] In his essay "The Ministry of the Holy Spirit in Evangelism," Brasher argued that the "baptism and indwelling of the Holy Ghost" was the "supreme equipment" necessary to every preacher for the task of evangelism: "Finney said, 'God will hold us responsible for every soul we did not save because we did not seek and obtain the baptism of the Holy Ghost.' We must have the Holy Spirit or fail of our task."[8] Most holiness folk perceived two classes of preachers—those not sanctified, whose efforts faltered for lack of the indwelling Spirit, and those with the baptism of the Holy Ghost, which enabled "heavy-draft" preaching, drawing in a large harvest of spiritual fruit.[9] "If all our Methodist preachers and members in North Alabama had this enduement of power of the Holy spirit," Brasher declared, "we could capture this whole North Alabama, give the devil the lockjaw, and hang crepe on the doorknobs of hell in a little while."[10]

Brasher typified most holiness preachers in remarking the unusual power, "with new and larger results," that attended his preaching after his sanctification.[11] This change, in part, was related to his abandoning the habit of preaching from a manuscript.[12] Holiness preaching, maintaining the traditional, though declining, Methodist practice of the spontaneously delivered word, was always extemporaneous. For most nineteenth-century evangelicals, extemporaneous or "spiritual" sermons with colloquial, animated utterance best evidenced the sincerity and inner religious experience of the preacher, and thus appealed to the hearts of the hearers.

Stories of camp-meeting audiences that quickly became disenchanted with the preacher who attempted to read his sermon abound in Methodist lore.[13] Such preaching, according to William Arthur, secured "a gain of elegance, at the cost of ease; of finish, at the cost of freedom; of precision, at that of power; and of literary pleasure, at that of religious impressiveness."[14] In essence, sermons that were read "insured utterance by natural means, instead of trusting to help from above."[15] One of Brasher's stories displays his similar disapproval of using a manuscript: "A preacher was preaching from his manuscript. There was a boy up in the gallery watching him. Finally the preacher slipped the last page over, and the boy knew it was the last one. The preacher said, 'Friends, I could just go on and on in this.' And the boy said, 'You couldn't either, you slipped the last piece of paper over.' Hurrah for the boy."[16]

In holiness meetings, the chief concern was that nothing hinder the freedom and spontaneity of the message directly inspired by the Spirit. A truly spiritual sermon was not determined or fettered by a previously composed manuscript. "The greatness of preaching the gospel," Brasher declared, "is in providing a circumstance on which may be precipitated the Holy Spirit."[17] At times, the very language of the sermon was directed by the Spirit. Brasher recalled: "Sometimes when you thought you failed in your preaching, you did your best preaching. I've had times when I've had to hunt my words and pick them down here [gestures downward]—good little stout words—and wondered why the Lord didn't turn me loose that morning. When I got through, some fellow came up and said, 'I thank you for that sermon. That's the best one you've ever preached. I understood every bit of it.' Now, if He had turned me loose two hundred words a minute, he couldn't have got it. But He hobbled me."[18] Even the Scripture text and the theme of the sermon were often suggested to the preacher by the Spirit. In a sermon on the rich young ruler, Brasher typically stated: "I'm sure the Lord gave me this text and gave me this message four or five weeks ago, as plain as anything in the world."[19]

Wary of confusing human messages and motives with those of the Spirit, Brasher continually reminded his auditors of the sovereignty of the Spirit: "The great power of the Holy Spirit is not something that you control; it isn't something that you direct. The Holy Spirit is not

someone to be used; it is someone to use you."[20] Holiness audiences
were considered uniquely qualified to determine the authentic presence of the Spirit both in the preacher and in his sermon. The Southern Methodist holiness evangelist Beverly Carradine maintained that
a sanctified audience could easily distinguish between the spiritual and
the merely human: "They can tell at once the difference between an
oration and a sermon, between the fluency of one and the liberty of
the other, between orthodoxy and spirituality, the throat-shout and the
soul-cry, rhetorical flowers and holy fire, the noise before and the noise
after Pentecost, the flutter of spread-eagleism and the hovering of the
Holy Dove."[21]

The holiness ideal of complete reliance on the Spirit for powerful utterance notwithstanding, substantial elements of the sermons of
Brasher and his colleagues were not truly spontaneous but carefully
crafted in advance. In reality, the distinction between the language of
humans and that of the Spirit was far less clear than Carradine claimed.
A chapter on preaching in William Arthur's *The Tongue of Fire,* a book
that hastened the American shift to Pentecostal interpretations of sanctification, illustrates the confusion. Arthur condemned as unspiritual
any sermon that depended not on immediate inspiration but upon
manuscript or memory: "In neither case are the thoughts and feelings
gushing straight from the mind and clothing themselves as they
come."[22] Yet on the same page, without any recognition of paradox,
Arthur advised that before delivery of a sermon, "in the study, attention to style ought to be with a view, not to beauty, but to power."[23]
Clearly, attention in the study to style had to do with a preparatory
choice of particular words, phrases, and images—what Arthur disparaged as "pre-composed" preaching.[24]

The blurring of spiritual and human agency in preaching becomes
evident in a consideration of Brasher's sermons. Desiring to be used
by the Spirit for the eternal benefit of his auditors, Brasher before
preaching always prayed for the leading of the Spirit, and he often referred to his sermons—even their language—as "given" to him. Yet
much of his preaching was also of his own skill and design. After his
sanctification, his new preaching purposely cultivated a traditional style
of rhetoric that proved powerful in evoking religious experience in its
hearers.[25] In Brasher's thought, just as "spiritual feeling" could and
should be "well-directed" by the human recipient, so also language inspired by the Spirit—"sacred eloquence" or "divine rhetoric"—could
be enhanced by a preacher's education or careful choice of words.[26]
Thus Paul Rees, a fellow holiness evangelist, could describe Brasher's
spiritual preaching as "disciplined eloquence," a product of spiritual
and human action.[27]

Some holiness folk believed that the language of holiness preaching issued directly from the Spirit. In any event, the carefully fashioned, often formulaic, rhetoric of holiness preaching mediated a sense of the Spirit's presence to the listeners, much the same as repetitive liturgical language, form, and symbol convey an awareness of the holy to worshippers in high-church traditions. In this sense, much holiness religious experience departed from what Samuel Hill describes as the norm of evangelical Protestantism—"a theology of unmediated encounter," in which "conviction of the Lord's reality, direction, and presence is self-confirming, unmediated," and *"without significant reliance on worship forms."*[28] In the camp meetings served by Brasher and others like him, a powerful, often sublime, stylized rhetoric mediated the *visio dei.*

Formulas and Themes

In 1970, Bruce Rosenberg published his ground-breaking book *The Art of the American Folk Preacher.* Although his research—both its subject and origins—at first appears to have unlikely connections to Brasher's preaching, Rosenberg's work illuminates some central aspects of Brasher's holiness rhetoric. Rosenberg studied the style of chanted sermons, a distinct, traditional form of spiritual preaching found among both southern blacks and whites.[29] Treating primarily the black tradition, he based his investigation on the earlier research of Milman Parry and Alfred B. Lord, Harvard scholars who had studied the oral epics of Serbo-Croatian "guslars," or epic singers.[30]

Parry and Lord had discovered that the epic singers of Serbo-Croatia composed their oral poems "by the judicious manipulation of metrically consistent phrases, some memorized and some spontaneously composed, which enabled them to spin out stories at great length."[31] Parry and Lord named these phrases "oral formulas" and defined them as "a group of words regularly employed under the same metrical conditions to express a given essential idea."[32] In his American research, Rosenberg discovered that southern preachers who chant their sermons compose them spontaneously using formulaic techniques similar to those employed by the guslars.[33] Alan Jabbour aided Rosenberg in his fieldwork and described his hearing of a typical chanted sermon, this one delivered by the Reverend W. T. Ratliff of Durham, North Carolina:

Rev. Ratliff begins his sermon in normal, though stately and carefully measured prose. As he gets into his subject, he gradually raises the intensity of his delivery (though with well-timed ups and downs). About one third of the way into his sermon the prose has verged into a very rhythmical delivery, punctuated into periods (more or less regular) by a sharp utterance which I suppose might be called a vehement grunt. Within the rhythmical framework, the rises and falls eventually build to a climax when he lapses into a sort of chant, still with the same punctuation, but with a recognizable tonic (tonal center). Some of the congregation (who respond *ad libitum* throughout) here lapse into humming along with him. After this climax he breaks off dramatically into normal prose, then builds back again, and finally tapers off into a subdued normal delivery at the end.[34]

Citing the practice of chanting as the critical component that determines the extensive use of formulaic language, Rosenberg divided all spiritual, or extemporaneous, preaching into two distinct categories—either chanted or prose sermons. In the former, the music of the chant creates the formulas when the preacher attempts to "fit his language into a metrically consistent pattern."[35] In these sermons, the majority of verses are formulaic, and extended passages appear with parallel syntax. In contrast, Rosenberg maintained that in the more common prose sermon where chanting is absent, "the length and metrical consistency of each uttered line is not regularized."[36] Prose, or "nonrhythmical," sermons, claimed Rosenberg, contain very few or no formulas; groups of formulas forming narratives are thus even more rare. Parallel syntax appears infrequently and the preacher's disinterest in rhythm results in irregular sentence meters.[37] In effect, all prose sermons, as described by Rosenberg, are like "conventional oratory or conversational speech."[38]

Recasting Lord's concept of "formula" to fit American folk preaching, Rosenberg redefined "formula" as "groups of words, which, when recited, are metrically and semantically consistent, related in form by the repetition and identical relative placement of at least half the words in the group." Loosely, "formula" has come to mean "a group of words approximately repeated."[39] Some formulas may be repeated in the same sermon, while others, known as "systemic formulas," are repeated at least once in other sermons or narratives.[40] The following transcriptions are three variants of a formula, in their semantic contexts, as used in several sermons by the Reverend J. Charles Jessup of Gulfport, Mississippi:

> They couldn't find ten holy dedicated
> separated consecrated people

That were walkin' before God and living a
holy life.

And it can only come
Through the medium of consecration and
dedication and separation
From the world.

It's gonna take a clean holy consecrated
sanctified dedicated separated life
Hidden away with Christ in God.[41]

Some formulas, Rosenberg discovered, are memorized, while most, as those above, are not strictly so but are recreated with variations to fit the meter.[42]

Individual formulas may stand alone but often appear with others in clusters to form a "theme," defined as "a sequence of formulas, nearly memorized, used to describe recurrent scenes, ideas, or actions within the sermon."[43] Jeff Titon, who studied the white tradition of chanted sermons in the preaching of the Reverend John Sherfey of Virginia, noted the following typical, recurrent, formulaic themes in Sherfey's sermons: the battle between God and the devil for souls, the wickedness of the world, the hypocrisy of certain types of preachers, appropriate Bible stories, stories of Sherfey's personal experience, pleas for the unsaved to convert, and the joys of the Christian life in this world and in heaven.[44] In chanted preaching, themes help give coherence to language and serve to hold the sermon together. They are, in Rosenberg's words, "the chassis upon which the vehicle is mounted."[45] Other connective narrative passages and exempla flesh out the sermons, but the rhythmical themes are clearly the most important components.

These formulaically consistent narratives or descriptions also serve as convenient memory aids for the preacher, their familiarity freeing the preacher to deliver them with special drama or pathos.[46] The rhythm of formula and theme, as much as dramatic delivery, stimulates the audience emotionally, moving hearers to religious ecstasy. Chanted formulas and themes possess an unusual ability to evoke religious experience through their combination of the emotional power of music and the rational power of words.[47]

Preachers who chant their sermons state that during chanted passages they often feel that the Spirit controls and fills them completely. The change from speaking to chanting is a sign of a "superior blessing" or a "special anointment."[48] "At such moments, some preachers say, the words come so fast that they have to pause to straighten them out in their minds."[49]

In tracing the uncertain American origins of this primarily southern genre of preaching, Rosenberg cited evidence of possible beginnings among the New England "New Light" Congregationalists of the First Great Awakening, many of whom became Separate Baptists. They were noted both for their "freely expressed passion in worship" and for the peculiar "musical tone" of their preaching. Rosenberg also drew parallels between the development of the chanted sermon and spirituals, both of which employ repetition and similar rhythms, and sometimes share texts.[50]

Indeed, a "musical tone" called the "holy whine" was a trademark of Separate ministers and a probable point of origin of the chanted sermon. A contemporary criticism of the preaching of James Davenport (1716–57), a New Englander, described his holy tones: "He preached in an unnatural singing tone, which mightily tended to raise or keep up the affections of weak and undiscerning people, and consequently, to heighten the confusion among the passionate of his hearers. Which odd and ungrateful tuning of the voice has become one of the characteristics of a Separate; that sect being almost universally distinguished by such a tone."[51] Rosenberg, however, showed no awareness of the direct and ubiquitous influence of the New England Separate Baptists in the South.

In 1755, Shubal Stearns (1706–71), a Separate Baptist minister from Connecticut, migrated with family and friends to Guilford County, North Carolina, and established a church at Sandy Creek. Stearns brought with him the Separates' uninhibited emotionalism in worship and their characteristic "singular tone of voice," both "musical and strong." Not long after Stearns's arrival, a contemporary historian, Morgan Edwards, observed that "all the Separate ministers [in the South] copy after [Stearns] in tones of voice . . . and some few exceed him."[52] Stearns's church quickly became the center of an astonishingly rapid Separate Baptist expansion. In the 1760s alone, at least 125 ministers trained under Stearns fanned out from the Sandy Creek Association to the farthest reaches of the known South.[53]

One would expect that the popular, geographically pervasive holy tones and rhythms of the Baptists had influence on the sermon styles of such competing evangelical sects as the Methodists, whose emotional preaching and worship forms rivaled those of the Baptists. E. B. Teague, in his reminiscences of religion in antebellum central Alabama, took special note of the striking tones and cadences of the generation of preachers who were Brasher's models: "The Baptists and Methodists in those days had their peculiar intonations in speaking and in prayer. The former had a singsong, a good deal like, though less artistic, the intoning among the Catholics and high-church Episcopalians;

the latter an original unctiousness [*sic*] of accent, not to be described, however, well-remembered. Some leading men among them had given the key note and the whole pack took up the cry and echoed it throughout the hills."⁵⁴

This chapter will show that aspects of the rhetorical style described by Rosenberg in terms of rhythm, formula, and theme were adopted and persisted in preaching traditions beyond that of the chanted sermon. There are significant exceptions to the strict dichotomy that Rosenberg drew between the styles of chanted and prose sermons. The use of formula and theme is not always dependent upon chanting; such traditional forms of sermon composition do appear, even thrive, in the absence of chanting. An examination of Brasher's preaching shows that his spiritual sermons represented a transitional style between the chanted and prose sermons studied by Rosenberg. Although not chanted, Brasher's sermons made extensive use of formula, theme, rhythm, and parallel syntax—all with relationships and rhetorical functions similar to those noted by Rosenberg in chanted preaching. The preaching style of Brasher and his colleagues—a rhetoric informed by tradition and incorporating rhythm and formulaic language—flowered in the distinctive constituency of holiness camp meetings and the emphases of holiness theology. This sermon style, in turn, was powerful both in evoking and in shaping holiness religious experience.

A Rhetoric for Holiness Folk

Any preacher worth his salt knows that the style and content of a sermon must take into account the makeup of the audience. From his experience, Brasher observed that he had ministered more to the saved and sanctified than to "beginners," that he preached most "freely" to holiness camp-meeting audiences, and that for him nothing equaled "the gladsome swing of a full-salvation service."⁵⁵ The camp meetings that Brasher served were holiness meetings—attended primarily by the sanctified or the regenerate who were seeking the second blessing. Well before Brasher's ministry, much of holiness revivalism had become specialized in its concentration upon evangelizing second-generation holiness folk and calling the devout to perfection. After the Civil War, according to Charles Edwin Jones, holiness meetings became "the evangelism of the already convinced."⁵⁶ Preaching to one such camp meeting, Brasher metaphorically addressed his audience as an already spiritually fruitful orchard: "You hire two or three men to come every year for ten days to give you all the light they have on how you can grow more fruit on the same acreage."⁵⁷ In Brasher's eyes, Hollow Rock

Camp Meeting in Toronto, Ohio, was "from the gate to the workers' cottages on the hillside . . . a glad, happy, praying, and rejoicing throng. . . . A little heaven on the road to heaven."[58]

Christian perfectionists frankly defined themselves as a select or "separated" people.[59] A sense of special calling and higher status than that of the average Christian possessed holiness devotees. A letter to Brasher from the evangelist Robert G. Pike in 1920 expressed fears that a lack of spiritual power would render holiness folk "nothing more than the common run."[60] At about the same time, when some second-blessing adherents objected to what they judged the outlandish soul-saving tactics of the revivalist Billy Sunday, the holiness leader H. C. Morrison reportedly advised, "Let's not fight him. He is cutting logs above our mill."[61] Morrison's "mill" turned Sunday's rough-cut converts into finely planed perfectionists. The holiness evangelistic task was a specialized one.

This tendency to specialize did not escape criticism even from within holiness ranks. The evangelist Joseph Owen in 1919 warned that in recent holiness meetings that he had attended the preaching of regeneration was being neglected and that the meetings had little appeal to people not already committed to holiness doctrine.[62] Brasher, in answering the charge that holiness evangelists were "hobbyists," argued that in order for sanctification to be reached convincingly, all the attendant doctrines—the Fall, depravity, repentance, justification, regeneration, witness of the Spirit—must also be preached. Nevertheless, he admitted that holiness preachers did have a tendency toward "specialization."[63]

Although a large contingent in all holiness audiences claimed to be sanctified, there always remained some converted seekers after perfection and some unsaved. The same sharp distinctions of grace as in Brasher's childhood church persisted in the holiness meetings, only now dividing the congregation into three categories—sinners, saved, and sanctified. "A sinner comes to God with both hands uplifted and empty," Brasher preached. "He's under conviction. He's under sentence of death. He has nothing to offer God. He can't consecrate [seek sanctification] because he's dead in trespass and in sins, and nobody could consecrate a dead thing to God. When one is made alive by the new birth, and born of the Holy Spirit, then he has something that he can give to God, and that is consecration."[64] In his sermons, Brasher clarified and elaborated the different levels of grace through terse theological comparisons that reinforced the status of the sanctified and encouraged seekers on to holiness. The following couplets from a sermon preached at Hartselle Camp Meeting constitute a rhythmic, formulaic theme probably used many times by Brasher to illuminate the proper *ordo salutis* (steps in the way of personal salvation and the theology that undergirds the way):

> SINS were cleansed away when we were
> conVERted.
> SIN is cleansed away when we are SANCTified.
> In the FIRST place we got rid of GUILT.
> In the NEXT we got rid of depravity.
> In the FIRST we receive PARDON for what
> we've DONE.
> In the NEXT we receive CLEANsing from the
> NATURE we inHERited.
> In the FIRST we get GUILT cancelled and
> LIFE imPARted.
> In the NEXT we get carNALity cleansed away
> and a more ABUNDANT life.
> In the one we are BORN of the Spirit.
> In the other we are BAPtized with the
> Spirit.
> The one is SANCTification BEGUN.
> The other is sanctification comPLETed.
> The ONE is done judicially FOR us, by which
> we are pardoned for our PAST offenses.
> The other is done in a PRIESTLY fashion, by
> which we are C-L-E-A-N-S-E-D from an
> evil nature.[65]

In another sermon in a lighter, colloquial style, and with appropriate facial expressions, Brasher attributed characteristic appearances and behaviors to each level of grace: "When you turn your case over to Him, He will so shine inside of you that it will shine out through you until your face will have a different look from a sinner. A sinner looks down and up through his eyebrows. A converted man looks level, like that. A sanctified man lifts his head up, like that."[66]

Dwelling on distinctions of grace led to a popular conception that each increment of grace on the path to holiness was accompanied by new spiritual privileges, blessings not available at subordinate levels. Such a hierarchic picture of the added perquisites of each level was a favorite theme in the sermons of the celebrated Texas holiness folk preacher Bud Robinson, and represented (albeit humorously) an understanding of sanctification probably widespread among holiness folk. Brasher, who preached with Robinson at many camps, considered Rob-

The evangelist "Bud" Robinson (1860–1942) and "his fine bass," ca. 1930. Brasher Papers.

inson's exemplum too crudely drawn for use in his own preaching, but he delighted in reciting it on informal occasions:

Here's his "fatted calf": "'They shall go forth and grow up as calves of the stall'" [Malachi 4:2].

Brother, a long time ago I learned there were c-a-l-v-e-s, and then there were c-a-l-v-e-s. I had a little calf named "Raleigh," and a man lived in the settlement and he had a calf named "Lord Chesterfield." And I sold my calf for FIVE DOLLARS, and he sold his for FIVE T-H-O-U-S-A-N-D dollars—just four thousand nine hundred and ninety-five dollars more than MY calf. And then I learned there were c-a-l-v-e-s, and there were c-a-l-v-e-s. Then, there're three kind o' cattle. The l-a-n-e-runners that run along the lane. They got no pasture. Some of 'em with their tails chawed off by the dawg and one h-o-r-n knocked off. That's a SINner. He thinks he's a-livin' well when he's just a l-a-n-e-runner.

Then there's a crowd over in the pasture, of cattle, and they're livin' pretty w-e-l-l, look pretty fat, and they're havin' a pretty good time. That's a reGENerated man.

Then there's a calf in the s-t-a-l-l, a s-t-a-l-l–f-e-d calf, with HAY on his HORN, and MEAL on his NOSE, and a PINK RIBBON around the MIDDLE, and a WHITE BOY to lead 'im, and a colored boy to keep the FLIES off 'im. He's just so fat he shakes as he w-a-l-k-s. That's a sanctified man.[67]

The sanctified expected to receive at times a superabundance of grace, "hay on horns and meal on the nose," what Wesley described as joy upwelling in the heart from the indwelling Holy Spirit, what Brasher called "love having spells."[68] For Robinson, this ecstasy first occurred at his sanctification after the preaching of W. D. Godbey, when "God wasted grace enough on him to save the State of Texas."[69] It was primarily to these sanctified folk and seekers after perfection that Brasher and his coevangelists preached—an audience ever expectant of extraordinary bestowed power and blessings, that spiritual fruit which was both sign and sustenance of personal holiness.

A Rhetoric for the Way of Holiness

In a sermon explaining the event of Pentecost, preached in 1962, Brasher called for a revival of preaching that would bring "light, power, and grace" to the hearts of the people.[70] In so pleading, he named three dynamic features of the way of holiness as experienced and preached by him and his colleagues: Sanctification was first an act of divine grace that signified both a cleansing of the sinful nature and a "filling with," or "baptism with," the Holy Spirit. This cleansing and baptism then empowered the sanctified to live with holy integrity and joy amidst the ambiguities of life. Holiness folk appropriated anew this spiritual power whenever they witnessed God's "glory," also referred to in terms of "light," "vision," or "blessing."

Brasher and many of his contemporaries described holiness experience more often in terms of sight than of feeling. In the eyes of the sanctified, the world became transparent to the divine: "With a pure heart," Brasher proclaimed, "you are in a different world; the whole world is glorious. You are alive to all of God's creation. All of it is poetry to you."[71] Creation, for the pure in heart, could be transfigured into "a foretaste of heaven itself."[72] Such vision, or visions, properly belonged first to the sanctified, whom Lovick Pierce described as those "dead *indeed* to sin" [emphasis mine].[73] The sanctified could "see God," said Brasher, "because there isn't anything in [their] heart with a tendency away from Him."[74] Thus after the baptism with the Holy Ghost, one could expect "numerous fillings of the Holy Spirit" in which "the Holy Spirit would swing back the horizon of one's faith and give an extended vision."[75] Brasher significantly chose as the text for his hundredth-birthday sermon "Blessed are the pure in heart, for they shall see God."[76] Sublime perceptions of "glory" and "light," special "visions" and "blessings" served the sanctified as evidence of the Spirit-filled life, but proof of perfect love was not, according to Brasher, the important function of visions.[77]

The first purpose of visions experienced subsequent to sanctification was to grant a fuller perception of Jesus Christ. "When you were converted," Brasher explained, "you got introduced to Him, and when you were sanctified you became vitally and entirely His. But after sanctification there are deeper revelations of Christ [of which] your immature spiritual personality could not take hold."[78] Thus the first purpose of visions was to enhance spiritual growth—especially after sanctification.

Brasher ardently proclaimed the necessity of continuing spiritual progress after the moment of the second blessing. He warned the faithful not to "become petrified after they were sanctified," and he complained bitterly of "so-called holiness folks that one time got blessed at a camp meeting and have been sitting in the same drip nigh unto twenty-five years."[79] "When you are sanctified, mark the spot," he exhorted, "and then take the trail."[80] "To the old Methodist saints," Brasher argued, "sanctification was not a goal"; it was "something they got on the road. They were everlastingly on the stretch—out, up, on—hunting deeper revelations of Christ."[81] "Some think that when you get sanctified that's a terminal station. No, it's one of the stations on the way. The terminal is in heaven after you've been there several thousand millenniums, if there BE any terminal. And I doubt not that when you've been in heaven so long that you count the millenniums by the stars, you'll be growing in the glory, and knowledge, and wonder of God."[82]

In holiness meetings some visions stirred sinners to repentance and moved the converted to full salvation. But it was the already sanctified who most eagerly yearned for the special visions and blessings that would lift them on their ascent toward heaven and glorification. Like Bunyan's Christian, sanctified pilgrims grew increasingly perceptive of the heavenly vision, until they, too, inwardly dwelled in the Land of Beulah and looked upon the Celestial City: "Some of God's children have caught visions of the city's gates that swing open over streets of gold, to contemplate the beauties and glories of the habitation of God, and in the midst of life's strain and struggle they were ever engaged by the glimpse they had had of the things supernatural."[83]

"It takes more than regeneration to fit you for heaven," Brasher declared.[84] The clearer revelations discernible to the sanctified were the dynamic that prepared holiness folk for eternity; and to be made "fit for heaven" concurrently gave the sanctified power to prevail on earth. Preaching to his students at John Fletcher College, Brasher counseled, "You need to get blessed sometimes with visions big enough to swat the devil."[85] It was partly through such visions that the sanctified, "in the midst of life's strain and struggle," succeeded in what they called "keeping the blessing."[86]

Although the sanctified might receive "a blessing" in private, visions most often occurred under the influence of the "heavy-draft" preaching of holiness meetings—times, according to Brasher, for holiness folk to "get apart from the rest of the world and get a glimpse of Him."[87] Such preaching—distinguished by familiar, formulaic themes delivered in intensified tones—allowed "things supernatural" to be seen and felt. Under such preaching, as in Brasher's youth, "sinners saw their sins, and saints saw their inheritance."[88] It was a rhetoric that, in the words of Perry Miller, "filled the minds of its listeners with compelling images."[89] These sublime vistas led to holy ecstasy, sometimes accompanied by shouting, holy laughter, or holy dance.[90]

Full-salvation preachers conceived their sermons as instruments designed to awaken such experience. Encouraging a preacher who was having difficulty preparing sermons, Brasher reassured him: "The Lord will hand you a tool that will fit your hand."[91] Beverly Carradine cautioned holiness camp meetings against hiring unskilled artisans—"soft pulpit pedalers"—under whose preaching "the ecstasy is not so much put in as put on." With such preaching, Carradine warned, "there is no real vision of the people, and when there is no vision, the people are fallen and dead."[92] Continually begetting life in the sanctified, spiritual visions ensured that those "dead indeed to sin" would not "lose their experience" and slip back toward death in sin. At camp meeting, it was the "divine art" of the preacher to "keep the people blessed" and help "maintain the power and glory."[93] Brasher accordingly promised the sponsor of a forthcoming revival, "I will preach the truth firmly, lovingly, clearly, and do all I can to bless the people."[94]

That Brasher's holiness audiences were not so much looking for conversion as for the beatific vision is nowhere more obvious than in one of his reflections in later life about his own preaching: "It has been given me to pioneer this [doctrine of sanctification] in so many places where they hadn't heard it. And that knocked all my oratory out, nearly, because I had to go to teaching . . . from the stump up. And I therefore couldn't use my wings because the folks couldn't go with me."[95] The congregation indeed had to know the holiness experience in order to "go with" him, in order for the special rhetoric to have its intended effect. Brasher felt free to launch into the eloquence of formulaic themes primarily in the camp meeting, where they were desired and thus bore fruit. Writing home of his preaching the day before at a nonholiness midwestern revival, he wistfully reported, "I got on well yesterday, but, oh there is nothing like a full-fledged holiness camp."[96] An admirer who heard him at the Laymen's Holiness Association in Detroit probably was responding to Brasher's use of a more eloquent style: "That sermon . . . greatly blessed my soul. In fact, it seemed to me you did have 'the wings of the morning' in your imaginative faculty, and your words leaped like flames of fire. Halleluiah to the Lamb that takest away the sin of the world."[97]

The audience determined the degree of eloquence and imagery. Some holiness folk felt cheated in its absence. Brasher's daughter reported after she attended a meeting at John Fletcher College: "Dr. Owen preached Sunday afternoon and the Glendening tribe went off and had a prayer meeting against him. He preached an awfully deep sermon, and they told the Lord they didn't need anyone to explain the scripture. What they wanted was someone to preach hellfire and etc.!"[98] The most highly prized sermon imagery sparked visions that lingered beyond the confines of the meeting to inspire the heart amidst worldly stress. Such eloquence was treasured. A Kansas holiness layman lamented to Brasher that his church had a "fine educated preacher who can fairly paint the picture, but the paint is so thin it will rub off before you get home."[99]

Brasher's imagery lasted. "Oh, the power of your pulpit messages!" wrote one listener. "They live in my heart and bless me daily."[100] The images employed by Brasher touched and revealed the deepest sentiments and desires of their holiness auditors. In one of his favorite themes, for example, which portrayed sanctification as a "birthright" or "inheritance" consequent upon conversion, Brasher called forth a vision that "lived" by employing a version of the myth of the Old South:

> I've had people who WANTED this experience, and YET they'd say, "I've given up all, and seems like I've trusted all, but somehow I can't FEEL it" [laughs]. I can think of a fellow who had been WILLED a GREAT ESTATE. And he said, "They tell me I'm rich. Everybody says I'm rich. That my inheritance would make anybody rich. But I can't FEEL rich [laughs]. I'm not going to BELIEVE I'm rich 'til I FEEL rich." Can you imagine him talking like that? Oh, I could tell him how to FEEL rich.
>
> Take the WILL. You've been willed a certain estate. It has been PRObated. There have been no CONTESTants to the will. It's YOURS for POSSESSion. How are you going to feel rich?

Take that will and the deeds and go over on the land and tell
those fellows over there that you are the new owner [laughs].
That henceforth they'll deal with YOU in the matters of rental
and the like of that. Go down through the field and see those
great fields of WAVY GRAIN, and FLEECY COTTON, and
GREAT HAY MOUNDS, and over a pasture fence and find
great herd of Whiteface, and Durham, and Shorthorn, and, fat
as [?]. DROVE of them. Then go further and see those FINE
SPOTTED HOGS, and those big red ones over there, GRAZ-
ING in the alFALfa, squealing out their satisfaction. LOTS of
them. THOUSANDS of them. A little over in the pasture there,
and there is a WHOLE HERD of TENNESSEE-KENTUCKY
THOROUGHBRED HORSES. Eyes look as intelligent as a
human, and their nostrils extend and they PAW the ground, say,
"I'D LOVE TO RUN." Worth a THOUSAND DOLLARS a
hoof. Go on back to a GREAT FOREST of HARDWOOD that
would MAKE YOU RICH IF YOU DIDN'T HAVE ANY-
THING ELSE BUT THAT. Look at those great trees lifting
their lofty limbs there, s-w-a-y-i-n-g in the breeze.

Come back to that old colonial mansion, that wonderful old
manor house, S-O b-e-a-u-t-i-f-u-l as it stands out there among
the magnolias. And you enter in. Everything there is beautiful.
You're in the kitchen, and everything from ham to honey there
to eat. Go on in the drawing room, and on through the parlors,
and up into the stairways, and into the bedrooms full of antiques.
There's a rollotop [*sic*] desk and it's got your name on it. Take the
key and open it and roll back, and there's enough entered in the
First National that you couldn't live the interest up. How are you
FEELING now [laughs]? If you wouldn't FEEL RICH then you
are DEAD [laughs].

Well, that's a hint of what I mean when I say it's an INHER-
ITANCE. And when the fellow said, "I would like to HAVE it,
but I can't FEEL like I GOT it," well, I'll tell you how to FEEL
like it: "THIS IS THE WILL OF GOD, your sanctification."[101]

The romantic image of the Old South—fields of cotton, manor
house and magnolias, antiques and family pedigree, superabundant
wealth—flowered amidst postwar deprivations. A product, as all myths,
of "deep-seated group yearnings,"[102] the theme of the Old South as portrayed by Brasher still had a telling effect on early twentieth-century
southern holiness audiences, heirs of a tradition of social dissatisfac-
tion. Their plain-folk parents and grandparents, of marginal economic
and political power, aspired to the status and wealth of the planter.[103]

As farmers, artisans, and tradesmen, most holiness folk experienced life as toil, and the familiar myth of ease and the "big house" beckoned. Drawing upon memory and imagination, the image of the plantation offered Brasher's southern audiences momentary retreat to an idealized existence. Listeners "could forget present complexities and fantasize a simplistic vision, often calming, romantic, and dreamlike. Fantasy sometimes completely replaced reality."[104] Through this theme, Brasher called his audience to "go with him" in its imagination, but the myth ultimately elicited emotional response. Successful images, according to Joseph Campbell, are "ecstatically experienced in life-empowering visions."[105] Out of context and in its transcribed form, the plantation image may lack power and appear crass. However, such a theme, Braden correctly argues, "at the moment of utterance . . . [can be] highly moving, particularly before . . . [its intended] audiences conditioned by its frequent repetition."[106]

In the context of the sermon, moreover, Brasher invested the myth-theme with even greater power when he transposed it to the spiritual realm. He directed the emotions evoked by the vision of the plantation to "the inheritance in Christ—this cleansing of the heart, this purity of soul, this fullness of the Spirit, this gracious abundance of peace and joy" that is the will of God.[107] Already captivated by the graphically portrayed myth, the listeners then were caught up by a vision of the spiritual riches of the sanctified life and, implicitly, of the glories of heaven. For the common folk of southern holiness meetings, sanctification promised riches surpassing even those of the myth—present and eternal rewards that banished anxiety about limited worldly resources: "He will give you an atmosphere of heaven right down here while you walk the soil of earth. Make you feel that you're rich. You are an HEIR to his crown and throne . . . to a destiny that will grow brighter and greater as you grow in the glory of God."[108] By means of the myth, humble saints could see their lasting inheritance.

Descriptions of and testimonies from camp-meeting worshippers best prove the centrality of spiritual visions in holiness meetings. Some evangelists claimed that while preaching to their congregations they could see the very souls of people looking back at them, and the preachers often saw ecstasy therein.[109] In fact, the distinguishing trait of the sanctified perhaps most frequently cited by turn-of-the-century evangelists was that of the "faraway look"—what Brasher sometimes called "the New Jerusalem light":[110] "The Holy Spirit pencils on the face of the sanctified a sweet faraway look. It looks beyond hills and vales to a city whose foundations are built of God, and there gathers in the face a reflection of . . . Glory."[111]

Letters from Brasher's listeners testify to "eyes opened only in spiritual vision"[112] during his preaching. After hearing him in 1907 at White Cross Camp Meeting near Oneonta, Alabama, Eloway Hurst wrote, "The sermon you preached Sunday was the *richest* I had heard for awhile. It seemed to me sometimes my poor little narrow contracted soul would just burst out of its fetters . . . and soar into the heaven-lies." A listener in Conneaut, Ohio, told Brasher that his eloquence brought her "face to face with God Himself."[113] A broadside advertising the camp meeting at Sharon Center, Ohio, announced: "Brasher's flights of oratory carry his hearers very near the gates of heaven."[114]

Auditors recorded their "life-empowering visions" in other places besides letters. The evangelist Raymond Browning was transfixed by Brasher's graphic theme of the crucified Christ, particularly by the statement "The blood of Christ reaches deeper than the stain has gone." Browning preserved the vision by composing the gospel hymn "Deeper Than the Stain Has Gone."[115]

Occasionally folk were so entranced by their visions that they failed to return with the preacher to the more practical part of the sermon. Sister Glock, whose husband was a wealthy German farmer in Oskaloosa, Iowa, sometimes lingered too long at the celestial gates and consequently disrupted the preaching. When she "got happy" she would shout "Gloreee!" and twirl her handkerchief. She often did this at inappropriate times during the sermon, "reveling in her own fancies."[116]

The power of familiar, eloquent themes seemed to increase with the size of the audience. During the Depression, D. W. Haskew, a Southern Methodist minister from Dothan, Alabama, reported on the sessions of Indian Springs Camp Meeting at Flovilla, Georgia. In 1933, when there were nearly a hundred ministers present, and congregations numbered above two thousand, he described the effects of Brasher's and H. C. Morrison's preaching:

> Wisdom fell in car-load lots in the epigrams of Dr. Brasher, and when he neared the close of his sermons he never failed to ring out in clear oratory that swept men to their feet, and filled them with uncontrollable joy. But the climax never came until Sunday morning when Dr. Morrison preached the horns off the altar and swept every star from his vision, when he pulled down the walls that surrounded the celestial city and let heaven flood his congregation. The silver-haired apostle flung heavenlike star-dust over his audience, and when he closed a thousand people leaped to their feet shouting, laughing, and rejoicing, while hundreds fell at the altar and sought for pardon and peace.[117]

Such displays of ecstasy attracted some folk whom Brasher disparagingly called "the purely sensualists, even in religion."[118] Holiness

White Cross Camp Meeting, Blount County, Alabama, 1905, with the tabernacle in the background. According to Eugene A. Maynor (interviewed in Oneonta, Alabama, August 1982), "The women who wore hats didn't shout. Most left their hats at home and shouted. Nearly every service ended in shouting." Brasher Papers.

Sister Glock, standing, center, sometimes shouted at the wrong times during preaching, "reveling in her own fancies." Many holiness women dressed in white for camp meeting to signify their readiness for the Second Coming in accordance with Daniel 12:10. Brasher Papers.

language suggested the presence of spiritual pleasure seekers. The same broadside that advertised Brasher's "flights of oratory" announced, "Many are looking forward to this spiritual treat." In his initial sermon at an Ohio camp meeting, Dr. Warren McIntyre reportedly "charmed" his hearers with the theme "Where will you spend eternity?" And in Nashville, J. O. McClurkan's daughter called the Annual Convention of the Pentecostal Mission "a big juicy slice of religious experience."[119]

Visions evoked by holiness rhetoric were relished by some auditors for immediate effect, but Brasher insisted that the purpose of such revelations was never simply "to give us something that we can talk to the folks about."[120] As a dynamic of growth after sanctification, visions rightly received resulted in lives changed and empowered, usually for the good of others: "Some men have [experienced] such a weight of glory that their body was too weak to carry it, but when they did get on their two feet they went straight for a task that was worthwhile." Brasher's theology of visions was neither escapist nor narcotic.[121]

The Sermon Style of John Lakin Brasher

Structure

A collection of sound recordings of thirty-one sermons, seventeen Bible studies, and one autobiographical narrative—all extemporaneously delivered by Brasher—enables the study of his spiritual preaching style. Nineteen of the sermons, all of the Bible studies, and the life story were delivered at holiness camp meetings. The remaining twelve sermons were preached in local churches. All of the sermons and Bible studies were recorded in Alabama; the autobiography was presented at Hollow Rock Camp Meeting, Toronto, Ohio. Delivered from his eighty-first through his one-hundred-first year, the messages belie Brasher's age. Even the twelve sermons and seven Bible studies recorded after he was ninety-five demonstrate remarkable vigor of delivery, cogency, and richness of content. A repertoire of familiar formulas and themes helped Brasher preach effectively at such an advanced age. This study of his preaching also draws upon his extemporaneous Bible studies and his autobiographical account because they contain much of the same narrative material he employed in his sermons.

In his later years, recordings show, Brasher preached sermons from thirty to sixty minutes in length. In his prime, it was not uncommon for him to preach one and a half hours.[122] He had, according to Gordon Michalson, "an excellent homiletical method, far more orderly than that of many of his contemporaries. He would have an interesting introduction, state a proposition with three or four headings, have the body of his sermon, and then a conclusion. He drew heavily on history and literature, and even philosophy, to make a reasoned case both for the need of the cleansed heart and the possibility of it. His conclusions were not the hyperemotional conclusions that many of his contemporaries had, but they were moving and convincing."[123]

Brasher's sermon structure usually followed the "text-context" pattern traditional in America since its use among seventeenth-century New England Puritans.[124] Beginning in ordinary narrative prose, he would cite a quotation from Scripture ("text") and then explain it ("context"). Early in the explanation, he would raise one or more doctrines from the text and proceed logically to explain and prove the doctrine, using various exempla to underscore his points.[125] Building upon this "reasoned case," he next applied the doctrines to the lives of his listeners, fixing their attention through his use of increasingly emotional exempla.

Formulaic themes, replete with rhetorical devices, rhythm, and dramatic delivery, might be introduced at any point after the first "opening of the text," but their concentrated display was reserved for the second half of the sermon, especially for the concluding "exhortation." Through these themes, Brasher won the final emotional as well as intellectual assent of his audience. His best sermons always moved from an initial logical argument to a "moving and convincing" conclusion.[126] Two of the brief sermon outlines that he used in the pulpit illustrate his method:

Text: Matt. 16: 24–26.

Theme: The Value of a Soul.
Introduction: Phrase, the *whole world.*
1. You have a soul.
2. That soul is valuable from,
   a. its cost
   b. its scarcity
   c. its ability to endure
   d. its ability to enjoy
3. You can save your soul: co-operation.
4. You can lose your soul.
5. What it is to lose one's soul: Judas, others.
6. Illustrations: a disembodied spirit, its surprise, horror, dying in darkness. What the soul would mean then. The pleasures of heaven, the horrors of hell. [127]

Text: Luke 13: 1–5.

Theme: Repentance.
1. Nature of it.

2. Necessity of it.
3. Fruit of it.
4. Extent of it.
5. Divine assistance necessary in order to it [*sic*].
6. Time for it.
Exhortation.[128]

The familiar, partially memorized themes that clustered toward the end of the sermons (the pleasures of heaven, the horrors of hell, the time for repentance) served as secure trellises from which Brasher's creative eloquence could branch. The themes also freed him to concentrate on intonation, gesture, and expression, and to speak more rapidly, thus creating a sublime effect. Brasher self-consciously reserved his most impassioned delivery for these passages, cautioning one beginning preacher against using "the same tonality, pressure, and vocal powers in relating an incident as are used in stressing a point of great importance."[129] When he described the sermons of a fellow holiness evangelist, Joseph H. Smith (1855–1946), Brasher summarized the movement and effect of his own: "In his preaching he was like a great ship coming into view—at first the mast, then the deck, then he came into port with full power ahead and a great cargo of heaven's merchandise."[130]

Although logical and organized in a broad sense, Brasher's style also could be called "natural" or "organic." Any extemporaneous sermon lasting an hour or more, often based on only one verse of Scripture, necessitates digressions. Exempla and themes used by Brasher might be essential to the progress of the sermon or merely "ornamental," drawn from a large stock of free-floating, optional themes. Rosenberg compares the preacher's use of essential and ornamental themes to a jazz musician's improvising (ornamental themes) on a standard score (essential themes).[131] Another interpretation likens the style of "natural" preaching to a tree from whose trunk random branches unexpectedly challenge and delight the imagination.[132] Such sermons never struck the listener as stuffy or severely logical.

Formulas

In order to understand fully the effect of formulas and themes in spiritual preaching, one must hear a live performance. The transcriptions that follow will attempt to reflect some of the oral qualities of the sermons. By observing the directions found at the front of the book, readers may approximate the original delivery (either silently or aloud) and thereby "hear" the narratives.

Most of Brasher's formulas appear in clusters creating narrative themes. Many such formulas can be observed in the subsequently cit-

The evangelist Joseph H. Smith (1855–1946) at a camp meeting, Romeo, Michigan, 12 August 1934. His sermons were "like a great ship coming into view." Brasher Papers.

ed examples of themes. Since Brasher uses a given theme only once per sermon, the component formulas also usually appear only once, and hence are "systemic," nonrecurrent within a single sermon. Some formulas, however, stand alone. Although most of these solitary formulas, unconnected to a longer theme, are also systemic, some do repeat within a sermon. These latter recurrent formulas Rosenberg categorized as "refrain" or "stimulant" formulas.[133]

Refrain formulas, usually short and memorized verbatim, do not "advance the narrative" of the sermon in any way; they may serve as a pausing place for the preacher to think, as a way to emphasize the immediately previous passage, or often in Brasher's sermons as a mark of transition between themes or sections. Stimulant, or "hortatory," formulas function variously to arouse a listless congregation, to encourage assent, or to elicit decision, action, or verbal response from the listeners. In contrast to the chanting preachers in Rosenberg's study, who in their entire repertoires employed at most four or five examples of stimulant or refrain formulas, Brasher drew upon a large stock of such formulas. Following are selected refrain and hortatory formulas from Brasher's repertoire, some of which occur several times within one sermon:

Refrain Formulas

Amen.
Hallelujah.

Thank God.
Praise the Lord.
Blessed be God.
God help us.
That's the Book.
The Lord help us.
Glory be to God.
Oh, it's wonderful.
Serious business, friends.
That's good, isn't it.
Well, I like that.
That's so. You know it's so.
Oh, I can only hint at it.
Well, I must hasten.
Well, amen. I guess that's enough.
I could go on, but I mustn't.
Thank the Lord. I'm enjoying this a little bit.

Stimulant Formulas

You know about that?
Ain't that worthwhile?
Have you got the blessing?
You know what I'm talking about?
You don't like that, do you?
Well, what have we done about it?
I'd shout if it wouldn't shock you.

Examples of two of Brasher's favorite solitary formulas that do not usually repeat within a single sermon appear below. Several versions of the formulas, each from a different sermon, are presented. Formula A treats the economy of sanctification. Formula B describes holiness folk.

Formula A

1. So the FATHER WILLS it
The SON BOUGHT it with his BLOOD
The Holy Spirit CONsummates it
When you meet the conDItions

2. His blood BOUGHT it
His Spirit WORKS it
His Father WILLS it.

3. Why should I when God
WILLS it
And his son DIED for it
And the Holy Ghost
CONsummates it.

4. The blood BOUGHT it
God WILLS it
The Spirit
LIVES to CONsummate it.

5. God WILLS it
His son has BOUGHT it for you
The Holy Spirit is right here
   ready to give it to you.

6. What the Father WILLS
What the blood of the son BOUGHT
Is in the hand of the Holy Spirit
To administer.

7. But he sent the Holy Spirit
And he's to do for us what
   the Father wills
And what the son bought
And there's no other person
   can do it.

8. God WILLS it
The blood BOUGHT it
But these don't do the work
He works it in you
He's the SANCTifier
The Holy Spirit.

9. That's HIS work
God WILLS it
Christ ProVIDed it
The Holy Spirit BRINGS it.[134]

Formula B

1. And they can GO FURTHER and
STAY LONGER and
SHINE BRIGHTER and

SHOUT LOUDER and
PAY MORE and
LIVE ON LESS
Than any crowd on earth.

2. They'll GO FURTHER and
SHINE BRIGHTER and
SHOUT LOUDER and
LIVE ON LESS
And GIVE MORE
Than any gang above ground.[135]

Brasher left evidence of his delight in and self-conscious crafting of formulas, especially those that he and his coevangelists called "epigrams," "nuggets," or "flashlights."[136] These clever, tersely expressed thoughts—actually formulas—were relished, even requested, by holiness audiences. In 1914, J. O. McClurkan wrote Brasher asking for "a good epigrammatic, philosophic, rich and juicy article" for his newspaper, *Living Water.* D. W. Haskew at Indian Springs Camp Meeting extolled the "wisdom which fell in car-load lots in the epigrams of Dr. Brasher." And when listeners lauded the "wonderful sayings" and "quotable epigrams" of Sam Jones, they were talking about formulas.[137]

"Epigrammatic" formulas, which could be used separately or in groups within themes, occur frequently in Brasher's sermons. These selected examples appear in two versions of his theme of the Crucifixion:

It was the heartbreak of deity.

It was the pathos of divinity.

It was God's best meeting Hell's worst.

Infinite love met demoniac hate.

Truth had its controversy with lies.[138]

Brasher both crafted and collected this type of formula. His date books, which he carried with him at camp meetings, contain not only jottings of his own contrived sayings but also "nuggets" mined from his colleagues' sermons.[139] Brasher revealed his considered use of such formulas in his corrections of a stenographic copy of an extemporaneous sermon he preached in 1916. In the margin, he wrote, "add epigram."[140]

Themes

Content and Style　　The diverse content and style of Brasher's formulaic themes make it difficult to divide them into discrete categories. The two ensuing transcriptions demonstrate his use of repetitive themes or "set passages." This theme, which we shall call "God's requirement of holiness," is actually an extended periodic sentence. The two versions contain some verbatim formulas, shown by single underlining, and some formulas with similar syntax and content, shown by double underlining:

Version A

You can't think of a HOLY GOD
Sitting in a HOLY HEAVen
Surrounded by HOLY ANgels
Giving out a HOLY LAW
Sending out a HOLY SON
To provide a HOLY reDEMPtion
By his HOLY BLOOD
And instituted [sic] a HOLY CHURCH
With HOLY HYMNS
And HOLY SACraments
And HOLY COVenants
And sent [sic] his HOLY SPIRIT
Into the world to
EFFECT that very purpose,
You can't think of THAT God
Expecting LESS of us
Than holiness [voices: Amen].[141]

Version B

It's unTHINKable to think of a HOLY GOD
Sitting in a HOLY HEAVen
Surrounded by HOLY ANgels
And sent [sic] his HOLY SON
To provide a HOLY reDEMPtion
Through a HOLY SACrifice
Who sent his HOLY SPIRIT
To teach us the way of life
ANgels to GUARD us
A CHURCH in which to
Put our MEMbership
Of HOLY VOWS
And HOLY SACraments
And HOLY FELLOWships
And ordained a HOLY MINistry
To proclaim a HOLY GOSpel

And invites ALL WHO WILL LISTEN to the Gospel to come
home at last to himself,
It's UNTHINKable that THAT God would require
LESS than holiness [voice: Right].[142]

With some exceptions, the contents of Brasher's themes fall
roughly into several groups: biblical narratives graphically portrayed,
often dramatically acted, and sometimes fancifully embellished; memorized sequences of Scripture verses; historical narratives of salvation
history such as the progress of "the glorious church"; delineations of
the *ordo salutis*—steps in the way of personal salvation; spiritual incidents from the lives of holiness saints and heroes; autobiographical spiritual narratives; and descriptive exempla such as the perception of God
in nature.

The style of the themes varies widely. Some consist of straight-
forward prose, containing, however, numerous memorized words and
phrases. An example is the theme of the inherited plantation incorporating the myth of the Old South. Regular prose is found most often
in the biblical narratives and biographical and autobiographical incidents. In all the categories of themes cited above, however, some passages may be set in highly fashioned florid language, bordering at times
on grandiloquence. Within each group of themes there appear examples crafted and delivered in a decidedly metrical style. Sometimes
Brasher intones the dramatic conclusions of his metrical themes.

A theme repeated may contain approximately the same number
of formulas and words as a prior version, as in "God's requirement of
holiness." Or a repetition may be greatly reduced or expanded, especially in themes built upon formulas with parallel syntax. In the theme
"the sovereign work of the Spirit" in the sermon "Let Us Make Man
in Our Image," Brasher uses anaphoric formulas, each beginning with
the clause "He's the only one . . ." to describe the work of the Spirit,
as in *"He's the only one* that can convict a sinner."[143] The theme employs the formula, with various endings, 8 times and contains 95 words.
The same anaphoric theme appears in Brasher's sermon "Quench Not
the Spirit," where the theme uses the formula 10 times and the narrative expands to 525 words.[144] Anaphoric formulas thus facilitate great
variation in versions of a given theme. The familiar phrases serve as
scaffolding from which the architect may construct a small or large
edifice, plain or highly ornamented. (See Appendix C.)

Variation within a formulaic framework allowed for the promptings of the Spirit. Although Brasher polished his themes, they were
never intended to be rote passages; rather, they were a combination

of preparation and inspiration: "That is the reason a young preacher . . . needs a circuit with seven or eight appointments, and a good ways apart, so he can preach that sermon all around his circuit and improve on it. I don't mean [he should] say the same thing every time, because if he does, that is played out. He has lost all the juice out of it. But if he adapts it to the occasion, and improves on what he has said, and looks back and sees the defects in the composition and delivery and mannerisms, and improves on it, that is better."[145] Brasher created and improved upon themes throughout his holiness preaching career. How many he commanded in his repertoire will never be known. In the limited number of his sermons and Bible studies preserved in sound recordings, there are hundreds of discrete, formulaic set pieces. These recordings preserve only a small fraction of what was his total sermon repertoire. (See Appendix D.)

A woman in Brasher's church in Boaz, Alabama, once remarked to him that "she never did know what his text was going to be, but she always knew what he was going to preach about."[146] Her statement artlessly recognized not only Brasher's penchant for Scriptures bearing upon holiness but also his use of a stock of themes about holiness that could serve a multitude of different texts. The theme "God's requirement of holiness," for instance, served equally well to illustrate both the text of Brasher's sermon "Be Ye Holy for I Am Holy" (I Peter 1:16) and that of his sermon "Let Us Make Man in Our Image" (Genesis 1:26).

Some themes formed the indispensable core of a sermon. Brasher's tracing of the historical march of the church in his sermon "The Glorious Church" and his dramatizing of the Passion narratives in his sermon "The Sufferings of Jesus" represent such themes.[147] Yet, even these central, extended themes could be modified or fragmented and used in other sermons. Brasher once borrowed, for example, substantial portions of the theme "the glorious Church," originally designed to expound Ephesians 5:25–27, to flesh out another sermon, "Dispensational Truth," based on the text Romans 9:22.[148] Other, shorter themes, such as "God's requirement of holiness," floated freely from sermon to sermon, employed where useful as illustrative or hortatory devices. Many sermons possessed no centrally prominent formulaic passage, containing instead many lesser themes scattered throughout the regular narrative prose of the preaching.[149]

Referring to his extensive repertory of folk tales and anecdotes, Brasher once remarked that he knew "bushels of incidents."[150] He also knew bushels of themes. Although a large stock of themes was a desideratum, it did not automatically guarantee effective preaching. The power of Brasher's preaching emanated not from his imaginatively crafted themes alone; it came equally from his choice and combination of them for each sermon. Both creation and selection of themes constituted his aesthetic. Such artistic judgment was a necessity—but unfortunately not the universal possession—of evangelists who preached extemporaneously for an hour or more. An evangelist named Adams in Knoxville, Tennessee, apparently lacked both sufficient repertoire and the necessary aesthetic discernment. One of his listeners, W. R. Murphy, wrote Brasher: "Brother Adams is a very peculiar preacher. He preaches from one-and-a-quarter to one-and-a-half hours each time, and he is the worst man to repeat I ever listened to. He don't sermonize at all. He scatters abroad. He says lots of good things, but you have to pick the *hay* out of the *briars*."[151]

Dramatics   Calling for a "new enthusiasm" in the holiness movement, Brasher, in 1921, urged its evangelists to proclaim "the atonement in Christ . . . until Calvary is made to drip in the hearing of the audience and its crimson gore to appear before the people."[152] In the tradition of the circuit rider J. L. Freeman, whose graphic themes had caused young Johnny to imagine that he saw "the ground tremble where the saints were getting up," Brasher vividly portrayed, even dramatically reenacted, biblical events.[153] His gifts as a storyteller enhanced his extraordinary dramatic performances, which, elaborate with gesture, facial expression, and variation of voice, defy adequate transcription.

Such themes, especially those of the Passion narratives, convicted sinners, urged the saved onward to the Canaan of rest, and offered the sanctified a vision that enabled them to "keep the blessing." The atonement, according to holiness theology, provided for sanctification as well as justification, but perseverance in either was never assured. Holiness language thus indicated the necessity to recall continually the vision of the crucified one: Brasher and his coevangelists exhorted those with the blessing to safeguard their experience by "sheltering under the blood" or by "keeping the blood of the atonement on their souls."[154]

His frequently used theme of the Crucifixion served for sinners and saved as a convicting agent. However, for the sanctified, the ritually recurrent vision functioned almost as a sacramental memorial. Holiness camp meetings and revivals uncommonly, if ever, observed the Lord's Supper. For the folk gathered there, the repeated, dramatized theme of the Crucifixion resembled, and virtually replaced, the solemn function of the usual Protestant celebration of the sacrament. The familiar graphic theme and the audience's appropriation of it fulfilled meanings and hopes similar to those expressed in traditional liturgical prayers of consecration repeated immediately before Communion: "Christ . . . did command us to continue a perpetual memory of His precious death until His coming again. In remembrance of His death and Passion, may [we] also be partakers of the divine nature through Him."[155]

Other incidents of the Passion and post-Resurrection appearances formed a standard part of Brasher's repertoire of dramatized themes.[156] He imaginatively embellished some biblical themes. Typically, and to the delight of his audience, he cast Job's tormentors as "three anti-holiness preachers."[157] Other themes portrayed biblical characters in narratives that were unabashedly fabulous, yet affecting: In hell, Judas ruefully counts his shekels, while Pilate desperately washes his hands in a basin of fire.[158] In other themes, the timeless Christ stands beside the empty tomb gazing at the folk in an Alabama revival,[159] or with penitents' names written on his outstretched, pierced hands, cries before the Father, "Spare them! Spare them!"[160] In heaven, Gabriel and his angels wait especially upon those who had had no earthly rewards.[161]

Brasher's vocal gifts complemented his creative dramatics. His voice normally was deep and resonant but possessed such a range of volume, pitch, and color that it could express any emotion or play any part.[162] Like John Jasper, the celebrated black folk preacher of nineteenth-century Richmond, Brasher at times was virtually "a theater within himself with the stage crowded with actors."[163] During his enactment of Abraham and Isaac, when at the last second the thunderous voice of the angel intercepted the downward thrust of Abraham's knife, audiences gasped and cried out in relief.[164] In the drama of Jacob wrestling with God, Brasher so affectingly imitated the limp that Jacob received while seeking a blessing that the theme, Brasher claimed, won more souls than any other in his repertoire.[165]

These themes, which in a moment shifted from description to drama, indeed held their listeners in a "thrall supernatural."[166] When Brasher suddenly seemed transmuted into Abraham, Isaac, or Jacob, the vision so overmastered the hearers that they, too, ceased to be spectators but literally participated in it.

In a favorite theme, "the immortal company," Brasher envisioned himself in heaven watching a mighty procession of glorified saints. Beginning with "Abel, the first martyr," Brasher gazed at or greeted over a score of immortals—biblical prophets and apostles, heroes of the church, holiness-movement worthies, and, finally, transfigured members of his own family. Breaking the spell only momentarily, he asked his audience, "Are some of your folks there?" and then returned to view the transcendent scene awhile longer, punctuating his visions with the

exclamation "Oh, to join them!"[167] The evangelist Tilden Gaddis heard
Brasher use the theme in a camp meeting at Jamestown, North Dakota, in 1938. He reported that the people, enraptured by the vision,
spontaneously came from their seats to the front of the tabernacle—
in fancy, joining their loved ones in the company of heaven.[168]

Brasher recognized that reenactment of the divine drama could
easily slip into, or be perceived as, showmanship. His widely revered
colleague, Henry Clay Morrison, who could devote the body of a sermon to an imaginary elevator trip to hell and to heaven (with no obvious debt to Dante), clearly trespassed in this regard.[169] A letter of 1922
concerning Morrison from his vice president at Asbury College spoke
of the "thousands who blindly follow him, intoxicated by his oratory
and heroic tone."[170] The matter of preaching style, however, was one
not simply of personal motives but also of taste. John Lakin early
learned the pitfalls of overdramatization when a wise layman discreet-
ly informed him, "Brasher, you are not impressive when you scream."[171]

Subsequent contemporaries attested that he used dramatics "never for display" but always "to fasten divine truth upon hearers."[172] He
described his own experience of preaching as "soul travail exhausting
in the extreme," times in which he felt as if he could "wring tears out
of his fingers."[173] In 1919, Joseph Owen, a fellow evangelist, commend-
ed Brasher's "pulpit decorum" and contrasted it to the changing style
of holiness preaching, which, Owen lamented, "largely emphasized the
gymnastics of the gospel."[174]

Eloquence and Elegance   In August 1897 the Waco, Texas, *Tele-
phone* reported the recent session of the burgeoning Waco Camp Meeting. The writer, though not a holiness adherent, admired the preaching of the featured evangelists—southerners whom Brasher five years
later would claim as his close friends and colleagues: "Their preachers
are powerful stump speakers and immense in tropes, figures, comparisons, metaphors, similes, and other figures which have captured the
imagination of the masses from time immemorial."[175]

Brasher and others in his circle of evangelists—Carradine, Mc-
Clurkan, Morrison, and Godbey (to an excess)—loved "eloquent
speech."[176] Brasher employed his own elegant, sometimes flowery, language in preaching, yet he also memorized gems of eloquence he heard
in the sermons of his colleagues—reciting them to inspire his preaching audiences as well as to entertain family and friends during storytelling times. H. C. Morrison, whose oratory "climbed over the Milky
Way,"[177] provided Brasher with some silver-tongued quotations: "This
is from one of Dr. Morrison's eloquent sermons on the pre-existence

The evangelist H. C. Morrison (1857–1942), with flowing white hair, often took long walks in the woods to relax between camp-meeting services. Brasher Papers.

The tabernacle of Waco Camp Meeting, Waco, Texas, 1904. The preachers were "powerful stump speakers." Note the sunshade near the eaves and the raised wooden floor to protect against snakes and insects. Brasher Papers.

of Jesus Christ: 'I have often wished that I might divest myself of materiality and dart back into eternity so quickly that the lazy-footed lightning would burn itself out and sulk in sullen darkness, while I hurry away to the feet of Jesus.'"[178]

Although Brasher ornamented his prose, he chose his fancy phrases with discretion and introduced embellished passages in moderation: "Some folks call a pie 'grand,'" he complained, "using all the adjectives they've got to describe something they swallow! What do they do when they go to talk about GOD and his works?"[179] "His eloquence was remarkably disciplined," wrote a colleague. "He was not interested in florid oratory for its own sake."[180] The compliment bespeaks familiarity with a type of southern preaching that failed when the prose gilded the lily. Brasher's son wrote of one Alabama evangelist: "Only when he forgets his grandiloquent pose and happens to fall into common vernacular does he say anything that is linguistically correct and intelligible."[181]

In some sermons, Brasher included themes interlaced throughout with polished phrases and imagery—for example, the conclusion of a version of his theme of the Crucifixion:

> He said, "I'm exceeding sorrowful and SORE
>   A-M-A-Z-E-D."
> Devils HAUNTED and MOCKED him, and
> FIENDS GOADED him.
> And here on the CROSS
> He cries,
> "The Father has hidden his face."
> There comes a moment when the sun is
>   darkened and the
> Earth reels like a drunken soldier on his
>   way home.
> Rocks break with crash of thunder.
> The sheeted dead stir in their pillows in
>   the graves and get up and walk about.
> He said, "It is **FINISHED.**"
> Earth
> And heaven heard that cry.
> Hell
> Had CHALLENGED GOD
> And been defeated.
> The CROSS was not God's plan.
> The cross was HELL'S CHALLENGE.

Infinite love met finite hate,
Demoniac hate.
Truth had its controversy with lies
Righteousness with unrighteousness
Injustice with justice
God's holiness with sin's exTRAVagance.
There could be but one issue.
GOD was triumphant.
TRUTH prevailed.
The blood BOUGHT the victory.
It was HELL's GETTYSBURG
And the first line of the devil's last,
    awful charge
BROKE at the foot of the cross
Like those pale legions broke
At the top of Roundtop.
'Twas over with.
Heaven was triumphant.
God was victorious.
Mercy had met with hate
And triumphed.
The SUFFERINGS of Christ.
Oh, I can only HINT at it.
I have neither strength nor time to give you
Any more of the
PATHOS and the divine tragedy of that scene.
The EARTH that he made for us and our
    comfort
REELING under his dying feet.
The sun rolling back his abode
From the SIGHT OF MEN,
Refusing to LOOK UPON HIM
Whose BEAMS he had borrowed.
Stars reeling in their orbits and the
    planets
DRUNKEN with exCITEment STAGGERED ON.
God had met hell's highest peak of hate
And triumphed.
God had met sin's deepest, darkest, most
    tragic attack
And conquered it [hits pulpit].[182]

Embellished themes often followed or preceded some mundane, folksy allusion, which through contrast heightened the inspiring, imaginative effect of the eloquence. In a sermon treating the beauties of the Spirit, Brasher in a routine manner told of his visit to a North Dakota camp meeting, mentioned the evening meal with its "big Wyoming potato," then immediately launched into the following prose:

> The sun rested behind the prairies and
> Then he seemed to say
> To the nightfall,
> "Stand back awhile
> I want to paint a picture."
> There were wisps of clouds out there in the
>   West
> And he etched them with silver and
> Sprinkled them with gold dust and
> Then he studded them with rubies and
> Flecked them with carbuncles and
> Then he made us lakes with azure and rivers
>   of azure to flow against cliffs of amethysts and pearl
>   and gold
> And their crests were caught aflame with
>   the beauty and
> Chariots of light raged hither and yon
> On the crest of the clouds
> And there stood in kaleidoscopic wonder for
>   three quarters of an hour
> And he took his hand and
> Rubbed it off into a dull purple and said,
> "I'll hang another picture tomorrow."
> And we worshipped
> The God of beauty [audience: Amen].[183]

Sometimes lofty phrases leaped out from the midst of otherwise ordinary passages. Asserting the doctrine of the indwelling Holy Spirit in the hearts of the sanctified, Brasher awakened his listeners to the magnitude of the claim when he reminded them that the same Spirit, "when all nature lay in chaotic confusion," had "hovered over nature until it began to assume form and order and beauty and symmetry and motion, until unnumbered worlds trembled into their orbits, and proceeded on their eternal journey."[184]

What elicited the elegant style? Brasher and those in his circle grew up in a tradition of southern oratory that put a premium on fancy prose as opposed to mere plain-style preaching. Aimed at audiences composed primarily of the already converted or sanctified, familiar flowers of rhetoric opened the door to the *visio dei* for those blessed with spiritual discernment.

In some holiness preaching, however, high-colored eloquence may have served to counteract pejorative stereotypes of second-blessing folk. The holiness movement was in part a reaction against an increasingly upper-class Protestantism with new theologies, formal religious practice, and rising standards of education. The common folk who comprised the movement had no less pride than those they criticized. They took pains to show that they were as intelligent as the "rich, proud ecclesiastics and skeptics" whom they opposed.[185]

In 1913, Beverly Carradine wrote: "If anyone thinks that because the holiness people are not multi-millionaires, are not found in swell society, and do not figure conspicuously in newspaperdom, that they are thereby lacking in intellectual force and mental acquisitions and cerebral quickness, such an individual has made a profound mistake."[186] For those who felt disadvantaged in education, threatened or perplexed by changing mores and new theologies, high-flown "cultured" language mitigated a sense of inferiority.[187] Eloquence helped refute popular stereotypes that stamped holiness people—and their preachers—as coarse and ignorant.

Brasher was happily at home in either the vernacular or refined speech. His love of embellished prose and his use of it in preaching reflected his experience that people could be won and inspired by the sublime. He also would have agreed in principle with the statement of his colleague A. P. Gouthey: "There is no language that can exaggerate the ministry of the Holy Ghost."[188]

Cadence and Other Devices   Brasher's themes achieved power through dramatics, elegance, and, finally, rhythm. By no means always present, metrical passages nevertheless appeared in every type of Brasher's themes. His frequent use of cadence and parallel syntax—especially anaphora—bears strong similarity to southern chanted sermons. Rhythmical themes, most frequent at the close of his sermons and accompanied by other special rhetorical devices, possessed greatest force. Rhythm helped win assent or "pull the net," as Brasher said.[189] Cadence also served as the catalyst of ecstasy and vision, perhaps in the way described by William Butler Yeats: "Rhythm . . . hushes us with an alluring monotony, while it holds us waking by variety, to keep us in that state of real trance, in which the mind liberated from the pressure of the will is unfolded in symbols."[190]

All of the transcriptions of themes thus far cited—especially those of "the proper *ordo salutis*" and "God's requirement of holiness"—display Brasher's fondness for rhythm and parallel construction. The following metric passage, also containing anaphora, is his opening of a theme on the Second Coming:

> The LORD's coming.
> He SAID so.
> I don't know why he brought it in
>   connection with that:
> "Any man love not the Lord Jesus Christ,
> Let him be anathema.
> The LORD is COMING."
> Coming to JUDGE.
> He is coming to RECEIVE.
> He is coming to HONOR.
> He is coming to EXALT.
> He is coming to take his OWN to HIMSELF.
> HE'S COMING TO BRING HIS OWN CHILDREN
> INTO THE EVERLASTING FELICITY OF A HEAVENLY
>   STATE
> WHERE NO SIN EVER comes [hits pulpit]
> And where no SORROW ever is known.[191]

In spite of similarities of style—and possible common historical roots—between Brasher's rhythmic themes and the tradition of chanted sermons, he and his immediate holiness colleagues claimed no kinship between their own preaching and the latter. Brasher did not truly chant portions of his themes, nor did he punctuate his rhythmic pauses with grunts as do chanting preachers. In 1920, one of Brasher's co-evangelists bragged to him that he recently "broke" a young holiness preacher "from grunting."[192] Moreover, Brasher's circle of holiness folk regarded chanting preachers—whom they called "Hardshells"—as ignorant, coarse, and biblically illiterate, and their sermons often as nonsense made up only to satisfy meter. Brasher's repertoire of narratives contained unflattering humorous tales about "Hardshells" and parodies of their preaching style, which he considered archaic and wished "had played out way back yonder."[193] He enjoyed chanting the following parody in a singsong fashion:

> Brethren, my text today
> Is as follows:
> "They shall gnaw a file

> Between the mountains of Hesperdam
> Where the lion roareth
> And the whang-doodle mourneth
> Over its firstborn."
> Brother,
> There are different kinds of files:
> There's a hand-saw file
> And a cross-cut file
> And a gnaw-file.
> "Ye shall gnaw a file
> Between the mountains of Hesperdam
> Where the lion roareth
> And the whang-doodle mourneth
> Over its firstborn."[194]

Brasher combined other rhetorical devices with cadence to increase the persuasiveness of his eloquence. The repetitive use of the clause "He is coming" in the theme of the Second Coming demonstrates his most frequently used device, anaphora, a series of sentences or clauses beginning with identical words.[195] Each repetition of the initial clause, "He is coming," increases the force of the message, while each new final infinitive opens, augments, and raises the audience's vision: "He is coming to judge . . . coming to receive . . . coming to honor . . . coming to crown . . . coming to exalt . . . coming to take his own to himself . . . coming to bring his children . . . to a heavenly state."[196] Throughout the relatively brief, half-hour sermon in which the theme appears, Brasher employs no fewer than ten distinct anaphoric passages—eight in the final half of the sermon—each sequence adding to the emotional intensity generated by the preceding one.

In the closing exhortation of the sermon, Brasher concludes with a powerful periodic sentence in which grammar and thought are not complete until the final phrase:

> Oh, when God's w-r-a-t-h is kindled,
> When the HOLY BLOOD
> That JESUS shed
> Has been TRAMPLED upon by RUTHless feet
>   [hits pulpit]
> Who disHONORED that blood,
> When that LOVE that
> NAILED him to the CROSS and wouldn't let
>   him GO [hits pulpit] 'til he was DEAD
>   [hits pulpit],

Took him to the grave and MASTERED it and
went to heaven to plead for us,
When that love AT LAST has been REJECTED
and RESISTED and DENIED,
And God's JUST-NESS
And his HOL-iness
And his RIGHT-eousness
And his LOVE,
InFLAMED to WRATH,
POURS ITS TORRENTS
Upon an **UNPROTECTED** SOUL,
UN-SHELTERED
And unbaptized,
Who can m-e-a-s-u-r-e the **DEPTH**
Of that destruction.[197]

Brasher was a master of periodic sentences and employed them often
in his sermons, especially at the climaxes. Remarkable in length, the
sentences constituted themes in themselves. The piling-on of clauses,
verbs, nouns, and adjectives augmented the force of rhythm. The single example above displays a quadrupling of the anaphoric clause beginning with "when"; incremental series of verbs: "rejected," "resisted," "denied"; and nouns: "justness," "holiness," "righteousness," "love";
and tripling of adjectives: "unprotected," "unsheltered and unbaptized."
The continuously increasing internal burden of such sentences, resolved
only in the final phrase, riveted the attention of the listeners and created profound emotional, if not entrancing, effect. A minister who attended the annual session of the Alabama Conference in 1916 sixty
years afterward recalled Brasher's use of additive language and its impact: "He was talking about sin. And he came out with a string of adjectives maybe two yards long—calling sin 'so-and-so, and so-and-so,
and so-and-so.' And that audience was spellbound. I believe there were
over a hundred at the altar . . . audibly groaning in the Spirit for deliverance from sin."[198]

In his exhortations, Brasher employed still other devices to win
his listeners. He sometimes used chiasmus—the crossing of words of
one clause by reversing their order in the next. The device made the
contrasts especially memorable:

He no longer LOVES SIN, he HATES it.
He no longer HATES HOLINESS, he LOVES it.[199]

God has his BEST for those who will not be
satisfied with the merely good.

God has his GOOD for those who will not pay
the price for the best.[200]

Another of Brasher's most persuasive instruments was his use of
antithesis. His doubling of the nouns in this passage enhances the cu-
mulative effect of the images:

You may stop to think what hangs on those
    three letters: n-o-w.
Chains and dungeons
Or thrones and mansions,
Darkness and despair
Or light and triumph,
Hell or heaven,
Association of devils and demons
Or the presence of saints
And the angels of God,
An eternity of woe
Or an eternity of glory,
Hang upon that word: N-O-W.[201]

Kenneth Burke, in *A Rhetoric of Motives,* argues that in the recitation
of long lists of oppositions, the form itself draws the audience into par-
ticipation and is a catalyst to assent.[202] Throughout the body of his sermons, Brasher also adeptly used series of rhetorical questions to en-
gage his audience personally—to move individuals to the threshold of
decision or to elicit testimony from the saved and sanctified. Here, in
a passage following a statement on conversion, he seems to call for both
decision and testimony:

All those dark movings of the human soul
CANcelled
To stand before him as if we never had
    committed a sin
In our lives.
That's a tremendous thing.
Has it happened to YOU?
You know ABOUT it?
Can you tell me WHEN?
Can you tell me WHERE?
Can you tell me HOW you reached it?
HAVEN'T you reached it?
Are you GLAD?
Do you let the world know you're glad?[203]

All of these devices augmented the power of rhythm. Finally, at points of greatest seriousness in his sermons, Brasher's preaching verged upon chanting. In these passages—often extended periodic sentences—he accentuated rhythm, intensified tone to an almost musical quality, increased volume, and gradually raised the pitch of his voice. (For an example with musical notation, see Appendix E.)[204]

This tonal delivery—undoubtedly traditional—matched the voice Brasher used when imitating the eloquence of Freeman and Parker, the circuit riders of his boyhood.[205] At these powerful moments, Brasher's preaching reached the level of the sublime. "Sublimity in eloquence," said John Witherspoon, suggests "not only the ideal of great force, but of carrying away everything with it that opposes or lies in its way."[206] These sacred moments blessed Brasher's listeners, and "visions of rapture burst on [their] sight."[207]

Repertoire

After the death of the "grand itinerant," George Whitefield, Benjamin Franklin observed: "By hearing him often, I came to distinguish easily between sermons newly composed and those which he had often preached in the course of his travels. His delivery of the latter was so improved by frequent repetition, that every accent, every emphasis, every modulation of his voice, was so perfectly well turned and well placed, that, without being interested in the subject, one could not help being pleased with the discourse."[208] Whitefield figured early in the continuing American tradition of traveling evangelists who preach a standard set of sermons. Brasher once admitted to a camp-meeting audience that he had "eighty-odd" sermons on the subject of holiness.[209] In fact, his personal notebook of sermon outlines shows that his stock of sermons was considerably more extensive. One hundred sixty-five outlines appear in the book, and dozens more fill cards and scraps of paper among his manuscripts.[210] Revivals that sometimes lasted twenty-one days and often required preaching twice daily demanded a large repertoire.

Brasher and his colleagues, like Whitefield, preached some sermons more often than others. Anticipating hearing Brasher at a nearby camp meeting in 1921, a friend, Jacob Harris, inquired if Brasher's "great sermon," "The Sufferings of Jesus," would be a part of his "regular series."[211] It probably was. Like the earlier renowned southern preacher John Jasper, Brasher had a group of "special sermons" within his larger repertoire—"sermons which had grown by special use and which embodied the choicest creations of his mind. These he preached over and over again . . . and without apology to anybody."[212] Just as

Brasher identified the circuit riders Freeman and Parker by one or two of their superlative sermons, so holiness folk associated him with a set of unusually powerful sermons: "The Value of a Soul," "Salvation—Its Content and Time," "The Mind of Christ," "The Sufferings of Jesus," "The Second Coming," "The Resurrection," "The Glorious Church," and others.[213] Holiness evangelists such as H. C. Morrison, J. O. Mc-Clurkan, and J. B. Chapman each were renowned for one or more extraordinarily popular sermons.[214]

Brasher's extensive repertoire notwithstanding, he recognized its limits. In 1922 he had agreed to hold a two-week fall revival in south Baltimore. When he received a call to preach at a similar revival in west Baltimore during the same season, he answered the invitation with some hesitation: "You perhaps know . . . that effective sermons that bring things to pass are not owned by us ordinary preachers by the hundred. I should hate to run stale on the audiences of Baltimore—not for my sake, but for the meetings' sake. But I think if some might be willing to hear a sermon again, that I might be saved from the embarrassment, if I had a second meeting. Not that I have just so many sermons, but then the truth of the gospel is largely contained within a certain compass."[215] Early in his career, when Brasher was still building the major themes and sermons of his repertoire, he took a self-imposed leave of absence from Hartselle Camp Meeting: "I served it for ten or eleven years in succession until I'd preached everything, and they knew I had preached everything, and I ran away from them. And I waited 'til they'd forget some of it, so I could come back and preach it again."[216]

In one sense, Brasher never preached the same sermon twice. Even in such a frequently used sermon as "The Sufferings of Jesus," where set themes of the Passion constituted the body of the sermon, there was ample room for variety through choice of nonessential themes and other exempla. Remarkably, Brasher never ceased to formulate new material and to incorporate it into his old sermons. In his final years, he still was composing affecting themes and interjecting contemporary exempla.[217]

Brasher probably fashioned a major portion of his sermons—and thus many of the formulas and themes that he employed in them—in the years immediately following his sanctification. He preached these more-or-less fixed creations, as well as more recently composed sermons, for the rest of his life. For example, when he was ninety-three years old, he told a camp-meeting audience that a "section" of what he had preached the previous day was "at least sixty years old."[218] It was not written, of course, but extemporaneous.

One can trace some formulas, themes, and sermons that Brasher preached in the 1950s and 1960s all the way back to 1900 and before.[219] In light of their relatively fixed content, their early dates of composition, and their patterning after nineteenth-century models, Brasher's sound-recorded sermons represent a unique survival in culture—a window on turn-of-the-century holiness preaching and even upon earlier southern evangelical preaching style. Both the freedom to repeat sermons and their style, which included set formulas and themes, enabled sermons to remain "intact" for over half a century.

A retentive memory helped. Brasher's childhood training in storytelling and in recitation at school prepared his mind to store innumerable themes and exempla, and to call them forth effortlessly. His fellow evangelist Paul Rees related the following incident: "When he was past 100 [1968], I called on him, and after an hour together when I was ready to drive away, he said, 'Paul, have you ever heard these words?' With that, he recited a whole passage, which when he got well into it, I recognized as coming from a sermon of mine that he had heard me preach in the 1920s."[220]

The tradition of repeating sermons cannot be judged by values applied to the weekly preaching of settled ministers in today's mainline churches, where congregations expect each Sunday to hear new exposition and exempla that bring the gospel to bear on complex social and personal issues. In Brasher's tradition, "effective sermons" were primarily instruments—artistically fashioned—designed to "bring things to pass": the experiences of conversion and sanctification.[221]

Although holiness evangelists repeated sermons, often with the hearty approval of the audience, there nevertheless remained a tension between the custom of relying on a stock of sermons and the ideal of receiving each message fresh from the Spirit. Brasher observed the tension that some holiness preachers felt: "I have seen evangelists . . . make a dramatic entrance to the service, with their overcoats thrown over their arms, with a pale shadow over their face, as much as if to say, 'I've just come from a deep profound search of new truth,' when I knew it was one they had preached a hundred times."[222] Brasher did not seem to be troubled with such feelings. Always ready to adapt and improve upon earlier versions, he left ample room for— and prayed for—inspiration on every preaching occasion.[223]

More important, holiness folk looked forward to familiar sermons and themes. When in a sermon Brasher stated, "I wish you could see that man on that cross!" veteran listeners eagerly anticipated the imminent theme of the Crucifixion by voicing an emphatic and expectant "Yes!"[224] The polish that Franklin noted in Whitefield, gained by repetition, gave some themes an aesthetic appeal similar to that of a pleasing tune, but the repetition of transcendent images elicited a far more profound response. Audiences never tired of hearing what was most meaningful to them. In 1938, an evangelist described the preaching and the listeners at Indian Springs Camp Meeting in Georgia: "Brother Morrison has preached with a vigor and an effectiveness that astonishingly belie his eighty-two years and his recent afflictions. He has preached the Abraham sermon and the one on the Rich Young Ruler in which he takes us on an elevator trip to hell and heaven. One doubts if Brother Morrison himself knows how many times he has preached those two sermons right here. Yet the people hang on his words."[225]

Some special sermons were delivered repeatedly because they were favorites of the audience. Preached in a relaxed setting removed from normal daily distractions, they reawakened and focused the deepest experiences, beliefs, and meanings of the listeners' lives. Such moments, said Brasher, provided "perspective—an outline of His purpose. Blessed be God for an occasional glimpse!"[226]

In 1933 at Indian Springs, the Reverend J. P. Gilbreath heard Brasher deliver his ever-popular sermon "The Glorious Church." In it Brasher traced the doctrine of holiness throughout the great epochs of church history, showing that the experience of perfect love as proclaimed by the holiness movement was neither innovation nor fanaticism but had been the center and goal of the true church in all ages. Gilbreath invited Brasher to preach the sermon at his church and was "anxious" to hear it again, just as Jacob Harris hoped to hear once more "The Sufferings of Jesus," a sermon that had already "permanently helped and inspired" him.[227] Throughout his long career, Brasher continued to bless the people with these, his "choicest creations," delivering them time and again in the power of the Spirit and, thus, as other preachers in his tradition, "without apology."[228]

8

Sanctification and the "Foolishness of Folks"

STORIES OF RELIGIOUS EXPERIENCE

I'm trying to write and the three preachers are telling stories on the porch. . . . I had to stop and listen to the preachers and it's too late to write more and get it off so will have to wait and tell you the rest when I get home.

—MINNIE EUNICE MOORE BRASHER,

    INDIAN SPRINGS CAMP MEETING, AUGUST 1926

Once, after telling stories for two hours, Brasher slapped the arm of his chair and said, "I've got bushels of incidents. I've had more funny things happen in my revival meetings that would fill a book."[1] Then he began another story. His children and grandchildren remember countless such evenings at home listening to favorite tales that were always accompanied by some "new" stories from his seemingly inexhaustible repertoire. Only the mantel clock striking a late hour could send him reluctantly off to bed. More often than not he would return, wraithlike in nightshirt and stocking cap, to tell one more.

Brasher spiced his sermons with many of the same stories. His sound recordings alone contain about a thousand tales, his manuscripts hundreds of others, and acquaintances still living recall other narratives that regrettably were not recorded during his life.

Brasher's earliest memories were of storytelling at the fireside, where "light and shadows created ghostly forms on long winter evenings."[2] His maternal grandmother, two older brothers, and father were all gifted storytellers. His father knew a great stock of tales including

Revolutionary War legends of *his* grandfather, humorous stories of the Old Southwest, Civil War narratives, and a host of preacher anecdotes gleaned from his itinerancy.[3] The "big house" served constantly as an overnight lodge for a diverse group of travelers—and storytellers—livestock drovers, settlers pouring into Sand Mountain, and itinerant preachers. Brasher remembered their tales as well as the legends and lore that circulated in his wider boyhood community.

Joining the ranks of the ministry, Brasher rose from apprentice to master storyteller. Methodism required the gathering of all preachers at the annual conference—a time when fellow itinerants exchanged a fresh harvest of both secular tales and narratives—many humorous—relating to the itinerancy: stories about bishops, cantankerous laity, unpaid salaries, remarkable providences, and sermon parodies. However, it was Brasher's holiness evangelism that provided him an immensely larger supply of narratives than was routinely available to standard Methodist preachers. Each camp meeting or revival that Brasher served—and there were dozens each year—matched the storytelling opportunities of an annual conference. These continual meetings augmented his treasury of personal experiences and multiplied his sources—both preachers and lay folk—of new tales.[4] On another occasion, Brasher again summed up his repertoire with a traditional metaphor: "There's a lot of game up that creek."[5]

Like all narrators, Brasher did not keep in stock all the tales that he had heard. More to the point, he chose not to repeat some. For instance, he is not known to have told any tall tales, even though they must have been common in his early community. Nor do his numerous supernatural legends include many stories of the dark side of the spirit world. Tall tales may not have suited his self-image as a respected—and truthful—gospel preacher. A desire not to recreate his own childhood fears in his offspring made him reluctant to repeat tales of black magic and evil spirits: "When I was a little fellow, I had to have somebody sit in the bed with me until I went to sleep. The folks were to blame for it. They told witch stories until I was afraid of a crack in the floor."[6]

Sound recordings of Brasher's extemporaneous sermons allow us to hear some of the very exempla southern evangelical audiences heard in nineteenth- and early-twentieth-century preaching. We can discover the types of narratives from his larger repertoire that Brasher chose for sermons. There is little direct evidence elsewhere of the exempla employed in the preaching of nineteenth-century Methodist itinerants. Printers and preachers censored it.

Throughout the long and tedious history of the printed sermon,

Dinner during a revival in Birmingham, Alabama, ca. 1930, at the home of Mr. and Mrs. M. C. Thomas. Such meals were always storytelling times. Brasher is seated at right. Brasher Papers.

Brasher (right) and a fellow evangelist, Charles M. Dunaway of the Methodist Episcopal Church, South, swap tales (and hats) at Hollow Rock Camp Meeting, Toronto, Ohio, 1923. Brasher Papers.

well into the twentieth century, editors and preachers conspired to delete illustrative narratives from printed texts, turning the lively word into dull disquisitions. Convention decreed that the anecdotes that enlivened extemporaneous preaching, especially personal ones, were unfit for publication. For instance, of the many printed volumes of George Whitefield's sermons, only one posthumous collection of stenographically recorded sermons dared include some of the anecdotes that made him famous. Contemporary readers complained that these sermons were "like the ravings of a madman" and should never have gone to press "without considerable alterations." Luke Tyerman, Whitefield's late-nineteenth-century biographer, disparaged their style as "familiar . . . free and easy talk, intermixed with anecdotes, personal reminiscences, and quaint quotations."[7]

Even Peter Cartwright, the nineteenth-century "backwoods preacher" legendary for his yarn-spinning in preaching, has left us only indirect evidence of the narratives in his sermons. He crafted his autobiography around a hundred skillfully polished stories, but which ones he used—and how he used them—in his sermons, we will never know. If they survive at all, handwritten sermon notes that ministers carried into the pulpit provide little clue as to what stories they told in preaching. Printed and manuscript sources simply did not record the rich variety of traditional narratives and figures of speech present in extemporaneous nineteenth-century evangelical preaching. The sound recordings of Brasher's sermons do.

Brasher's preaching style essentially copied that of his father's generation. He in fact compared the "colorful experiences" of his "father in the gospel," J. L. Freeman, to those of Peter Cartwright, and he once planned to write down "the many rich anecdotes" that enlivened Freeman's sermons.[8] Brasher received many of his exempla from his elders, and he, alone, of his generation, lived long enough to have dozens of his extemporaneous sermons preserved on sound recordings.

Since his formulaic sermons tended to become fixed early in his career, their exempla open a window on a tradition heretofore difficult to document. Here are the "anecdotes, reminiscences, and quaint quotations" omitted in printed sermons.[9] Here is the robust language admired by the Waco Camp Meeting observer in 1897: "immense in tropes, figures, comparisons, metaphors, and similes."[10] These tropes and anecdotes incarnated the doctrines, values, and mores dear to Brasher's listeners, reawakening and focusing their deepest experiences. More than any other of the rhetorical devices Brasher used, they tell us about holiness folk.

Remarkable Providences

A crowd in the tabernacle of the holiness camp at Jamestown, North Dakota, listened raptly to "the great southern orator." Camp leaders were praying for conversions—for the "first break" in the meeting—and the sermon, "Now Is the Day of Salvation," elicited visions of souls trembling in the balances. At the climax, the preacher cried out: "Jesus might come in the clouds before morning. Yield to God and be saved!" He then related a story:

> A group of young people came to a Virginia camp meeting, taking the outing as an excuse for attending. They did not want religion. We pled with them and urged them to give hearts [sic] to God. I then gave a warning which I have never given before or since, but God seemed to put it upon me. I said, "Now a coffin is already built that will hold some of your forms, the carriage is ready, and the preacher licensed." Sunday afternoon one of the gayest of the girls went to the operating table for appendicitis, and blood poisoning set in and she died. On the afternoon, four days after my declaration, she was dead. And it came to pass that the coffin was in the county seat at the time I made the speech, the carriage was in readiness, and the preacher lived just across the hill. In five days every word of it was fulfilled.[11]

Such testimonies of supernatural intervention of the Spirit—sometimes in warning and judgment, more often in blessing—interlaced Brasher's preaching. The tale—at once a warning, a judgment, and an incidence of clairvoyance—is a striking example of a remarkable providence, an ancient genre of story that discovers God's providential action in "extraordinary exceptions to known natural sequences."[12] These narratives of divinely ordered judgments, conversions, deliverances, encounters, dreams, and omens trace their origin to early Christian belief in God's direct guidance of the universe, both in ordinary and extraordinary occurrences. And the tales portray a Providence that allows extraordinary events to occur either as blessing or judgment upon human moral action. Hence, the untimely death of the young woman in Virginia.

Remarkable providences have appeared as legends and sermon exempla throughout the history of the church, often sharing subjects and sources with Old World folk religion. In the New World, Puritan spiritual autobiography most notably revealed believers' intense interest in extraordinary signs of divine favor or condemnation. Byrne has demonstrated the vigorous persistence of remarkable providences in

HOLINESS

CAMP·MEETING

. The Eleventh Annual Meeting of the Buckingham Branch of the Virginia Association for the Promotion of Bible Holiness, will be held at the Tabernacle, about 3½ miles southwest of Buckingham Court-House, in the County of Buckingham, Va.,

From August 13th to 22nd, 1911

The presence of every Christian, of every denomination, is cordially solicited, and such will be sincerely made welcome.

The purpose of these meetings, after these ten years of earnest endeavor, is too well understood to demand further comment, by those who have attended; but for the information of any who have not attended these precious meetings, we would say, that the "old time religion," the acceptance of "the faith once given to the fathers' and earnestly endorsed by all of the orthodox churches:—repentance of sin, regeneration of the heart, establishment in the faith, or sanctification, are the doctrines taught, and earnestly insisted upon.

The meeting this year, under the providence of the Holy Spirit, will be conducted by the following human leaders:—

Rev. J. L. Brasher, of Boaz, Alabama.

Rev. Jno. M Oakey, of Danville, Virginia.

Bro. Brasher comes to us most highly endorsed as a gifted worker in the Master's vineyard, and an able expounder of His everlasting truth

Bro Oakey is too well and favorably known to our people to need any further introduction.

We will also have with us Mrs. C. W. Hudgins, of Portsmouth, Va., who is a lovely gospel singer, and who will be our soloist during this meeting.

Then too we expect Master Kohle Burton, of Radford, Va., who renders the gospel so sweet and touching by his productions from his cornet.

We expect the music to be a most attractive and effective part of this year's service.

There will be the usual three regular services each day this time, as in former meetings. Then we hope also to have the bible lessons early in the morning services as heretofore.

Rally to the Master's flag Christians of every name. There is a work for each of us to do in these meetings, in this earnest effort to save the lost, establish the faint-hearted, and win many sheaves for the garner of heaven.

Ample cottage accommodations are to be had on the large shady grounds, for all visitors from a distance. Those coming from a distance would do well to provide themselves with quilts, sheets and towels.

Plenty of splendid water on the grounds.

Come all and enjoy a spiritual 'feast of good things." Any information desired may be had by addressing either of the undersigned.

Meals on the ground at practically cost.   Yours faithfully,

J. E. CONNOR, President

A. C. GARNETT, JR., Sec'y.

☞ PLEASE POST

A broadside advertising Brasher as an evangelist at a Virginia camp meeting. Was this where the young people seeking an "outing" suffered a remarkable judgment? Brasher Papers.

the lore of nineteenth-century Methodist itinerants.[13] Brasher's frequent use of such stories again places him in the tradition of the circuit riders of his youth, but it especially marks him as a preacher of the holiness movement.

A religion that emphasized the indwelling of the Spirit engendered stories of the supernatural. Holiness presses ran advertisements for collections of remarkable providences that were harvested often from oral sources and sown again by readers. In 1901, the Chicago holiness publisher Samuel B. Shaw promoted two such books, *Dying Testimonies of Saved and Unsaved* and *Touching Incidents and Remarkable Answers to Prayer.* Each, he claimed, had already sold a quarter of a million copies. Shaw also hawked a special children's edition of the latter.[14]

Fascination with accounts of extraordinary spiritual encounters was part and parcel of the holiness movement's reaction to the waning of supernaturalism in nineteenth-century, middle-class Protestantism. Liberal Protestantism, which holiness adherents condemned as denying the freedom of God, distrusted sharp discontinuities in the religious life and spoke instead of continuous spiritual growth and of the natural unfolding of religious experience.[15] Thus William Arthur, the midcentury theologian popular with the holiness movement, argued, "Instead of seeking to keep down spiritual movements to the level of natural explanation . . . we ought rather to pray that they may put on a more striking character of supernatural manifestation."[16]

Early in the twentieth century, controversy between the holiness movement and fundamentalism again reinvigorated the former's tradition of remarkable providences. Holiness folk stood with fundamentalists in adhering to a standard set of doctrines that constituted orthodoxy.[17] However, they faulted fundamentalists for emphasizing the authority of Scripture to the exclusion of the work of the Spirit. Holiness leaders argued that fundamentalist rational assent to Scripture was a powerless substitute for the living Christ. "Mere soundness of doctrine, as such, is not enough," declared one holiness convention. "The life of God must be imparted to the soul."[18] "Watch your step," Brasher warned, "lest while you yet have your head orthodox, your heart loses its music."[19]

In the South, tales of extraordinary spiritual manifestations already held a venerable place in traditional religion.[20] In addition, premillennialists looked for spiritual outpourings to occur immediately before the rapture. They, more than any others at the turn of the century, maintained the supernaturalism of the past.

Holiness biblical interpretation, which discerned the doctrine of the second blessing everywhere in the Scriptures, complemented and sustained stories of the Spirit's activity in daily life. After sanctification, believers, including Brasher, typically reported receiving "new light" on the Scriptures whereby references to the second blessing stood out "as conspicuously . . . as the Rockies."[21] Holiness expositors described their "new" Bible as "a gospel with a sunburst."[22] Second-blessing holiness was their canon within the canon. Brasher even crafted a theme on the ubiquity of holiness in the Scriptures:

> It thunders in the LAW
> It whispers in the NARratives
> Sings in the PSALMS
> It's uttered in the PROphets
> It's proclaimed in the GOSpels
> It's exPOUNDed in the EPISTLES.
> It closes its apocalyptic glory in the
>   ReveLAtion
> And runs OVER and says Holy Bible.[23]

Stories of remarkable providences—testimonies of the Spirit's activity among the sanctified—went hand in hand with the scriptural doctrine of second-blessing holiness.

Remarkable Conversions and Sanctifications

Stories of remarkable conversions and sanctifications served as paradigm and inspiration for members of the audience seeking those experiences. It was the second blessing that also provided special vision to discern the Spirit's workings in daily life. Every sermon preached by Brasher featured accounts of sanctification.

Given his preoccupation with holiness, tales of remarkable sanctifications occur in his preaching far more frequently than stories of conversions. But his sanctification stories follow patterns similar to the standard structure of his conversion accounts. In the latter a wicked or resistant person is overcome by the influence of a believer or an extraordinary event. The more iniquitous the subject, the more startling the conversion. Such stories, according to H. C. Morrison, could "remind people that Jesus can save great sinners."[24]

Thus the woman who swindled Jerry McCauley nineteen times was shamed into salvation after the twentieth and became a "main worker" in his mission.[25] After his wife's death, Uncle Sam Dillard, who formerly "drank and fought and fooled with women," repented and "no longer looked like the same man."[26] Likewise, "bottle-scarred" Charlie Morrison professed religion and converted his neighbors' still houses into sorghum pans.[27]

Brasher's sanctification tales, like his conversion stories, empha-

size the opposition between human will and the Spirit, but in a remarkable variety of characters. His stories were inclusive of gender, race,
age, health, educational level, social status, and geographic setting. In
one sermon alone, Brasher wove together the unusual sanctifications
of these seemingly unlike folk: Mary McAfee, a rustic Kentucky tollgate keeper; Beverly Carradine, an aristocratic New Orleans preacher; Bud Robinson, a stammering, epileptic Texas plowboy; Aunt Catherine Bynum, an aged saint of Blount Mountain, Alabama; Betty Cook,
an invalid in a New York City apartment; and himself.[28] The stories
demonstrate the egalitarian tenor of the holiness impulse. All were one
in the Spirit. Anyone could receive the blessing.

The ritual locus of the experience was the camp-meeting mourner's bench, in holiness parlance, the "altar." In Brasher's stories, however, the blessing also came to the faithful in the woods or in a corn-
field, in the kitchen, on a sickbed, even to a seeker sitting on a fence.[29]
The Spirit was not bound to time and place.

The form of the experience was equally varied. Although sermon
accounts of the blessing served as models for seekers, there was a range
of accepted types, and Brasher respected, even affirmed, the idiosyncrasies of individuals' contact with the Spirit. In testimony meetings,
saints sometimes tried to legitimate their status by comparing their
experience with that of others. "Tell your own experience," Brasher
admonished them.[30]

Descriptions of the blessing ranged from Minnie Brasher's "quiet peace" to Bud Robinson's "oceans of glory and billows of fire" when
God "wasted grace enough on him to save the state of Texas."[31] Receiving the blessing was sometimes "easy." Simple assent to the scriptural promise of sanctification (Phoebe Palmer's "way" of holiness) enabled some seekers to claim the gift.[32] More often, sanctification came
only after intense struggle to yield the will entirely to God. Palmer's
terminology of "placing all on the altar" produced probably the favorite formula for remarkable sanctifications—sanctification in the form
of a test. A choice example of this type from Brasher's repertoire includes voices, a vision, and—to gain audience sympathies—images of
the Lost Cause and the Cult of True Womanhood:

> I held a meeting down in Doleete [?], Alabama. You wouldn't
> find it now on the road. It's gone. I went down there and preached
> ten days. Stayed in the home of Captain DUDley. He was a Con-
> federate soldier with an EMPTY SLEEVE. GALlant old chap. His
> wife was a fine, cultured woman. I don't know why I went unless
> it was to help her some, or her to help ME. She told me the sto-
> ry of her FULL salvation.

She had been conVERTed. She felt the need of a DEEPER work of grace. She saw it in the Book. She WANTED it. No TEACHER, human teacher. The Spirit gradually led her on and, gave up THIS, and she gave up THAT, and she gave up THAT, and she gave up THAT. Finally this suPREME test came: "Will you leave your husband and children forever and serve me?" Why, that's a BLOW. That's DEATH, you know, for a faithful loving wife and mother. "Leave my husband and my children and go off and serve God? A WANDERER?" She wrestled with it a MONTH. She grew thinner in BODY. Her little boy saying his prayers at her knees that night said, "Oh God, bless Mama and make her cheerful and happy like she used to BE." She said, "Lord, I never can leave him now." But the Lord said, "Will you leave ALL for me?"

She got the breakfast one morning. Put on her best dress and took her Bible under her arm and walked out at the front door and the old Captain was standing there, said, "Where are you GOing?" "I'm going away to leave you and the children, forEVER, to SERVE GOD." He took her by the arm and pushed her down in the chair gently and said, "Son, run over to the mill yonder and call brother so and so. My wife's lost her m-i-n-d." He held her and she struggled to go, and then she said she saw, as in a vision, Abraham offering up Isaac. And God said, "Now you needn't go, since I've seen you didn't keep back anything."

For twenty-five years she had been the best of wives and mothers and never had to be worked over yet. She PAID the PRICE. God want her to leave her husband? No. He isn't separating folks. He wanted HER. He wanted the THRONE. HE HAS TO HAVE IT. No HUMAN can have it. No posSESSion can take it. No PASSion can control it. HE WANTS IT. He must have it.[33]

Setting and subjects, process and content of remarkable sanctifications were multiform. Nonetheless, the human prerequisite for a clean heart was always what Brasher called "utter yieldedness."[34] With vision unclouded by "possessions and passions," the saints could identify the providential working of God in the here and now.

Dreams, Voices, Visions, Clairvoyance

Although some branches of Christianity have always viewed dreams as direct contact with the spiritual world, early American Methodism's evaluation of dreams and visionary experiences was ambiguous. Wary of charges of "enthusiasm," circuit riders were reluctant to claim supernatural origins for dreams; yet dreams and related phenomena figured prominently in their lore.[35]

Later, Brasher and his holiness colleagues showed little hesitation in accepting dreams, visions, and impressions as supernatural. The important question for them was whether an impression was of the Spirit or of the devil. Holiness interest in signs of the Spirit bolstered credence in all sorts of unusual manifestations.[36] Brasher's family tradition also placed great store in dreams and signs. His father once risked a trip home through rebel "bushwhackers" on the basis of a dream.[37] His wife's grandmother viewed and spoke to the revenant of her husband.[38] After their young daughter's death, Brasher and his wife were tormented by "preternatural" knockings in their house.[39]

In his preaching, Brasher employed narratives of visions, voices, and clairvoyance quite freely, but at the same time he offered listeners a standard test for ascertaining the divine or other origins of their own experiences.[40] The dreams that Brasher related in his sermons were not types that conveyed specific warnings or directions. They were instead inspirational visions similar to those the sanctified might have during the wakeful ecstasy of a camp-meeting service. Their primary function was to concretize doctrine. His dream of heaven described "roofs of gold and beautiful red jewels."[41] A dream of his son's violent death at a camp meeting helped him—and his audience—to "see a new meaning in Calvary."[42] In another sermon, Brasher related Bishop Bowman's near-death vision of his daughter in heaven. She had died an infant, but in his vision she had become a "beautiful grown young woman."[43] The account corroborated Brasher's belief in growth in grace—and body—after death. Two of his own children had died in infancy and no doubt many children of his listeners had also.

Several tales recount incidents where a "voice" instructs or directs a sanctified person.[44] Brasher's usual emphasis, however, was upon the subtle leading of the Spirit, and in these tales he may have been using "voice" metaphorically. More characteristic was Brasher's comment that the Spirit "hasn't absolutely just flat-footedly told me anything, that I remember."[45]

His own denial of hearing voices notwithstanding, Brasher did believe in spiritual clairvoyance. In some narratives a person was given a clear premonition of the future: Dr. McLaughlin told his Bible class, "I'm saved up to the last tick of the watch. Sudden death would be sudden glory." The same day an earthquake crushed him; his broken watch recorded the moment of his demise.[46] Dr. Godbey and a friend had identical premonitions of Godbey's death: "At eighty-eight, down at a camp meeting, God said [to Godbey], 'Come up to the Mount of Blessing [God's Bible School, Cincinnati, Ohio].' Said to Mrs. Stanley in New York, 'Go back to the Mount of Blessing.' She got back in time for him to pillow his head on her shoulder and go up to meet the Lord."[47]

In some stories, the faithful received providentially inspired knowledge of faraway events. In a story not in his recorded sermons but written for the same audience, Brasher related that while in Birmingham, he "knew" the situation of a friend in Atlanta:

> One day I had a strong impression that Brother Pike needed help, so I gave up my pastoral visiting . . . hurried to the parsonage, and wrote him a letter. I had only one dollar at the time, but I enclosed that one dollar and hurried to mail the letter that afternoon. It reached him the next day as he and some of his boys were picking blackberries. He did not have a dime, so my dollar reached him in the nick of time. Before the food was gone which he bought with it, he got a call to an Indian mission out West. With the call was money to pay expenses and take care of his needs. As far as I know he was never so tried again in that way. For years he sent me five dollars each Christmas to buy some turkey, saying he was "paying interest on the investment."[48]

Brasher took seriously encounters with the Spirit in dreams and clairvoyance, but he never emphasized stories containing verbatim messages from the Spirit. Such stories contradicted his belief in both the mysterious sovereignty of the Spirit and the freedom of the human will. His refusal to tell such stories also reflected the deliberate distance he and holiness folk placed between themselves and pentecostals who claimed at times to utter the very words of the Spirit. Brasher's tales of clairvoyance did demonstrate his belief in a special spiritual protection and care that was available to the sanctified.

Remarkable Deliverances

In storytelling at home, Brasher riveted his grandchildren's attention with a large repertory of deliverance tales—generations of family heroes who by their own grit and wit had narrowly escaped savages, panthers, Confederate "homeguards," and enemies of the Methodist Episcopal Church. In Brasher's sermon narratives, however, it was the Spirit who delivered the sanctified from financial want, illness, and opposers of holiness doctrine.

Holiness evangelists depended on free-will offerings from the meetings they held, and income was unpredictable, sometimes nothing. Brasher's correspondence with his wife, even in the period of his greatest popularity, reveals that they were often without cash. Tales of contributions that delivered him at the exact moment of need evi-

denced the Spirit's stamp of approval on his evangelism and witnessed
to a God who cared for the poor.[49]

The late-nineteenth-century holiness revival placed considerable
emphasis on healing. Brasher's holiness folk believed the prayers of the
faithful could be effective in bringing physical healing by the Spirit but
they disagreed with the pentecostals' claim that particular individuals
possessed the spiritual "gift" by which to heal others.[50] Brasher often
told of his wife's healing at the time of her sanctification[51] and of his
own several years later.[52] Here, the context was a preliminary delinea-
tion of the various sufferings borne by Christ:

> I know there is such a thing as physical suffering because I've had
> rheumatism. If you'd put your finger in a vice and screw it up as
> long as you can bear it, that is neuralgia. Take a full turn on the
> handle after that, and that is rheumatism. In January and Febru-
> ary nineteen and five, I was afflicted with articular rheumatism.
> Had to have a feather pillow under my ankles to keep my heels
> from touching the bed, bow frame over my toes to keep the cov-
> er from resting upon them. Every movement was agony. I couldn't
> turn over. But the Bible students came into my room and laid hold
> on the Lord for a couple of hours, and my recovery was as steady
> as the rising sun. And for fifty-odd years I never had a rheumatic
> pain but I know what PHYSICAL suffering is.[53]

Stories of deliverance from financial woes and illness gave the
sanctified hope and comfort. A third group of tales sealed their conviction that the holiness way was peculiarly God's own. The Spirit delivered holiness folk from enemies of their religion. Dr. Godbey and
other pioneer holiness evangelists in the South made great homiletical mileage out of stories of escape and protection from angry antiholiness mobs.[54] Brasher told of the confounding of Methodist bishops
who designed to stop his holiness evangelism.[55] One of his favorite accounts of deliverance from opposers was that of old Aunt Catherine
Bynum, who proved second-blessing doctrine and thereby helped rescue Brasher from a crowd who believed he was preaching heresy:

> I was holding a meeting over here on Blount Mountain in a tab-
> ernacle that the boys built over there. And there was a crowd over
> there that thought I was preaching all sorts of heresies. And they
> got Aunt Catherine Bynum to come. They knew she was a great
> saint, and wanted her to come over and refute what I was preach-
> ing. And she came. I preached several sermons. One day she said,
> "Brother Brasher, may I talk?" I said, "Certainly." She said, "I

mind very well when I got this blessing you are talking about. I'd just been converted and I loved the Lord so good that I didn't want to ever backslide. And I went down in the woods back of the house and got down on my knees and said, 'Lord, I love you so good I want you to bless me so I'll never backslide.'" And she said, "I gave up just like I was going to die, it seemed like. And He gave me PERfect PEACE, and I've had it for forty years, and I didn't know what to CALL it, but I see it's now what you call 'sanctification.' Bless the Lord."[56]

Remarkable Judgments

The Spirit both delivered the sanctified and brought judgment to bear on their opposers. Out of the pulpit, Brasher told a range of tales in which personal setbacks and calamities were perceived as direct divine judgments. Sins that surely precipitated judgment were avarice and pride. His father left the itinerancy "to make something for his old age . . . and lost everything he had."[57] Yet, fire desolated the valley where comfortable farmers had been too stingy to feed his father on his deathbed.[58] Holiness song-leader John Harris held out for a higher price on Florida real estate: "The boom busted, and he had to move into a garage and his wife take in music students to live."[59]

Pride reaped the same rewards. On Brasher's first multichurch circuit, the humblest congregation saw a heartening revival. At a wealthier, snobbish church, an attempted revival was "a total flat failure."[60] At Indian Springs Camp Meeting, Brasher preached in the morning on a certain text. In the afternoon, another evangelist, thinking he could outdo him, tried to preach on the same text. A violent thunderstorm drowned out his message.[61]

The sanctified not felled by avarice or pride could witness the unhappy recompense of sinners. In Brasher's sermons, remarkable judgments centered on folk who scoffed at holiness and on those who heard the message but failed to yield their will for the blessing. Witness the fates of two scoffers:

I was holding a meeting down in a country church and a woman got up when I dismissed and said, "I'm not coming back there anymore to hear that STUFF." But she came back in two weeks in a COFfin.[62] When you reject God, He is through with you.

Good old friend of mine rode nine miles one frosty night to hear me preach before I got the blessing and said, "John, if you ever get mixed up with this second-BLESSing business, I'm DONE with you." And he proved TRUE [hits pulpit]. One day

he said, "I wish to God I could never HEAR this second-blessing stuff anymore." And he took caTARRH; it destroyed his
HEARing; he couldn't hear the loudest peal of THUNder. He
never had to hear it anyMORE.[63]

Those who heard and rejected the Spirit's offer of full salvation
brought sure doom upon themselves. A preacher in Texas earnestly
sought the blessing, but when he "came up close to surrender, he'd
back off." He finally decided that sanctification would hurt his financ-
es and his standing in the conference. Brasher reported: "There never
was a record of his winning another soul. I last heard of him, he was a
vagabond, out of the ministry, a miserable backslider."[64]
The failure of holiness folk to sacrifice for the holiness cause also
brought judgment: "A lady promised me $500 for my school, and had
$1,300-Persian rugs on her floor, and never paid it. But she died a pau-
per and was BURIED in the charity of friends who one time admired
her."[65]
In the harshness of these judgment tales, Brasher appears to have
lost his usual restraint. But neither the tone of their delivery nor their
context reveals a sense of gloating or vindictiveness. There is instead a
mood of pity for the victim. The judgment was clearly that of God, not
Brasher. In the middle of another judgment tale of a minister who resisted the blessing, Brasher interjected, "My heart ached for him."[66]
These stories illustrated belief in the profound seriousness of the
Spirit's call to holiness. They emphasized the limited number of opportunities a listener had to hear the call clearly. They announced the
holiness conviction that to reject an inward call to sanctification constituted the sin against the Spirit—for which there was no cure: "When
the light fully comes, and you reject it, you have committed a willful,
deliberate act against God and the blood of the Atonement. The light
will come some day so clear, the call so clear and distinct, that if you
don't walk in it, you will get darkness."[67] Remarkable judgments warned
against that night.

Remarkable Saints

Critics of the holiness movement reproved it for its supposed ar-
rogance. Answering them, Brasher counseled his audience, "Some folks
say, 'You must think you are better than other folks.' Don't be bashful,
say, 'Certainly.'"[68] The sanctified claimed, however, that their only boast
was in the power of the Spirit. Most of the stories of remarkable providences thus far cited have identified judgments or blessings of the
Spirit from without. Those stories are part of the tradition of remark-

able providences dating back to the Puritans and beyond in which the Spirit descended and disrupted the natural order on behalf of the saints. The Calvinist emphases on human depravity and divine transcendence never allowed the Spirit to keep close quarters with the saints for long. In the holiness tradition, however, certainly in Brasher's preaching, interest shifted to stories of remarkable spiritual activity from within. The Spirit indwelled the saints.

Stories of the remarkable faith, obedience, and sacrifice of the saints predominated in Brasher's preaching. His sermons were a veritable catalog of holiness hagiography highlighting the actions and attributes of nineteenth- and early-twentieth-century sanctified worthies: holiness folk "go further, and stay longer, and shine brighter, and shout louder, and pay more, and live on less, than any crowd on earth."[69] These tales patterned holy traits and deeds along the lines of the Pauline fruits of the Spirit.[70] Some saints reportedly displayed powers that bordered on magic.

These unusual spiritual enduements—beginning with the second blessing itself—equipped the saints to do battle with what they believed were the evils of the End Time.[71] As a coping response to disruptive social and cultural changes, the holiness movement proclaimed a need for special spiritual support to help individuals "keep pure" in an age of peculiar trials. "The grace that took our fathers to heaven wouldn't take us to market," Brasher declared.[72] Stories of the saints both inspired and mirrored the ideal self-conception of Brasher's audiences.

His narratives of holiness heroines and heroes do not fall neatly into categories, but they can be divided into stories that emphasize either deeds or attributes. As for deeds, stories about the sanctified cite extraordinary abilities and feats enabled by the Spirit. Second-blessing folk allegedly possessed special insight into the meaning of the Scriptures, an insight not naturally (usually, rarely) available to "scholars" but present even to unlikely people who "had the Spirit":

> I go into the kitchen where Aunt Mandy is getting dinner and say to the old colored woman, "Mandy, what does this passage mean in the Book: 'My soul longeth, yea, even fainteth for the courts of thy house'?" "Why," she said, "Chile, don't you know what dat means? That's the Psalmist havin' a spell o' homesickness fo' de house o' de Lawd [audience laughter]. I wish I could go right NOW," she said. And off she goes singing [sings]:
>
> > I'm sometimes up, I'm sometimes down,
> > Comin' to carry me home,
> > My soul, my soul feels heavenly bound,

Comin' to carry me home.
Swing low, sweet chariot, comin' to carry me home,
Swing low, sweet chariot, comin' to carry me home.

"Bless de Lawd" [audience: "Amen"]. God didn't put any premium on ignorance. She just got the blessing and had it in her HEART. And she knew what the thing MEANT because it was just like she FELT about it.[73]

Recipients of the blessing received remarkable powers of creativity. After her sanctification, Mrs. Morris, a farmer's wife in Ohio with only a sixth-grade education, wrote hundreds of hymns: "She would have lived and died a faithful farmer's wife, and been buried by the village preacher, in the village cemetery, and nobody would have sung, 'Sweet will of God still fold me closer, 'til I'm wholly lost in Thee,' if she hadn't got the blessing."[74] After his eightieth year, the holiness evangelist Dr. Godbey (a neglected model for today's academics) "dictated ten books in three days . . . and their accuracy has never been called into question."[75] For holiness folk such marvelous tales inspired reverence for the power of the indwelling Spirit. Brasher's primary emphasis in such stories was to demonstrate that only the Spirit could fully enliven human potential.[76]

Some deeds bordered on magic. The prayers of the sanctified yielded extraordinary results. One hero was L. P. Brown of Meridian, Mississippi, in whose home Ira D. Sankey reportedly was sanctified: "L. P. Brown was a miracle in prayer. He prayed a man off of the gallows and into his home and into a decent man's death bed, when he was CONVINCED that he wasn't guilty. And he wasn't guilty, and they hung him, but the rope slipped. And they never got him back on the scaffold after that."[77]

After the blessing, recipients could commonly expect an ability to interpret Scripture, heightened creativity, and efficacy in prayer. Yet other tales suggest that beyond these basic powers the blessing enabled a hierarchy of spiritual deeds: self-sacrifice for the cause of holiness, "soul-winning," and the combination of the two—preaching holiness in foreign lands.

Brasher gave great importance to tales of average folk who exchanged personal comfort and luxuries for the promotion of holiness: "We can do nothing worthy of God, until we sacrifice."[78] A large sum of money, for instance, was given for a holiness school by a young man at a camp meeting. Brasher carefully related that the donor was just a "small-town grocer" and quoted him as saying, "I never eat a meal for fifty cents, if I can get enough for a quarter to sustain me, so that I can have that other to distribute."[79]

The holiness missionary and Alabama native Eloway Hurst, seated with Bible, at a camp meeting, ca. 1907. She "sleeps in the sand of Egypt." Brasher Papers.

The blessing made extraordinary soul-winners out of unlikely preachers. With the blessing, Bud Robinson, who spoke with a lisp, won over a hundred thousand souls, educated hundreds of youth, and died in triumph. Without it, Brasher declared, "He would have lived and died over [in Texas] cutting mesquite wood at fifty cents a cord to buy food for his wife."[80]

The ultimate in sacrificial heroism was missionary work. Holiness emphasis on the imminent second coming urged the preaching of full salvation to the heathen in foreign lands. Many camp meetings after the turn of the century set aside a special missionary day with services concluding with calls for missionary volunteers. Brasher was an early promoter of such services. His repertoire embraced many tales of sacrificial journeys to the "foreign fields": Will Huff, an Iowa evangelist, stated his call succinctly, claiming, "South America won't let me sleep."[81] Gertrude Howe feared that her aged mother would be hurt when Gertrude announced her missionary intent. To her amazement, her holiness mother sang the doxology.[82] Brasher's most poignant and polished tale was of young Eloway Hurst, a small-town Alabama girl sanctified and called to missions under his preaching. Her first and last assignment was to the Near East, where she "preached to those poor, wretched, vermin-ridden folks, took smallpox, and sleeps in the sand of Egypt."[83] These narratives of self-sacrifice modeled personal consecration for holiness audiences and raised before them again the inestimable value placed on the doctrine being preached.

Saintly deeds sprang from a holy disposition. Worldly folk might not recognize the sanctified, but holiness people identified each other by certain unmistakable marks: "Dr. Cell met a man in Dallas, Texas, one day, on the sidewalk. And he looked at him, and the fellow looked at him, and they smiled, and they passed, and then they turned around and both looked [audience laughter]. Dr. Cell said, 'Why, I'm a Methodist preacher.' He said, 'So am I.' Said, 'I'm sanctified wholly, praise the Lord.' Said, 'I thought so'" [audience laughter].[84] The faces of the saints supposedly manifested their status—what Brasher called a "sweetness," "glory," "radiance," and "joy" emanating from the inner presence of the Spirit.

With inbred sin eradicated, some holiness folk claimed to have no desire for worldly vices: "Bud Robinson went to New York City way back yonder, and they showed him around over the city, and took what he called a 'hack,' no cars then, and showed him everything they could in one day. And he could see about as much as anybody in one day. And he went back to his hotel that night and knelt down by his bed and said, 'Lord, I thank you that I ha'nt [*sic*] seen a thing today that I WANted'" [audience laughter].[85] This tale follows a section in which Brasher talks about "power to live straight in a strange city." It implies that "Uncle Buddy" viewed far more than the great churches of Manhattan. Second-blessing adherents recognized each other by shunning certain outward practices—drinking, smoking, gambling, dancing, and ostentatious dress or adornment. The modern city symbolized those perceived evils. Some preachers fixated on condemning such "vices" and, in fact, as the tale suggests, liked looking for them. In his own preaching, Brasher rarely engaged in such censures, considering them a waste of time better used to stress the major points of the gospel. A vigorously moralistic ethos nevertheless characterized much of the holiness constituency.

Brasher spent far more time exhorting his listeners in the positive ethics of holy living, especially in the practice of long-suffering love. True holiness issued in extraordinary concern for the welfare of the unfortunate. Education, temperance, and "rescue work" among "fallen women" took priority. This narrative comes from the time of Brasher's early ministry in Birmingham:

I've had some experience in RESCue work. I've found those poor, lost girls broken-hearted. And to give them a glimpse of HOPE was like a BURSTing of NOON at MIDnight. I'll give you this beautiful prayer one prayed. See if you can beat it in literature. The worker said, "PRAY, daughter, pray." "I don't know how to pray. I've never prayed. I've been a SINner." "Well, you pray. Tell him what you think, what you want." And here's her iDENtical prayer: "Lord, take these poor, tired feet and PLACE them in the way everLASTing. Amen." Isn't that beautiful? Poor, lost girl, kicked and hated and cursed and abused. "Take these poor, tired feet and put them in the way everlasting."

And I had her funeral. Preached it in a house of shame. Told them how Jesus could save anybody, and how she with that little prayer had walked up into the presence of the Lord.[86]

Holiness groups at the turn of the century did not concentrate on large-scale institutional social reform, but they excelled in zeal for humanitarian work with individuals. They credited their voluntary work to the compassion of the Spirit, which "never gives a man up."[87]

Perfect love disposed the saints to joy, strict morality, long-suffering love, and, some said, to long life. For years, Brasher cited his own life as example: "God GAVE me this experience. Thousands of folks have found the experience in the meetings I have helped to hold. Many of them are all gone to heaven already. If I hadn't had this experience I would never have been heard of out of more than two or three counties. I would have been dead years ago. A disease would have captured me. But I've seen THOUSANDS get the blessing. And hundreds of them have gone on to heaven. They will be on the committee when I get there."[88] Folk religion has always held that saintly lives were rewarded by longevity.[89] Brasher maintained that holiness was healthful primarily in the sense that the Spirit eradicated harmful passions, led the saints into the will of God, and gave perpetual strength for the work of holiness.

Sermon narratives of the saints often concluded with detailed accounts of their dying. Serene and sometimes joyful deaths vividly communicated the reality of sanctification. Such tales of "happy dying" have a long provenance in the evangelical tradition. In Methodism, a triumphant death symbolized personal victory over sin, a close relationship with fellow believers, and the expectation of future fellowship in heaven.[90] Accounts of pious exhortations from dying saints were designed to affect hearers profoundly—especially the unconverted.[91] As a boy, Brasher had witnessed the dramatic deathbed scenes of both of his parents, and for over eighty years afterward, he never tired of reciting polished narratives of his parents' last earthly moments.[92]

Since he was preaching primarily to the already converted or sanctified, Brasher recounted in his sermons only the deathbed scenes of the saints. The stories range from an enactment of a dialogue between

The triumphant death of a young girl. From S. B. Shaw's *Children's Edition of Touching Incidents and Remarkable Answers to Prayer* (Grand Rapids, Mich.: S. B. Shaw, 1895).

a dying John Fletcher and his wife to Bud Robinson's homely last statement of faith: "I think I hear the chariots a-comin'."[93] Such deathbed tales were always happy, celebrating the claim that "holiness people die well" and that the indwelling Spirit gave earthly saints a foretaste of heaven. In the ideal death, there was no fear or awkwardness as the sanctified approached heaven: "They don't have to be met at the door and introduced and told to get used to the habits of the folks. They don't have to be taken in a corner and told how to say, 'hallelujah' and 'praise the Lord' and 'amen' and 'glory.' They've been here [Hartselle Camp Meeting]. They got the training down here."[94] The sanctified were believed to be so well prepared for heaven that holiness people often discarded the word "death," stating instead that their late fellow believers had been "translated."[95]

Autobiographical Narratives

"There isn't anything connected with myself that's worth anything."[96] So Brasher testified in his sermon on his hundredth birthday. Yet in his preaching that day he referred to his own life experience at least six times. If holiness folk could "shout louder and go further," they said it was the Spirit who enabled them to do so. They never credited their remarkable feats and traits to native ability. Holiness preachers therefore felt quite free in their preaching to talk not only about other saints but also about themselves, or more precisely, the Spirit's work in and through them.

Autobiography was inseparable from Methodism, which grounded its theology in experience. Methodists made ritual the testimony meeting, and Methodists propagated their flock through organized class meetings that held up for close scrutiny the personal experiences of each member. Nevertheless, by the second half of the nineteenth century, many elite American Protestants frowned upon the use of personal narratives in sermons. Critics of their use accused preachers of "magnifying their attainments in grace under the guise of professing what the Lord had done for them."[97] The practice could easily lapse into boasting. Still, personal narratives were a venerable tradition in evangelical preaching. Many of Peter Cartwright's stories in his autobiography were quite likely tales he had told hundreds of times in sermons. John Broadus remembered that among Baptists in the early-nineteenth-century South "it was very common for the preacher to tell the exercises of his mind at the time of his conversion." Furthermore, he concluded, the practice "is natural, and lawful, and mighty if it is fitly managed."[98]

In almost every sermon, Brasher narrated personal experiences, sometimes with mighty effect. He ranged freely from the "inborn deviltry" of his youth, to the spiritual joys of aging, to jests about the difficulty (after ninety) of "living up to [his] reputation."[99] Some stories glorified the Spirit by contrasting its power to Brasher's natural condition.[100] His conversion and sanctification accounts served as models for seekers. All of these anecdotes created a unity between Brasher and his listeners. Here was a fellow pilgrim pointing out the way to his friends and equals.

His most powerful narratives were formulaic—polished set pieces describing the pivotal events of his spiritual journey. A fine example was an account of his conversion:

> I remember that August back yonder in 1886
> When I was a FARM boy
> Without anymore home than a GYPSY
> Living on a FARM with a good FAMILY
> Conviction came to my SOUL
> And I prayed in the BARN and
> Prayed in the STABLES and
> Prayed in the FENCE corners and

Prayed in the WOODS and
Prayed on the way to CHURCH and
Prayed in the blacksmith SHOP and
Looked like the heavens were DARK and BRASsy
Looked as though God had forGOTten me
But there came an HOUR
When the darkness rolled away
When the heavens CEASED to be BRASS
And PEACE come stealing into my SOUL
And I KNEW my SINS were forgiven.[101]

A tonal, almost chanted, exhortation to seek salvation immediately followed. Then in a similar tone, Brasher quoted a hymn that universalized the meaning and complemented the aesthetic of his own crafted testimony of conversion. All together, the three—narrative, chant, and hymn—produced a telling effect.[102] Most important, the conversion narrative, like many of Brasher's personal anecdotes, highlighted the tension between human nature and the Spirit, the painful prayer-struggle to yield his will to supernatural suasion. Holiness folk made complete consecration of the human will to the divine will a precondition of sanctification. This ethic in part manifested itself in puritanical mores, but contrary to stereotypes entire sanctification did not necessarily signify grimness. The very struggle to consecrate engendered a distinctive holiness humor.

Consecration and Humor

These are such sacred things, I don't want to smile about them
much. But the foolishness of folks, I can smile about that.
—JOHN L. BRASHER, 1960

Yielding to the Spirit was the common thread that knit together the celebrated traits and deeds of holiness hagiography. Phoebe Palmer's theology of "placing all on the altar" put willful consecration at the center of holiness folk's pursuit of the second blessing. Although consummated by the Spirit, the holiness way began and deepened through self-denial.[103] Holiness people took seriously the divine injunction "Be ye holy, even as I am holy."[104] They knew this was a humanly impossible ethic, yet for some no sacrifice was enough, no moral code too strict.[105]

The quest for a pure heart could cause anxiety over even minor infractions. In one sermon, Brasher morbidly warned: "Every sin that a person commits is in the direction of a sin against the Spirit from which there is no recovery. It may be the slightest kind of a thing."[106] His narratives urged remarkable sacrifices for the cause of holiness:

> I was in a camp meeting up in Louisville, Tennessee. And one of our missionary friends came from India and made a speech and told what twenty-five dollars would do for a school in India. And there was a little woman there that lived out in the hills. And the next morning we were waiting for the service, and I was talking with the missionary lady. And this little woman from the hills came up, and she was dressed in I think it was a cotton dress and a nice little apron and an old-fashion poke bonnet. And she took the missionary by her arm and led her off to one side and said, "My daughter and I live up here in the hill, and we've been saving some money to buy us a rug for our front room. But when we went home last night and prayed over it, we decided that we could do without the rug better than those people in India could do without their school, and we brought it to you." And she untied the corners of her handkerchief and dumped the contents in the lady's lap, with tears of joy, that she was able to SACrifice for GOD.
>
> Was it all right for her to have a rug? Yes, perfectly proper. Perfectly legitimate for her to try to make her little home beautiful. But she preferred that those dark-skinned folks on that other side of the earth might hear the teaching of JESUS, while she walked on the floor [voice: "Glory"].[107]

Stories such as this swelled camp-meeting missionary offerings, but they also produced continual guilt among hearers who worried that even small luxuries might be sinful.[108] No amount of self-denial seemed to satisfy the holiness ethic, which left a legacy of guilt surrounding money and pleasure that would haunt the children and grandchildren of the sanctified. Little wonder that the holiness ethos has been painted as shockingly grim.

Zealous in their striving for purity, Christian perfectionists nevertheless heard and affirmed that the sole source of perfect love was the Spirit. Wesley himself stressed that human nature this side of the grave always remained subject to sins of ignorance and error. Ultimate reliance upon the Spirit's power thus allowed for a robust humor that gave the sanctified distance and escape from their otherworldly ethic of self-denial. They could indeed laugh at human folly and weakness, and sometimes even at their own strictness. Most outsiders and later historians were unaware that within holiness circles flourished a humor that balanced puritanical tendencies.

Consecration

Since consecration was the cardinal virtue, holiness folk marked people according to their response to the call to yield all. Brasher's narratives of remarkable sanctifications and related stories revealed and focused holiness attitudes, stereotypes, and prejudices about various groups.

His stories present an ambivalent view of the role of women. Brasher and his auditors were caught in the tension between the nineteenth-century view of women's place and the new privileges of leadership available to women in holiness circles. He espoused wholeheartedly the Victorian ideal of true womanhood: piety, submissiveness, purity, and domesticity. Woman's task was to "keep men more human and less brute."[109] Suffrage "opened a door of freedom for which women were not yet prepared."[110] He even argued that it was the women's vote that repealed prohibition and "let the saloon back in."[111] Here is how one of his narratives of a remarkable conversion enforced the ideal of domesticity. Audience laughter connoted assent:

> At that camp [Caney Springs, Tennessee] a dear old couple who were RARE saints, white-haired old folks, CAMPED in their tent. And they had a daughter who was a businesswoman, I suppose twenty-five years of age, if they ever get that old [audience laughter]. And she came to the camp, and they introduced her to me, very politely. And she said, "I told Father and Mother I'd come if nobody'd talk to me about religion." "Well," I said, "I WON'T talk to you about it. I'd as soon you'd go to hell as any woman I ever saw in my life." That knocked her off the Christmas tree. And I'm here to tell you that every time that she got in contact with me she talked about religion [audience laughter].[112]

The holiness goal of complete consecration meshed nicely with the broader cultural ideal of female piety, submissiveness, and purity. Narratives cited above show that Brasher's preaching highlighted women as models of consecration and sacrifice. However, in the new leadership roles that holiness groups granted women—especially preaching—holiness norms clashed with social dictates and traditional religious sanctions.

The radical doctrine of the indwelling Spirit drew no distinction between male and female. In their institutions and ceremonies, holiness groups practiced an equality of gender not found among other contemporary evangelicals. Holiness folk may have viewed businesswomen as improper, or at least with suspicion, but they applauded women missionaries, women testifiers, and women preachers.[113] Brasher was proud that after Minnie Brasher's sanctification in Birmingham she became for a while "a regular street preacher."[114] In other sermons, he approvingly cited Susanna Wesley and Catherine Booth as champions of women's right to preach.[115] Women, he believed, could bring special gifts to the work of evangelism. Brasher described his evangelist friend Leila Owen Stratton of Lebanon, Tennessee, as a gracious and cultured banker's wife, "yet so common that she could go in the homes of the mountain people just as easy as if she had been brought up on raw turnips."[116] In matters concerning the promotion of their faith, holiness folk suspended some of their ingrained cultural views about the role and status of women.

Holiness attitudes toward women were thus a conflicting mixture. They held to an ideal of female submissiveness and quiet domesticity, but they venerated publicly women's capacity to consecrate all in faith, and granted women the right to preach, the highest position of authority in their community.

Brasher's stories about blacks reveal similar tensions between cultural values and religious ideals. His attitude toward blacks was consistently cordial yet expectedly segregationist and paternalistic. He admired especially their humor and their music, but blacks, he believed, were in "the childhood of their race."[117]

Again, however, in his preaching he offered blacks as models of the consecrated life, equal in the Spirit: "Mandy Smith, that wonderful colored woman that sang and preached in the palace of Queen Victoria, sat down—and this was up North—by a WHITE woman. The woman MOVED. And Mandy said to herself, 'Child, you don't know who I am. I'm the King's daughter.' The King's daughter. Think of that. All of you good sisters are the King's daughters."[118] Brasher made the story palatable to his southern audience by setting it in the North and avoiding open confrontation between Smith and the white woman. He probably had used this account for decades, but it is remarkable that he could present it in Alabama in the mid-1960s. In the Spirit, cultural conventions regarding the place of both women and blacks were suspended.[119]

In fashioning his narratives of consecration, Brasher most often selected people, locations, and institutions similar to those of his plain-folk heritage. His exempla dwelled in the rural and the natural, camp meetings themselves a self-conscious return to preindustrial quiet. "Blessed is the fellow that's got a thicket to pray in; he'll never backslide."[120] It was the city that threatened to besmirch the spotless lily with soot.[121] The city spoiled religious sensibilities.

The common folk were often models of consecration. When the plantation-born preacher Beverly Carradine got the blessing, he first "laid down his gold-headed cane and silk hat."[122] In his sermon "The Mind of Christ," Brasher took the story of the woman who gave her hard-earned rug money to the missionary and juxtaposed it with the story of the rich woman who failed to give, died a pauper, and was buried through the charity of friends.[123]

Brasher was uncomfortable near riches. He felt "sorry and little" in homes where the dining table had "spoons and forks and hybrid spoons and forks"; he was "miserable" until he could "get back where they could eat all they HAD off of one plate."[124] He championed the virtues of plain living. Yet some of his exempla presented an undisguised regard for wealth. For example, one of his favorite theme-metaphors for sanctification was the set piece depicting the plantation inheritance, perhaps a vestige of the longings of his plain-folk childhood. He never extolled poverty or condemned riches for their own sake. When he criticized rising affluence he did so because its materialistic ethic quenched devotion to the Spirit.

Brasher was a spokesperson for education. As president of Central Holiness University in the 1920s, he envisioned the future of the holiness movement as dependent upon its colleges.[125] Quite well educated for his time, at midlife he nevertheless confessed to his family his "painful lack of the confidence which comes from a liberal library and scientific education."[126] Yet, in spite of his devotion to learning, many of his tales of the sanctified featured their lack of education.[127] Therein he appealed to some of his audience: "They roll the Chariot of blessing so low that anybody in the world can step IN it."[128] But his preaching emphasis on native intelligence over book learning was more than a play for audience rapport. It was a caveat against two perceived perils of formal education. First, any schooling that denied traditional supernatural beliefs was "false education."[129] Higher critics of the Bible were "ignorant as goats."[130] Second, any education that superseded the primacy of the Spirit was bankrupt. Brasher could say with complete candor, "I'd rather hear a one-gallus plowboy with the experience [sanctification] than the greatest doctor of divinity without it."[131]

A devoted churchman, Brasher was its harshest critic. He bemoaned the church's alleged substitution of wealth, education, art, and formality for holiness. Institutional Methodism had stifled the Spirit, no longer calling its members to a consecrated life:

I hear them wail out every Sunday morning while I listen over the radio: "All things come of thee, O Lord, And we bring back some of it." And then they sing "Amen" so long it looks like they are mighty sorry they gave it up [audience laughter].[132]

There are some beautiful altars in the country now. They call them "chancels," I believe. They are beautiful. I don't blame them for having them. But they're never WET with TEARS, tears of the penitent, the tears of the hungry for God.[133]

Supposedly bereft of spiritual preaching, members of the popular churches were the subjects of fervent intercessory prayer in holiness meetings. Most were assumed to be "corpses," unrepentant and ignorant of the life the Spirit offered.[134]

Humor

Hand in hand with the earnest soul-struggle of holiness meetings went humor. Consecration of the will was deadly serious—the sanctified called it "dying out"—yet some funny things happened on the way. The Spirit's work was sacred, but human nature was not, and Brasher could laugh at "the foolishness of folks" as they strained—sometimes not too successfully—to bend their contrary, often eccentric, ways to the norms of the holiness community. Confidence in the Spirit's victory allowed holiness folk to laugh at themselves.

Brasher gained audience consent to smile at others by first poking fun at himself. He accented his humanity, demonstrating his oneness with his listeners, deliberately deflating any loftiness in the legends that eventually clustered about him. Often at the beginning of preaching, he won quick rapport with his audience through humorous self-deprecation. At Hartselle Camp Meeting, he simply pointed to his mortality: "I came to you sixty-seven years ago under that new tabernacle. It was new and I was. I'm back here now and it's old and I'm old. But it's standing up, and I'm doing my BEST to do it [audience laughter]."[135] On another occasion, he spoke sarcastically about the value of a prayer he had prayed: "Brother Johnson has had me over twice to pray for the dear friends over in the courthouse, and they made records of it, and they BURIED it—that was very sensible, maybe [audience laughter]—they buried it in some cylinder that will be dug up 100 years from that date."[136] Another time he pretended that his pride was hurt: "How many never heard me before? Put up your hands [many hands]. Look at that. Look at that. Boy, where have you BEEN [audience laughter]?"[137] Sometimes he made a deliberately absurd statement: "It's been a good while since I have preached in this church, since I'm close to ninety-four and I've never been here before [audience laughter]."[138] With this opening humor, Brasher established a bond with the audience even before he read his Scripture text. His listeners met a fellow traveler. They knew in advance he would be entertaining as well as serious on the sermon journey, and *together* they would hear the text and discover its import for them.

Brasher frequently salted his preaching with humorous tales about others. Some of these stories, properly defined as "local character anecdotes" by folklorists, emphasized incongruous or peculiar character traits of individuals within and outside the holiness community.[139] Brasher sported with his audience when he reminded them: "The Lord never made but one like you, thank the Lord. We couldn't stand two."[140] Many of his narratives dwelled at length and with delight on the personal quirks of the saints. In one sermon he drew this colorful sketch of the pioneer southern holiness evangelist William B. Godbey:

> He used to come to the school when I was president down here at Boaz [Alabama]. He would drop me a card looked like a FLY had dropped on the ink and run across: "I will arrive at your college a certain date, to be there so many days. Arrange the services according to your godly judgment. Amen" [laughs].
>
> I sent Brother Murphree one day to meet him, told him how he would look. I said, "Don't look for a finely dressed old gentleman. Look for a fellow with a linen duster on rolled up to his elbows nearly. He will have a bundle of books in each hand, wrapped up in newspapers, about all he can carry. And there will be an umbrella under his arm tied up with a piece of rope, and his Greek Testament tied up with a red bandana handkerchief. That will be Dr. Godbey."
>
> And he got off the thing and was gone a rod before Brother Murphree overtook him: "Is this Dr. Godbey?" Said, "Praise the Lord, when's the first service?" That was the introduction. Brought him over to the school, and he knelt right down in [sic] the floor in the hall and said, "O God, bless these juvenile immortals and grant that they may be blowing the silver trumpet of the gospel while I'm playing on the golden harp" [laughs]. Had him over for dinner and he baptized our daughter. And we had soup for the first course, and everything else we gave him he put it in a bowl and ate it with a spoon. But he was POURING out LEARNING and GRACE all the time.[141]

Tales of the idiosyncrasies of the sanctified entertained audiences, but on a deeper level they reassured would-be saints that the Spirit respected personality, that the holiness way did not erase all favorite habits, pleasures, or peculiar preferences. These anecdotes affirmed the

The pioneer southern holiness evangelist W. B. Godbey (1833–
1920) in his customary linen duster. Humorous anecdotes about
such sanctified eccentrics affirmed the right of individuality within community. Asbury Theological Seminary.

right of individuality within community—a community with strict norms yet with healthy room for divergence. Such stories question stereotypes that portray conservative religious groups as the locus of forced, monotonous conformity.

Brasher also employed local character anecdotes virtually to laugh people into sanctification. Personality quirks—"the foolishness of folks"—could be harmless, even endearing, as those of Godbey; in some instances, however, they were serious impediments to entering the community of the blessed. Some traits were "foolishness" because they kept seekers out of the best.

Many of Brasher's humorous anecdotes center on a seeker impeded by some habit or desire. It might be unusual vanity, inordinate love of possessions, or a petty vice such as smoking or gossiping. The stories typically resolve happily when the subject gives up the foolishness. Thus Bud Robinson responded to the gossip who cried out, "I have everything on the altar but my tongue": "Sister, this altar is about sixteen feet long, looks like you could get it on that" [audience laughter].[142] In another tale, a man kneeling at the altar at Indian Springs finally got the blessing when he reached in his pocket and threw his tobacco as far as he could throw it. Brasher concluded with comic hyperbole: "All the riches of divine holiness, all the glory of an indwelling Holy Ghost, and all the prospect of an eternal heaven for the holy— it'd been hangin' on a plug of tobacco" [audience laughter].[143]

Sometimes the foolishness was simply nearsightedness when it came to recognizing and appropriating permanent beauties. Occasionally Brasher baptized a traditional secular tale and used it to make a theological point, as in this local character anecdote: "Now a man with a pure heart opens up to the world. This is GOD's world. . . . Can you look on these hills and not be thrilled? Some folks never see anything beautiful. A man took a fellow up on Lookout Mountain to show him that MARvelous view, and retreated so he could see it. And he turned around after a while and the fellow said, 'I've seen something today I never saw beFORE.' 'What was it?' He said, 'I saw the back of a BUZzard and him a-FLYin''" [audience laughter].[144]

Many of Brasher's exempla poked fun at outsiders. These tales demarcated the bounds of his holiness community and reinforced group solidarity. Used as weapons in the contest with competing sects and theologies, these stories wielded the power of ridicule, deflation, and sarcasm. Other tales laughed at variant theologies and extreme practices *within* the holiness movement.

In almost every sermon, Brasher related humorous incidents that ridiculed and described the downfall of antiholiness adversaries. Brasher enjoyed playing up the opposition almost as much as reporting his victories over it. "They've done everything to me, I reckon, except whip me and skin me," he boasted.[145] Highlighting the adversary roused the troops like nothing else. Many of his humorous tales, like those of Peter Cartwright and his circle, were structured according to dramatic oppositions, and the typical comic ending saw the adversaries converted or discomfited. In these comic stories, Brasher always won.[146] Two companion tales he used often were incidents that occurred early in his holiness itinerancy:

> I've had to bear three or four prejudices, living as I have. My father was an INTENSE UNION MAN. . . . And then when I got SANCtified, I got a double dose, you know. Yeah, "that fellow Brasher." I was holding a meeting once and I wondered what in the world this CROWD's come toNIGHT for. I never saw such a crowd at that place. And the next day I found out that it had been rumored that I was going to organize a Mormon CHURCH there that night [audience laughter]. And they had come to put a FIXing on me.
>
> I held a camp meeting at another place, and they told it on me that I took three beautiful women up there, and every woman I got SANCTified I got five dollars a head and shipped them to Utah [audience laughter]. White Cross Camp. I told them that was a GRAVE mistake, because I didn't take but TWO beautiful women along [audience laughter]. One was my WIFE, and her COUSin.[147]

In other sermons, Brasher concluded the same stories by telling how the opposers brought in the saintly Methodist Aunt Catherine Bynum to refute him, but she, to their surprise, testified to the very holiness experience he was preaching (see above).[148]

Another tale typically ridicules an opposer by reporting his lawlessness: "I have KEPT THE FAITH [audience: 'Amen']. Whether people LIKED it or not. Whether I was POPular or not, whether I was CRITicized or not, and I had plenty of it. Accused of breaking up churches. Man wrote me a letter I was disturbing his church. It was so peaceful that he was carrying a double-barreled shotgun for his FATHER-in-law [audience laughter]. They needed somebody to stir up that church [audience laughter]. Might have had a funeral. He saw his mistake later. He was deLIGHTfully fixed to hear what I preached, and to support it."[149]

The popular churches and their membership often received the brunt of Brasher's satire. Not all of his humor took the form of structured incidents; he loved to jest in descriptive analogies and metaphors such as the following scene depicting jaded church members: "The Lord wants to be properly represented, advertised. A lot of people don't advertise the Lord very much. Their life is so LAME, so WEAK, so IMPERFECT, so inconSIStent, that the profession of religion at all, doesn't add one thing to God's cause. . . . If you saw a big sign somewhere on a great white-fenced farm, 'Stock Farm: Fine Thoroughbred Stock,' and all you saw inside the fence was an old yo-necked horse, and a swayback cow with long horns, and a poor little sheep or two, would you think he had recommended his farm?"[150]

Less frequent but still enticing targets for Brasher's ridicule were Modernists, who, according to holiness folk, based their criticism of traditional doctrine on mere suppositions and who grabbed at any scientific theory that punctured supernaturalism: "Modernists amuse me like a little dog 'Trip' I had once, that anywhere you'd point a gun up, he'd tree a squirrel."[151]

Competing sects, especially Baptists—primary contestants with Methodists for the soul of the turn-of-the-century South—were the losers in a number of anecdotes. Brasher was careful, however, in his preaching to restrict his humorous barbs primarily to matters of doctrine. Although the following Baptist tale hinges on bad language, most of his humor in the pulpit refrained from slurs on the character or habits of other religious groups. This story ridicules the Baptist belief in "eternal security," which decreed that once a person was converted ("established") he could not fall from grace: "I heard of a man once who told his boy to go on to Sunday school, and the boy said, 'Well, why don't you go, Father?' He said, 'I don't need to. I'm established.' The boy didn't know what that word 'established' meant, but he kept it in his mind. Some days after that they were driving the team and it balked and wouldn't pull a pound. After the old fellow had used a lot of language that wasn't very good, the boy said, 'Pa, I know what's the matter with that horse.' Said, 'What is it?' Said, 'It's ESTABLISHED.'"[152]

Disciples of Christ, popularly called Campbellites after their founders, Thomas and Alexander Campbell, were ridiculed for the heavily rational, antiexperiential tendencies of their doctrines: "An old colored woman was by the Campbellite when he said there was no such thing as heartfelt religion, and she said, 'Not as YOU knows of'" [audience laughter].[153]

Roman Catholics, though never serious competitors with holiness groups, were the butt of an occasional story. In this case, the "vain" doctrine of purgatory served as a foil for the holiness view of sanctification: "One fellow was a member of that Church and kept paying year after year until finally the priest said, 'I think I've got him now in about eight feet of the bank.' 'HAVE you?' 'Yes. I need a little more MONEY now, and we'll have him OUT.' 'Well,' he said, 'Dad's been ALWAYS a great jumper, and if he's THAT close he can JUMP out'" [audience laughter].[154]

Ridicule and satire also controlled deviations from norms within the holiness community. Above all, the holiness movement stood for an instantaneous second blessing, immediately available. Nevertheless, a small minority of Methodists who participated in the movement emphasized growth toward perfection more than instantaneous blessing. A tale set at Asbury College, a center of southern holiness, curtailed the minority view through humor: "Asbury [College] had a president there for a week or two [laughs], and he preached going on to perfection as 'always approaching it.' And the boys found an old horse out there on the commons, and caught him, and tied a bundle of fodder and a couple of ears of corn in front of its nose. And by having a stick along his body, hung it so he couldn't reach it at all, you know. Then they gave him a larrup and told him to 'go on to CORN' [audience laughter]. The more he went, so much the further the CORN went. Now God isn't FOOLING with folks."[155]

Brasher and his circle also tried to set boundaries on the behavior of worshippers who became filled with the spirit during their meetings. Listeners were given a generous tether in acting out their ecstasies, but evangelists discouraged extreme—perhaps nonspiritual—manifestations and condemned spiritual thrill seekers. By mimicking those who sought the sensation of spiritual power but not the substance, Brasher put them in their place: "For some folks it's 'POW-a.' They say, 'POW-a. I want the POW-a' [laughs]. It's not noise and fuss, nor gesticulation, nor how loud you can holler, nor how high you can jump. It's how WONDERFUL you can LIVE."[156]

As conservators of traditional mores and as advocates of direct communication with the Spirit, holiness groups usually harbored at least a few fanatics. While all holiness people favored modest dress, some evangelists made straitlaced attire a badge of orthodoxy and harangued camp-meeting audiences until, as Brasher lamented, "the people slipped away from the camp just like they were ashamed."[157] Annoyed that some evangelists could "hang the kingdom of heaven on the length of your hair or a pink ribbon around your middle," Brasher and his close colleagues never spent much time preaching on dress codes and through humor like the following story tried to discourage fanatics who did: "Brother [Joseph H.] Smith always had a question [time]. One morning one fellow roared out, 'Ought we not to preach POINTED-

LY and FREQUENTLY on women's DRESS?' What was his reply to that? 'Not too POINTEDLY, there's too little of it [audience laughter]. Not too FREQUENTLY, lest they think we THINK too much about it'" [audience laughter].[158]

The performance and content of preaching itself was judged by humor that was sometimes shared with a preaching audience. Brasher carefully styled the delivery of his own sermons (described in the previous chapter) and promoted a preaching norm by telling his audiences tales about inexperienced preachers. He enjoyed describing Arthur Moore, who later became more polished and a bishop: "No more awkward preacher ever started out than Bishop Arthur Moore. Why, he'd run to the edge of the platform and scream and throw up his hands and stomp like a mule would at a fence. He'd relate an incident with his hands stretched out like that [gestures] and squalling at the top of his voice" [audience laughter].[159]

A light, self-regulating humor featuring poorly chosen or overextended sermon exempla thrived among holiness evangelists. Brasher related stories about his evangelist friend Andrew Johnson, whose illustrations sometimes "took him far afield" and whose congregation "did not always get back after one of his 'runs.'"[160] A notable instance of Johnson's choice of exempla was his vivid comparison of judgment day to a wagon wheel running over a frog's head.[161]

At a camp meeting in Iowa, Brasher and his coevangelist T. C. Henderson sat together on the front preachers' platform behind another evangelist, Charles Babcock. Babcock was preaching on depravity. In an unfortunate climax, he shouted, "The parasites of damnation are in our blood!" Henderson quickly sketched a cartoon depicting "the only parasite of d_____ in captivity." He handed it to Brasher, who refused to look at it until after the service was over, knowing that he could not control his laughter. Brasher saved the cartoon for fifty years. Such humor embodied an aesthetic judgment about proper exempla, but perhaps more important, it bespoke a confidence that the human condition was not that grim.

Although Brasher deemed frogs' heads and parasites inappropriate figures, he often employed traditional, rustic, or clever imagery to delight his hearers and, in the words of one, to "fasten" divine truth upon them.[162] On the one hand, Brasher was a child of the southern style that put a premium on flowery rhetoric, and he used it (as described in the previous chapter) to evoke the beatific vision. On the other hand, he was the immediate heir of the antebellum tradition of Old Southwest humor, which turned on wordplay, the homespun, and use of vernacular. William Henry Milburn, a nineteenth-century student of rhetoric (himself a

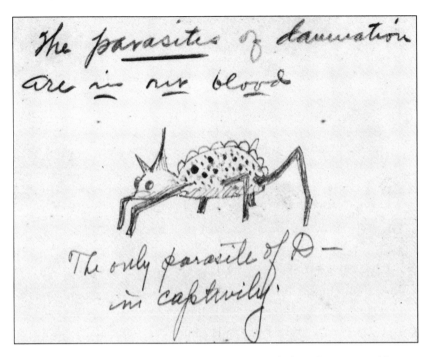

The evangelist T. C. Henderson sketched this cartoon of "the only 'parasite of damnation' in captivity," while another evangelist, Charles Babcock, employed the image in a camp-meeting sermon. Brasher Papers.

Methodist circuit rider), described Peter Cartwright, who stood in the same tradition: "He was the best lexicon of western words, phrases, idioms, and proverbs that I have ever met."[163] Brasher was a master of colloquial phrases, traditional similes and metaphors, which he interjected to entertain, to fix a point, and sometimes to toss a barb. In some places, Brasher juxtaposed the two styles—elegant prose and rustic image—thus magnifying the effect of each:

> How cheap it is
> For a person to be a sinner.
> Go on in sin when
> Heaven BECKONS you and
> God CALLS you and
> The blood was SPILLED for you and
> Eternity awaits you [audience: "Amen"].
> Crowns and thrones and harps and harmonies
>   eternal await you,

> Then take a few things and then die and be
> put in the ground like a hog
> [audience: "Bless the Lord"; "help him"].[164]

He occasionally dropped in colloquial pronunciations, words, and phrases:

> God's Son cleanseth us from ALL sin. How much is left when all is gone? I said to some little boys up on Blount Mountain, "Son, if you had twelve oranges and gave them all away, how many do you have?" "Nairn."[165]

> God wants us to have peace. Help yourself to peace. Don't come with a gill cup, come with a hogshead.[166]

> Oh, you can take and make a great preacher out of a scrub.[167]

> We oughtn't to wait 'til people get six feet high and cuss, before we get 'em converted.[168]

> Now then, they're workin' me pretty stiff today [preaching twice in one day].[169]

He drew upon a stock of traditional similes:

> Don't be stiff as a stick. This is not a graveyard. This is a church.[170]

> I get so tired of [church ritual] every Sunday morning, from Sunday to Sunday the same things that have been worn as slick as an otter slide.[171]

> If [the Spirit's] gone you don't care. You can go like a blind ox to hell, without any reproof.[172]

> Those ungrateful folks are like hogs who eat acorns and never look up to see where they came from.[173]

He excelled in and made most frequent use of traditional—and original—metaphors. A few examples hint at the range and color of his enormous repertoire:

> On a church that had relocated: "I've been associated with this church since before it SWARMED from Oneonta."[174]

> On committing sin: "Of course you can, if you are goose enough. I'd sell every right to sin I could for a nickel and throw the nickel in a mud hole."[175]

> On the danger of nonspiritual impressions: "That's Split-foot. You can hear the crack of Lucifer's whip in it."[176]

On people who resist sanctification: "How many, many, many have I seen come right up to the border, and look over in the green pastures, and the beautiful orchards, of delightful fruit of the Spirit; and turn back to crab apples, and cucumbers, and onions."[177]

On people who lose their spiritual experience: "An old boneyard don't look good anytime."[178]

On false testimonies: "Some folks talk about love that never have gotten in gunshot of it."[179]

On sanctification: "After a while, you'll get to wishing it was a yard long and you could taste it all the way."[180]

On temptation: "You can't keep the devil from laying his brats at your door, but you can refuse to raise 'em."[181]

On Enoch, who was translated: "He walked off into glory without any funeral expenses, and beat the coffin trust, and shouted his way through the gates of pearl."[182]

As the reporter on the 1897 Waco camp meeting wrote, such graphic figures indeed "captured the imagination of the masses."[183] The images delighted the sanctified and demolished sinners. The rustic and colloquial expressions attested to Brasher's plain-folk roots and won rapport with his rural-born audiences. Here, side by side with elements of high-flown oratory, lingered traces of the "backwoods preacher," the native stump speaker, a southern original, a rough-and-ready country humorist whose preaching drew heavily upon oral sources.[184]

Rich as it was, Brasher's sermon humor was culled out of a much larger stock of humorous religious tales that he relished telling. Not all of them, he believed, were fit for preaching. Many of his more detracting and delicious tales, told in family and other social gatherings, were not preserved on sound recordings, yet even a sample of some that were shows that he used restraint in his selection of humorous exempla. Out of the pulpit, Brasher, with tongue in cheek, told of Baptists who would eat dog fennel (a noxious weed) if liquor were poured on it; and he impersonated a half-wit determined to eat a roasting ear rather than celebrate his wife's conversion.[185] His preacher tales that documented his long itinerancy ranged over a colorful array of snuff-spitting termagants, voracious bedbugs, rancid food, stingy congregations, and women who tried to seduce him at his camp-meeting tent. None of these made it into his sermons.[186] In preaching, Brasher's showmanship and prowess as a taleteller took a back seat to his sense of the sacred and to his primary desire to present the holiness gospel in words and images that would appeal to all.

John Lakin Brasher in his hundredth year. Brasher Papers.

His use of exempla placed Brasher in a venerable tradition. Cotton Mather wrote that the proper work of ministers was "to *observe* and, much more, to *preserve* the remarkable dispensations of Divine Providence towards themselves or others."[187] Three rich traditions converged in Brasher that endowed his preaching with an exceptional variety of narratives: plain-folk taletelling, Methodist preacher lore, and holiness fascination with the Spirit's activity in this world. The bishops' appeal that speeded Brasher to his sanctification in 1900 reminded him that "Methodism began in experience."[188] As a child of that church, and as Mather had enjoined, Brasher both observed and preserved stories of religious experience. His curious gaze took in the secular and the sacred, the tragic and the comic, but it fixed most intently upon those incidents that he considered of universal and eternal import. Like a gloss on the margin of a text, he once mused amidst taletelling, "There are some experiences that belong to our humanity, the solution of which is very important."[189]

Preaching on his hundredth birthday, he again told his own story:

> I saw a LIGHT back yonder
> It was the GLEAM of a HEART that could be
>   made PURE
> It was the GLADness of a fellowship that
>   could be made CONstant
> It was the HOPE of a life that never ENDS
> It was the promulgation of a gospel that
>   saves men from being sinners to being
>   SAINTS
> It transformed human SELFishness into human
>   beNEVolence
> It transformed SORrow into JOY
> It transformed BURdens into GLADSOMENESS
> Until you're GLAD you can BEAR the burdens
>   of others
> I've KNOWN something about it.[190]

This was his well-crafted theme, his credo on the Spirit's work, his solution to the experience of his humanity.

Afterword

Brasher's story confuses the stereotypes of holiness religion. He was not unique, in significant respects representing many other holiness folk in the South. He was, above all, a figure who in his complexity embodied the rich diversity and contradictions within southern religion and culture.

Popular views have depicted holiness folk at the margins of society, disadvantaged rurals trapped in agrarian poverty or the disinherited of urban ghettos. Brasher did know brief poverty as a youth, but he came from thrifty southern plain folk. He was essentially middle class, as were most of his colleagues and audiences. Nor was his religion a regionally insulated southern exotic. Brasher's preaching, in its style, in its stories, and in its stress on the supernatural work of the Spirit, exemplified southern traditions. But the articulated holiness theology that he preached came south with Reconstruction and remained intimately tied to institutions and political loyalties dominant in the North. His doctrine of holiness, though marked by nineteenth-century modifications, was essentially the inherited Wesleyan position held by the Methodist Church. His evangelism spanned the nation.

Although some of his listeners were not highly educated, Brasher's preaching demonstrated a marked literacy. He sometimes lamented the limits of his learning, yet his schooling and constant reading placed him on a par with well-educated Protestant clergy of his time. Although he delighted in the vernacular of his region—and used it with telling effect in the pulpit—he was cited, even by a Britisher, for his scholarship and wide culture.[1]

Brasher possessed a sensitive spirit and patterned his preaching to stir the passions of his audience, yet his style was not excessively emotional. In fact, the holiness movement won him by emphasizing sanctification as an experience not dependent upon emotions. Brasher affirmed the plain-folk traditions of warmth and freedom in worship, but at the same time, always wary of uncontrolled ecstasy, he required order and decorum in his meetings.

Holiness sectarians have been painted as grimly ascetic. Among the saints, however, a lively humor served as an incentive on the path to perfection, protecting individuality, strengthening the bounds and bonds of community, and assuring seekers of the Spirit's victory over human foibles. This assurance that holiness folk claimed was not a narcotic but a tonic. Believing they saw the Spirit at work amidst all of life, they enthusiastically took up the task of sharing that vision and of making the world holy. Brasher's sanctification met his inner spiritual need, integrated his personality, and gave him permanent purpose—undoubtedly providing the dynamic behind his unusual longevity.

Although stereotypes locate holiness religion in sects separated from and antagonistic toward the popular churches, Brasher called for a spiritual revival within established denominations. He condemned "come-outism." He never relinquished his vision of the church someday renewed in holiness. But as the twentieth century unfolded and the holiness movement splintered into an ever-growing number of sects and factions, there was sometimes a wistful tone in his voice, as in a letter he wrote in 1922: "If nobody had left the church, we might after awhile have gotten hold of the pilot house."[2] Perhaps through a remarkable providence, in August of his one hundred second year, at Hartselle Camp Meeting, he preached his last holiness camp-meeting sermon where seventy summers before he had preached his first.

Appendix A

Some books read by Brasher in the Conference Course of Study (1892–96) and in U. S. Grant University School of Theology (1897–99). Compiled from his own list from memory and from volumes in his library with accession dates 1892–99.

Ackerman, George E. *Man, A Revelation of God.* 1888.
Arthur, William. *The Tongue of Fire.* 1856.
Buckley, James M. *A History of Methodists in the United States.* 1896.
Butler's Analogy of Natural and Revealed Religion.
Crooks, George, and John F. Hurst. *Theological Encyclopedia and Methodology.* 1894.
Fischer, George Park. *History: Ancient, Medieval, and Modern.* 3 vols.
———. *History of Christian Doctrine.* 1896.
Foster, Randolph S. *The Supernatural Book: Evidences of Christianity.* 1889.
Handbook to the Grammar of the Greek Testament.
Harman, Henry M. *Introduction to the Study of the Holy Scriptures.* 1878.
Hebrew Grammar.
Hill, David J. *The Elements of Psychology, A Textbook.* 1888.
Hurst, John F. *History of the Christian Church.* 1897.
Jevons, W. Stanley. *Elementary Lessons in Logic.* 1892.
Kidder, Daniel P. *A Treatise on Homiletics.* 1894.
Ladd, George T. *Elements of Physiological Psychology.* 1887.
Miley, John. *Systematic Theology.* 1893–94.
Pope, William B. *A Compendium of Christian Theology.* 1880.
Rawlston, Thomas N. *Elements of Divinity.* 1847.
Stevens, Abel. *History of the Methodist Episcopal Church in the United States.* 1865–67.
———. *History of the Religious Movement of the Eighteenth Century, Called Methodism.* 1858–61.
Terry, Milton S. *Biblical Hermeneutics.* 1890.
Wesley, John. *Extract, Law's Call.*
———. *A Plain Account of Christian Perfection.*
———. *Wesley's Sermons.* 2 vols.

Appendix B

Minnie Eunice Moore Brasher's account of her sanctification from her autobiography in the Brasher Papers.

Papa graduated and we moved to B'ham. I gained health and was getting on fine until little Johnie was born. When he was about five or six months old we took whooping cough. I thought my time had come. Our doctor told me the best thing would be to change climate. I didn't see any chance for that and began to study about dying. I had been a Christian all along but still had temper. Would get mad and have to repent and ask forgiveness for things I'd do and say. I saw I was getting worse and one night when Papa had gone to attend a funeral, I began to pray for dying grace and was desperate.

It seemed I'd said all I could think to say and began to pray the Lord's Prayer when I came to "Thy Will be Done." It seemed I heard a voice say, "This is the will of God, even your sanctification." I said, "Lord, I don't believe in sanctification, but if it is Thy will sanctify me, or anything, just give me dying grace." I opened my eyes. It seemed I could see writing on the wall, questions I'd have to study to see if I could promise to do them. When I'd say, "Yes, Lord," another would appear. One was, "Are you willing to go to the hardest place in the Conference, wear clothes out of missionary barrels? Are you willing to beat a tambourine and preach on the street?" The last and hardest, "Are you willing to die now and let your husband marry again?" After a while, I said, "Yes, Lord, maybe someone else can raise the children better than I can, anyway give me dying grace." All the questions ceased and I was as calm as could be.

As I lay down, I felt so light and white I thought it was death. I thought I'd better call some one and tell them I was dying. Then I thought, "No, it doesn't make a bit of difference, I'm all right, I have dying grace." I went to sleep after a while and waked up the next morning, was hardly able to get up and get around. Had to hold to chairs to get around but had such a sweet sense of cleanness and readiness. I was ready to go, didn't have a thing to fix up.

I don't remember how long it was before we were to have a revival in our church. Bro. Ruth came and was to preach, and I was too weak to go but down by my bed praying for the meeting one night, and something said to me, "The

Lord has done so much for you, why don't you ask him to heal you?" I lifted my hands and said, "Lord if it's Thy will, heal me for Thy Glory." Something seemed to come over me like electricity, only it was pleasant. I jumped up praising God, dressed hurriedly, and went out to the church. Walked up to the front and sat down by your father. He asked, "Where are the children?" I said, "At home asleep." He said, "Who is with them?" I said, "The Lord is with them. He has healed me."

The next day I was like a new machine, oiled and ready to run. Still, I didn't think about my dying grace until Sunday afternoon in the testimony meeting I told how I had prayed for dying grace and hearing, "This is the Will of God[,] your sanctification." Then I realized that was what He gave me. He blessed me so I felt as light as a feather and as white as snow. I believe anyone has to be really sanctified to know how happy I was. It's indescribable. "The half has never yet been told." Glory to God.

The Reverend Beverly Carradine's account of his sanctification, from Graphic Scenes *(Cincinnati: God's Revivalist Office, 1911), 268–71.*

The evangelist gave general direction as to the obtainment of the experience that were true and Scriptural, but the Spirit, as He always does, led specifically.

As well as I can recall some of the steps taken which led me into Canaan, one involved my willingness to become an alien and outcast from the ranks of my brethren on account of the truth of holiness.

No one but a preacher who has lived for years in the midst of a congenial Conference or Church Brotherhood could appreciate the suffering and sacrifice attending such an experience. Yet this was clearly brought to my mind and remained pressing heavily like a conviction upon it, until I said, "Yes."

Next came another vivid-like impression almost like a voice—"Would I be willing to give up reputation for all time?"

So again I said, "Yes."

Following this was the inward query—"Would I be willing to be misunderstood, all my life, and tread a path of human loneliness to the very portals of the tomb?"

And yet with body prostrate on the floor and face wet with tears I answered the Lord once more—"Yes."

As I took other steps in the line of consecration, it soon became evident that I was rendering a full obedience to God as I recognized His will in His Word or heard His voice sounding in my soul calling to particular acts of sacrifice and service.

So I kept saying "Yes, Yes, Yes," to all of the divine will and Word, to every call He made upon me, and I found a sweet growing consciousness that I was getting somewhere; that I was on the right road; and was in a way where the light was growing steadily brighter, evidently to some perfect day. I was three days seeking the blessing, and in all that period kept saying "Yes" to God.

The earliest published account of the sanctification of John Lakin Brasher and Minnie Eunice Moore Brasher, Methodist Advocate-Journal 10 (31 May 1900): 4.

We are just closing a successful revival at Simpson Methodist Episcopal Church. Rev. R. G. Pike, superintendent of Pentecostal Mission (this city), brought his forces and joined in with us. Dr. C. L. Mann, pastor of People's Temple, and a number from his church rendered very valuable assistance. Evangelist C. W. Ruth, of Indianapolis, Ind., and his singer, Rev. Robinson, of Somerset, Ky., labored with us ten days. Ten were converted and thirty or more were sanctified.

The church is in better condition than in many years. To the Lord be the glory!

My wife and I were gloriously sanctified before the meeting began. She at home all alone and I at the Salvation Army hall in a meeting held by S. L. Brengle, a brigadier in the Army. My wife, who has been almost an invalid for years, was instantaneously healed, and feels as well as when she was a girl. I recommend the Blood of Christ, to all my classmates and friends, to whom I have opposed this view of the second blessing, as able to cleanse from all sin and remove from the heart all unholy tempers and desires, all selfishness, etc., and make you every whit whole. I am not crazy I trust; if I am, all the harm I wish you all, is, God make every Methodist crazy from the Lakes to Gulf. Halleluiah!

J. L. Brasher, Pastor.

Brasher's account of his sanctification in his A Simple Statement of Christian Experience (n.p., 1962), 7–11.

In 1899, I had been appointed to Simpson Methodist Church in Birmingham. Immediately upon graduation, I moved to Birmingham and began my duties as pastor there. I found the church in a low condition financially and spiritually and worked the first year with very little results. In April of the second year, I was stirred by an appeal from Bishop Charles H. Fowler to the whole church. The financial world had not recovered, nor the church either, from that awful hard time beginning in the early 1890s. The bishop said, "The ground is strewn with the dead, the Church is in retreat," and other like refrain [sic]. I was determined that my sector of the church should not retreat. I began to pray and fast. To deny myself pleasant food and eat only enough to give me strength for my work, which I did with all my powers but saw but little fruit of my labors.

There was a small holiness mission down town at 1st Ave., and 21st Street, of which Rev. R. G. Pike, of precious memory, was superintendent. He had engaged Rev. C. W. Ruth of Indiana, and a singer for a revival in his mission. I attended one service and was not pleased at Brother Ruth's style of preaching, and publicly criticized it and him. He went to Fitzgerald, Georgia, for a meeting with a return engagement with brother Pike afterward. In the meantime the Salvation Army on 1st Avenue had a 3-day holiness special, with Colonel Samuel Logan Brengle as leader. Captain Houchins came to my door with a bulletin announcing the services and invited my attendance at the meeting. It was stated that Colonel (afterwards Commissioner) Brengle was a graduate of Depauw University in Indiana, and had studied 2 years in Boston School of Theology, and I thought a man of that scholarship could be worth hearing.

It was mid-April. I went to the afternoon service on the second day. I went in and sat down and looked around. All of the holiness crowd was there and some beside. I had said of them that they were "good folks, but weak above their eyes." Well, they knew enough to be there. Smiling as if they had discovered a fortune (and they had), the Colonel and staff were on a front seat facing the audience. I was impressed with the brightness of his face. I could argue against doctrine, but not against his face. When he arose to preach his text was, "Follow peace with all men and holiness without which no man shall see the Lord." He did not rant or ramble. In the simplest statements he told us what it was not, and what it was. When he was through he asked "All who have a clean heart" to stand. All around me stood but I did not. I had often stood on similar propositions, but not then. "All who want to be converted stand"; after prayer the meeting closed.

I went forward and met the Colonel, and said, "Colonel Brengle, could you come to my study, I would like to talk with you?" He said, "I can be there tomorrow morning at 10 o'clock if that will suit you." "That will be fine," I said. The next morning he did not come at 9:55 or 10:05, he was in my study door at exactly 10 o'clock. I told him all my heart as I never told anyone else before or since, and all he said about it was, "I think sanctification will fix you." That was the last thing I wanted him to say! He said, "Let us pray, you pray." I prayed a little prayer and he prayed a short prayer, then we arose and shook hands. He said, "The Lord bless you. Come to the service," and I said, "I will be there."

I went that afternoon. I was a little late, like a lot of folks are when they are hurting. It was a bit chilly in the middle of April, and the door to the Hall was closed. I stood at the door a moment and turned around and walked back to 1st Avenue and 19th Street. There the battle raged. Chicamauga [sic] and Gettysburg were no more stubbornly fought! Now, I did not need anyone to tell me that I had two natures in me. One said, "Go back to the hall. You need help. You want a revival. You know he has something you do not have." Another was arguing, "You can't afford it. You are a graduate of a theological school, pastor of a city church, have prospect of advancement in the conference and of making a great preacher. Those holiness folks will crow over you. You can't afford it." But the Lord threw His weight on the hall side and I turned around and went back to the hall, turned the knob and the door was ajar.

A lassie saw me and I would not retreat so I went in and sat down. Same crowd, only more of them, and a motley crowd beside, and there sat another pastor that I thought would make fun of me. Col. Brengle arose and announced his text and gave his message. I do not remember his text or his sermon. A word I was trying to build up my defense against. I would build up at one side and it would fall again and again. He now had finished his sermon and was saying, "All who have a clean heart, stand," and I did not. "All who want a clean heart, stand." I pulled up by the back of a bench. "All who want to be converted, stand. Come to the penitent form," and I went forward at once and knelt at the "Penitent form." As I passed to the altar I heard a woman say to another, "That little preacher is in earnest."

I knelt down and began to seek a clean heart. I looked around in a moment to see who else was kneeling. On one side of me was a red nosed bum and on the other side was a woman of the street. It was somewhat like being crucified between two thieves, so to speak. They settled their matter before I did. Bro. Pike tried to give direction and counsel, but I was too much engaged to listen to him. I prayed on until after awhile there came a strange stillness in my heart and soul, and I hoped I had not lost interest or concern. But later have decided it was the rest of consecration. I had gone to the bottom. All was yielded, opinions and all. I got off my knees and sat on the penitent form. Col. Brengle said, "What has the Lord done for you brother?" I said, "I do not feel so different, but I have put all on the altar." "Do you take Him as your Sanctifier?" I said, "Yes."

At the night service I testified. "The blood of Jesus Christ cleanses me from all sin," and felt a little lighter and more restful. At the close of the service the Col. come to me and shook hands with me and said, "I am glad for that testimony. Do not be afraid of terms. Don't be afraid of 'the second blessing.' Let the Lord have His way with you. Goodbye." He gave me some holiness books, among them *Hidden Manna*, by Sheridan Baker. I was in that "no man's land," so to speak, for some days.

I had a call to the funeral of a friend in Chattanooga, and took along with me A. M. Hills' great book, *Holiness and Power.* Somewhere between Birmingham and Chattanooga, the Spirit came, gently, quietly, assurably and with such fullness of peace I had never experienced before, and what sweetness and rest! For days ahead the peace and sense of purity deepened, and I could but wonder, "How long this will last?" He seemed to whisper to me, "I have come to stay." What a change! What a new life and strength for the work at hand! What new zeal in my pastoral visiting! Now it was a delight, before it had been a task that had to be done. Now it was a privilege, a joy. Now freedom in service whether a few or church full or camp tabernacle. A new light on all scriptures and a new pleasure in preaching and new and larger results. That was April 16th, 1900.

Transcript of John Lakin Brasher's account of his sanctification extemporaneously delivered at Hollow Rock Camp Meeting, Toronto, Ohio, August 1954.

Then, from the school I was appointed to a church in Birmingham. You know the M. E. church down there was not strong. The Southern Methodist WAS strong. They gave me no kind of fellowship. They paid no attention to me, but I was doing some work over in one corner of the town. Church was nearly dead when I got to it. I tried to get a revival, but didn't get anywhere, and I went to hear Commissioner Brengle, and walked in and looked at that beautiful face, and my theories began to evaporate. Then He took the text "Follow peace with all men and holiness without which no man shall see the Lord." He didn't rant. He spoke about what it was and what it wasn't. Just as simple as a baby. "Everybody's got a clean heart stand up." For the first time I DIDN'T. THEY stood all around me there. Those holiness folks, I said, "were weak up here." Afterward I said, "Could you come to my study, I would like to talk to you?" "I can be there at ten o'clock in the morning." "All right, that'd suit me."

He wasn't there at 9:45 nor 10:05, he was there at ten. That impressed me. I told him all my heart as I'd never told anybody before nor since, nor never will again. And all he said was, "I think sanctification will fix you." But that isn't what I wanted him to SAY. But he SAID it. Then he said, "Let's pray." Said, "You pray." And I prayed a little prayer, and he prayed a little prayer. He didn't rant, pitch, and cavort. Got up and shook hands with me and said, "God Bless You. Come to the service." I said, "I'll be there."

I was late getting there. Lots of folks get late in the meeting, 'cause they are hurting. I went up to the door and STOPPED. It was closed. I turned and walked back up to Nineteenth and First Avenue. And then I had a battle. You talk to me about Chickamauga and Gettysburg. I didn't need anybody to tell me anymore there were two forces in me. One was saying, "You better go back. You know you've been fasting through this month and denying yourself of all pleasant food that you might have a revival." And there was another saying, "You can't afford it. You are a graduate of a theological school, and you've got a future ahead of you, and you will make a great preacher yet." But after a while, the Lord helped me, and I turned and went back, and opened the door, and somebody saw me, and I couldn't retreat, and I went in and sat down, and there they were, the same bunch only more of them, and there was a preacher over there. I knew he would make fun of me. And he preached. I don't know what he preached about. NOT ONE WORD HE EVER SAID. I, trying to make my theories stand up and they wouldn't. When he got through, he said, "Everybody that's got a clean heart, stand." And they stood. "Everybody that wants one, stand." And I pulled up by the back of the bench. "Everybody that wants to be converted, stand." And there was an old red-nosed bum over there, and a streetwalker over there. "Come to the penitent form." And I led the procession. I heard a woman say as I went by, "That little preacher's in earnest." And I knelt, looked around directly, and there was a bum on one side of me and a harlot on the other. My pride and my dignity was going down, down, down, down. And old Pike tried to tell me something and I resented it, little bit. I prayed awhile until a strange silence seemed to come into me. I got up and sat down on the altar. Commissioner came 'round and said, "What's He done for you, Brother?" And I said, "I don't feel so different, but I've given up all and trust in Him." "You take Him for your sanctifier?" And I said, "YES."

I know some of you high-faluting folks wouldn't have thought I was getting anywhere. But I was dying out, you know. I went back that night and testified, "The blood of Christ cleanseth me from all sin." Felt better. After service was out: "Glad you gave that testimony. Don't be afraid of terms. Don't be afraid of the second blessing. Let God have His way with you." He gave me some books.

I had to go to a funeral at Chattanooga of a friend. Took along A. M. Hills' *Holiness and Power.* I don't know where, nor when, but that "peace that passeth all understanding" came somehow, and somewhere along the road. Brother Ruth came into my church right afterwards. I'd made fun of him before. He had been in a mission downtown, and I'd heard him, and I went home and MOCKED him and made fun of him before my prayer meeting. But he had a return engagement, and in the meantime I had been in touch with Brengle, and Brother Pike said, "We might have our meeting in your church, have the meeting TOGETHER, in YOUR church." And the board said, "It's all right," and we had it. And Ruth came in, when it hadn't been three weeks 'til I had said, "I would no more have a second blessing preacher in my church than a mad dog." And he founded me in the doctrine. I owe more to him, perhaps, than any man that's lived, in the establishment of my doctrinal content of preaching. And we had Bud Robinson. Then I had Andrew Johnson. He was a boy-preacher, THEN. Fifty-two years ago he held a meeting for me in that church, and that church DOUBLED its membership, and QUADRUPLED its attendance, and PAID OFF its debts, and when I resigned to go into the evangelistic field, it was supporting two workers in the foreign field. Just RUINED that church, just ruined it world without end. Well, that's the way I started.

Appendix C

Two versions of an anaphoric theme on the work of the Spirit.

1.

He's the only one can bring you INTO liberty.
He's the only one that can
ConVICT a sinner.
He's the only one that can
Regenerate a
BeLIEVer.
He's the only one that can teach a
CHRIStian.
He's the only one that
Can bring you to conseCRAtion.
He's the only one that can
Give you FAITH
For the CLEANsing.
He's the only one that can bring the merits of Jesus'
    BLOOD and apply it to your HEART
Until your HEART is CLEAN
And your SOUL is aGLOW
With the love of GOD.
He's the ONLY one. (SR 58)

2.

He is the only one DEALing with us. The Father is upon the throne of universal empire. The SON is upon the throne of intercession. The Holy SPIRit is here. He proceedeth from the Father and the Son, and He has been com-MISsioned to DO all that GOD NEEDS TO DO in the reDEMption of a HU-Man soul.

The Holy Spirit is the only one that can conVICT a sinner. Not in a trial of a thousand years could the church or the singers or the preachers conVICT ONE HUMAN SOUL. He uses singers. He uses preachers. He uses the CHURCH. But He, alone, can convict. Conviction is one hundred percent divine.

He's the only one that can asSIST a sinner to rePENT. Sinner thinks he can repent any time he PLEASES. No, that's a FALlacy. You can only repent when He HELPS you, and if He is grieved and DOESN'T help, no one can repent. His GRACious asSISTance must be GIVen every SOUL or they must perish.

He's the only one that can GIVE a man or a woman a NEW HEART. Not all the sacraments administered by whomsoever can give any man a NEW HEART. It's a fallacy to think that you can get a man out of the world, and bring him and join him into your church, and administer to him the comMUNion, and make a CHRIStian out of him. The only POWER in the HEAVENS or the EARTH that can make a man a NEW HEART is the Holy Ghost.

He's the only one that can tell that man when he HAS done it that it IS done. Nobody can tell you when you are born of God, but the Holy Spirit ALONE can tell you that. For He's the only one that KNOWS, 'til He has reVEALed it to you.

He's the only one that can show a believer that deep, dark, hidden sin, lodged way down in his nature, that CARnal mind, that something that won't be GOOD, that something that can't be made good.

He's the only one that shows its DEPTH, its HEINousness, its UGliness, and its hell-worthiness.

He's the only one that can assist a believer to CONsecrate. Somebody said consecration is one thing, and sanctification is God's part, but it's only half true. You can't consecrate fully to God, DEATHlessly to God, without the assistance of the Holy Ghost. And GOD CANNOT SANCtify you without your choice and faith. It takes BOTH YOU AND GOD to meet these conditions and GIVE you a holy heart.

He's the only one that can tell you when you have GOT a clean heart.

He's the only one that can CLEANSE your heart.

He's the only one that can keep you from FALLing and present you FAULTless before the presence of His glory with exceeding joy. From the time you are awakened to the fact that you are a sinner until you are housed in heaven, it is HIS hand that guides, HIS hand that saves, HIS voice that awakens, HIS Spirit that teaches, for the WHOLE WORK of redemption is NOW in HIS hands. (SR 36)

Appendix D

Subjects and Locations of Selected Themes in the Sound Recordings

The following are selected, discrete themes, including Bible stories, church history, *ordo salutis* (theology and the way of salvation), general descriptions, and memorized sequences of Scripture verses. Formulaic biographical and autobiographical themes are treated in Chapter 8. In the list below, the number preceding the colon is the number of the sound recording. The numbers following the colon denote page numbers of the transcripts of the recordings in the Brasher Papers. In the second section of this appendix, themes with the same title are not similar.

1. Themes That Appear More Than Once in the Sound Recordings

The Glorious Church (from the Old Testament to the holiness movement)	42:9–16; 59:9–19; 65:3–14
God's Requirement of Holiness	53:2–3; 58:1–2
The Crucifixion	38:15–16; 40:5–6; 50:9–10; 53:5–6; 55:8–10; 57:6–7; 58:7–8; 67:2–8
The Work of the Spirit ("He's the only one . . .")	36:3–5; 58:12–13
The Company of Heaven	53:10–12; 54:14–15
The Plantation Inheritance	54:12–13; 56:10–11
The Unselfish Christ	38:2; 55:5
Job	46:10; 57:14
The Devil	54:5; 56:4–5
The Pensiveness of Twilight (Adam and Eve in the Garden)	57:4; 58:2; 64:2
If All Were Sanctified	47:2; 51:15; 52:13

2. Other Themes by Content

These passages are identified as themes by language that is florid and repetitive (anaphoric), by periodic sentences, and by delivery that may be metric, intoned, and dramatic.

BIBLE NARRATIVES

The Humility of Christ	38:5–7
Abraham and Isaac	38:14–15
The Garden of Eden and the Fall	40:2–3
The Birth of Christ	40:3–4
The Poverty of Christ	40:4
The Passion	40:4–5
The Ascension	40:6
The Lord Is Coming	40:10–11
Noah	42:8–9
The Second Coming	44:18–19
View of Heaven in Revelation	49:12–14
The Devil	54:5
The Pearl of Great Price	54:15–16
The Sufferings of Christ	55:6–10
The Peaceable Kingdom	55:15–16
Christ, the Pattern of Perfect Holiness	58:4–5
The Poverty of Christ	58:5
The Passion	58:5
Christ's Questions before the Judgment Throne	58:9
The Rich Young Ruler's Loss	62:16–17
The Splendor of Heaven	64:9
Did Christ Die?	67:2
How Many Saw Him?	67:8

ORDO SALUTIS (THEOLOGY AND THE WAY OF SALVATION)

The Eternity of God	19:4
The Fullness of God	29:2
The Holy Spirit as Personality	36:2
The Faraway Look of the Sanctified	38:4
God Made Us for Service	38:5
How to Be Humble	38:6–7
The Body of a Saint	39:6–7
The Beauty of God	39:7–8
Christ Requires Our Love	40:9–10
The Humanity/Divinity of Jesus	41:4–5
Conversion versus Sanctification	41:7–9

MEMORIZED SEQUENCES OF SCRIPTURE VERSES OR HISTORIC CREED

Appendix E

Brasher intoned the following passage from the theme of "the rich young ruler." Transcript and sound recording of sermon, "What Lack I Yet?," Clear Creek Methodist Church, Gallant, Alabama, 30 September 1957 (SR 48).

Wouldn't it have been wonderful if he could have had a

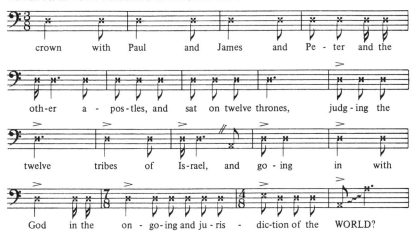

crown with Paul and James and Pe - ter and the

oth-er a - pos-tles, and sat on twelve thrones, judg-ing the

twelve tribes of Is-rael, and go - ing in with

God in the on - go-ing and ju - ris - dic-tion of the WORLD?

That was what was OFFERED him. What did he do?

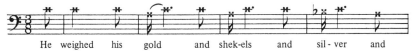

He weighed his gold and shek-els and sil - ver and

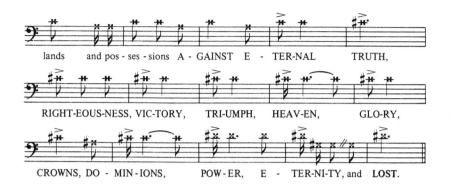

lands   and pos-ses-sions A - GAINST E - TER-NAL   TRUTH,

RIGHT-EOUS-NESS, VIC-TORY,   TRI-UMPH,   HEAV-EN,   GLO-RY,

CROWNS, DO - MIN-IONS,   POW-ER,   E - TER-NI-TY, and **LOST.**

Appendix F

Lineage of John Lakin Brasher

Thomas Brasiour (?)   m. ?
b. ca. 1644–d. 1710 (Md.)

William Brashier   m. Elizabeth _____
b. ca. 1674–d. 1708 (Md.)   b. England–returned to England 1708

Thomas Brashier (Brazier)   m. Hannah _____
b. 1701 (Md.)–d. 1784 (N.C.)   b.   d.

James Brazier (Brasher)   m. Cithea Cox
b. ca. 1748 (Md.)–d. 1834 (Ala.)   b.   d.

Rev. James William Brasher   m. _____ Hosey
b. ca. 1787 (S.C.)–d. (Ala.)   b.   d.

Rev. John Jackson Brasher   m. Milly Caroline Hafley
b. 1820 (Ala.)–d. 1887 (Ala.)   b. 1829 (Tenn.)–d. 1879 (Ala.)
                                        Daughter of:
                                        Cornelius Hafly
                                        b. 1785 Germany–d. (Ala.)
                                        m. Phebe _____
                                        b. 1801–d. 1878 (Ala.)

Rev. John Lakin Brasher   m. Minnie Eunice Moore
b. 1868 (Ala.)–d. 1971 (Ala.)   b. 1873 (Ala.)–d. 1959 (Ala.)

Notes

Abbreviations

BP: John Lakin Brasher Papers, Duke University, Durham, North Carolina.

SR: Sound Recording. Sound recordings are in the Southern Folklife Collection, University of North Carolina, Chapel Hill. Transcripts of the recordings are in the John Lakin Brasher Papers, Duke University. Full citations of the recordings appear after the Notes.

Preface

1. Transcript of funeral of the Reverend Wallace Allgood Murphree, Saint Paul Methodist Church, Boaz, Alabama, 1 May 1950, BP.

2. Liston Pope, *Millhands and Preachers: A Study of Gastonia* (New Haven: Yale University Press, 1942).

3. Wilbur J. Cash, *The Mind of the South* (New York: A. A. Knopf, 1941), 389, 290.

4. Erskine Caldwell, *Deep South: Memory and Observation* (Athens: University of Georgia Press, 1980), 53, 29.

5. SR 75.

Note on the Transcriptions

1. The format of transcription is a modification of those found in Dennis Tedlock, "On the Translation of Style in Oral Narrative," *Journal of American Folklore* 84 (1971): 114–33; and in Kenneth M. George, "'I Still Got It': The Conversion Narrative of John C. Sherfey" (M.A. thesis, University of North Carolina, 1978), 50–51.

Chapter 1: Fathers and Mothers Looking Down

1. SR 42.
2. John L. Brasher, "An Autobiography," 1, BP.
3. SR 16. Documentation for the family genealogy is in the Brasher Papers. See Appendix F for Brasher's lineage.
4. In South Carolina, the Brashers had attended Hopewell Methodist Church on the Greenville circuit. See the Reverend Samuel M. Green, "An Historical Outline of Greenville Circuit," typescript, South Carolina Conference Archives, Wofford College, Spartanburg, South Carolina. In the early eighteenth century, the family was Anglican, enrolled in the books of Saint George Parish, Harford County, Maryland, 1696–1753. See Saint George Parish Records, 1681–1790, Hall of Records, Annapolis, Maryland.
5. The Reverend E. B. Teague, "Sketches of the History of Shelby County" (1900; reprint, Tuscaloosa: University of Alabama Press, 1978), 14, 23. In the nineteenth-century South, the title "Uncle" denoted respect and was used regardless of the age or kinship of the recipient. See John L. Brasher, "How Can They Hear without a Preacher?," lecture delivered at God's Bible School, Cincinnati, Ohio, 1 Dec. 1947, BP.
6. Teague, "Sketches," 14. J. J. Brasher possibly was named after John Jackson, a Methodist circuit rider at that time in Alabama. See Marion E. Lazenby, *History of Methodism in Alabama and West Florida* (Nashville: North Alabama Conference, 1960), 115.
7. SR 10.
8. John L. Brasher to Delbert Rose, 13 Oct. 1964, BP; Milo B. Howard, Director, State of Alabama Department of Archives and History, to Ruth Corry, Georgia Department of Archives and History, 29 Dec. 1977, BP.
9. Letter of J. J. Brasher to Erasmus Q. Fuller, n.d., quoted in Erasmus Q. Fuller, *An Appeal to the Records: A Vindication of the Methodist Episcopal Church* (Cincinnati: Hitchcock and Walden, 1876), 366–67; *Minutes*, Alabama Conference of the Methodist Episcopal Church, 1867.
10. SR 15.
11. *Minutes*, Alabama Conference, 1867–79; Brasher, "Autobiography," 2; SR 9, 12.
12. Blount County Historical Society, *The Heritage of Blount County* (n.p., 1977), 99. In an interview (5 Jan. 1980), Blount County historian Captain Eugene A. Maynor stated that Brasher was offered the appointment by federal officials but refused it. See his poem "I Have a Silent Sorrow" and his "Composition on the Science of Music," BP.
13. Brasher, "Autobiography," 2.
14. John L. Brasher, "My Old Childhood Home," BP; Forrest McDonald and Grady McWhiney, "The Antebellum Southern Herdsman: A Reinterpretation," *Journal of Southern History* 41 (May 1975): 162, 166. McWhiney asserts that these drovers, long neglected by historians of southern culture, helped shape the character of the South. They made their living supplying lowland planters and markets with stock raised in the uplands. Brasher recalled:

"This road was the road for drovers to drive horses and mules. Sometimes they'd come with fifty to seventy-five beautiful horses, taking them down South where the plantations were." SR 10.

15. See Frank L. Owsley, *Plain Folk of the Old South* (Baton Rouge: Louisiana State University Press, 1949). Owsley states that "the core" of the southern "social structure was a massive body of plain folk . . . employed in numerous occupations; but the great majority secured their food, clothing, and shelter from some rural pursuit, chiefly farming and livestock grazing. . . . The group included the small slaveholding farmers; the nonslaveholders who owned the land which they cultivated; the numerous herdsmen . . . and those tenant farmers whose agricultural production . . . indicated thrift, energy, and self-respect" (7–8). Although the term is employed to describe the antebellum population, it also applies after the war. In fact, Owsley argues, "It was during the Reconstruction period that the plain folk revealed their real vitality and power of survival. Accustomed to every phase of work . . . related to farming and rural life, they had no such adjustment to make as the planter" (137).

16. For a brief but incisive summary of the culture and geography of the ridge and valley country of northeast Alabama, see Allen Tullos, "Tommie Bass: A Life in the Ridge and Valley Country" (M.A. thesis, University of North Carolina, Chapel Hill, 1976), 1–3.

17. Owsley states, "Much of the mountain and pine areas was, except for the absence of Indians, frontier country as truly as was the outer or Western frontier. Great portions . . . from Georgia to Texas were public domain until after the Civil War, and were sparsely settled." *Plain Folk,* 36. One of Brasher's narratives documents the migration to Sand Mountain:

> Our old home was right here on the trail that led from Georgia. They'd come from Georgia down the Georgia road to the county-line bridge out here and then come up through the Rocky Hollow to go out by Gregory Gap. And the road came right down the creek and then came right straight up the branch. There was a great big hollow poplar there which made the pivot 'round which they'd come and we'd hear 'em say, "WHA-HOY!" And say, "Another Georgian." And then we'd just go down to the gate and interview 'em as they passed: "HELLO! Where ya from?"
> "Georgia."
> "Uh, huh. Where 'er ya goin'?"
> "Sand Mountain. How far is it to Gregory's Gap? We've heard about it."
> "Three miles."
> "GIDDAP!"
> And that wave peopled the Sand Mountain. SR 13

18. SR 7; Brasher, "Autobiography," 6. Brasher's use of the term "quality folks" carries a moral connotation as much as an economic one.

19. John L. Brasher, "The Old Timer Rambles On: 'Gadsden in the 80's,'" manuscript copy for *Etowah News-Journal* (Attalla, Ala.), 1956, BP. C. Van Woodward spoke of the cotton-credit system as the "new evil" of southern

196 Notes to Pages 4–7

postwar agriculture, respecting neither class nor race; and which "judged by its economic results alone . . . may have worked more permanent injury to the South" than slavery. Since many farmers "had to have credit or starve," they signed mortgages that in effect forced them to grow cotton, the only crop that could be stored and transported without spoilage and easily turned into cash. C. Van Woodward, *Origins of the New South 1877–1913*, vol. 9 of *A History of the South*, ed. W. H. Stephenson and E. M. Coulter, 10 vols. (Baton Rouge: Louisiana State University Press, 1951), 9:180; Brasher, "Autobiography," 7.

20. SR 11.

21. John L. Brasher, "The Old Timer Rambles On: 'Oxen, etc.,'" manuscript copy for *Etowah News-Journal* (Attalla, Ala.), 1956, BP; SR 10.

22. Brasher, "Gadsden in the 80's."

23. Virginia Van der Veer Hamilton in *Alabama: A Bicentennial History* (New York: W. W. Norton, 1977) states, "Alabama was conceived in a folk migration . . . not exceeded until the Forty-Niners stampeded to California. Gripped by 'Alabama fever' . . . following the War of 1812, pioneers streamed out of Virginia, the Carolinas, and Georgia . . . to take over the last great Indian hunting ground east of the Mississippi" (3). On southern violence, see Dickson Bruce, *Violence and Culture in the Antebellum South* (Austin: University of Texas Press, 1979).

24. Teague, "Sketches," 21.

25. Shelby County Grand Jury, Fall Term, 1838, indicted Bailess, Jacob, and Thomas Brasher for a riot. John L. Brasher told the following story about his father's relatives: "His mother had some kinfolks, young men. They were not large, but brawny, just ponies. A young fellow was strutting around at a little gathering about what he could do, how he could throw anybody down on the ground. 'Anybody!' Well, nobody took him up. Finally this little fellow, weighed about a hundred and forty pounds, said, 'Well, if nobody else will, I will. I bet you ten dollars I can throw you down, and I bet you ten dollars I can kill you in the fall.' The fellow backed out and wouldn't wrestle with him. Some of Pa's kinfolks." SR 10.

26. Dickson D. Bruce, *And They All Sang Hallelujah: Plain-Folk Camp-Meeting Religion, 1800–1845* (Knoxville: University of Tennessee Press, 1974), 46–47.

27. Ibid., 123. John Jackson Brasher, as presiding elder, was responsible for overseeing all Methodist Episcopal churches in the northeast quarter of Alabama. As a youth, John Lakin was aware of his father's status: "My father being a minister of acknowledged ability placed our family in a very much respected scale, and gave my brothers and sister a social advantage which . . . they took too much for granted." Brasher, "Autobiography," 6.

28. John Jackson Brasher to the Reverend John W. Talley, 1 July 1869, BP.

29. SR 10.

30. SR 9.

31. SR 46.

32. Bruce, *And They All Sang*, 133–36.

33. SR 10, 9, 11.

34. Brasher, "Autobiography," 8. Brasher saw his father's financial ruin as a divine judgment resulting from his turning from preaching to secular employment. Shortly after John Jackson Brasher's death in 1887, the lawyer who held the mortgage foreclosed on the farm.

35. SR 72; Brasher, "Autobiography," 8.

36. SR 46. The colloquial usage "to live [something] on [someone]" was used here by Brasher to signify the moral influence upon him of his parents' daily life and interaction with their family.

Chapter 2: "In Poverty and Obloquy"

1. Blount County Historical Society, *The Heritage of Blount County,* 100; SR 16.

2. *Testimony Taken by the Joint Select Committee to Inquire into the Condition of Affairs in the Late Insurrectionary States* (Washington, 1872), 1:125.

3. "A Conference in a Tent," *The Methodist,* 29 Nov. 1873, 1.

4. *Testimony,* 1:784–85.

5. John L. Brasher, "History of the Alabama Conference of the Methodist Episcopal Church," 12, BP; John L. Brasher, "Memoir of Arad S. Lakin," BP. Lakin went with the newly created, all-black Central Conference in 1875.

6. Ralph Morrow, *Northern Methodism and Reconstruction* (East Lansing, Mich.: Michigan State University Press, 1956), 32, 248.

7. Ibid., 32–33.

8. *Christian Advocate,* 14 Sept. 1865, quoted in Morrow, *Northern Methodism,* 21–22.

9. Morrow, *Northern Methodism,* 47. The Alabama Conference, organized October 1867, was the eighth and final conference established in the South.

10. Ibid., 234.

11. Ibid., 235. Walter Fleming stated, "Every Northern Methodist was a Republican; and today in some sections of the State, the Northern Methodists are known as 'Republican' Methodists, as distinguished from 'Democratic' Southern Methodists." Walter L. Fleming, *Civil War and Reconstruction in Alabama* (New York: Columbia University Press, 1905), 639. A letter from fellow Methodist Episcopal preacher, T. R. Parker, Lineville, Alabama, to J. J. Brasher, 2 Nov. 1874, BP, lamented, "The prospect for us politically is gloomy. The Democrats have carried everything before them in this and adjacent counties by largely increased majorities."

12. *Testimony,* 1:430–32.

13. *Tuscaloosa Independent Monitor,* 1 Sept. 1868, 1. Among several northern papers that reprinted the cartoon, the *Cincinnati Commercial* published 500,000 copies for distribution as a campaign document for the Republicans. Fleming, *Civil War,* 612, n. 1.

14. "A Conference in a Tent," 1.

15. *Testimony,* 1:1207. Lakin's accounts of torture, mobs, and assassinations fill over fifty pages. Democratic minority members of the investigation, how-

198 Notes to Pages 11–13

ever, claimed that Lakin as a witness was "brimful of gall, bitterness, and false-hood, which he poured out before us in such a way that it is hardly possible to determine which of the ingredients predominated." *Testimony,* 1:493.

16. "A Conference in a Tent," 1.

17. Ibid.

18. *Testimony,* 1:126.

19. "Church Extension," *Methodist Advocate,* 12 Jan. 1887, 1.

20. *Nashville Christian Advocate,* 8 Dec. 1883, 1. All of these descriptions, presented by church leaders, of the membership of the M. E. Church in the South do not differ substantially from Owsley's definition of the "plain folk" discussed in the previous chapter. Conditions in the rural lower South, chronologically and sociologically close to the frontier, may have seemed more extreme to outside church officials accustomed to northern or urban landscapes and prosperity.

21. Approximately four-fifths of the membership of the Methodist Episcopal Church gathered from the former Confederate states were blacks. Morrow, *Northern Methodism,* 245.

22. Brasher, "History," 4.

23. John L. Brasher to the *Birmingham News,* 10 Dec. 1903, BP. The paper had published Methodist Episcopal appointments under the heading "Northern Methodist Appointments." Brasher wrote: "There is no such church on earth. There never was such a church existing, only in the mind of an ignorant or thoughtless class, who do not care for nicknames themselves and think little of nicknaming other people. We never have since the organization of our church in 1784 at Baltimore, seen fit to tack on a *tail* in the way of a sectional name. The world is our parish."

24. Brasher, "History," 5.

25. Fuller, *An Appeal to the Records,* 367.

26. John Jackson Brasher to the Reverend Erasmus Q. Fuller, n.d., quoted in Fuller, *An Appeal to the Records,* 366–67.

27. Brasher had to leave his family and flee for his life out of state behind the protection of the Union lines. On one occasion, his wife and children were locked up by the Confederate "homeguard" without food or water for an extended time in an unsuccessful attempt to learn his whereabouts. SR 1.

28. Sheriff Lee Murphree, from Tennessee, was lynched in 1867. Tape-recorded interview of Captain Eugene A. Maynor, Oneonta, Alabama, 5 Jan. 1980; *Blount County,* 99.

29. SR 11. Lakin reported a Methodist Episcopal local preacher of Fayetteville, Alabama, who was "shot dead in the pulpit while preaching in 1869." *Testimony,* 1:128. In reference to persecution, Morrow states, "Methodism's existence seemed most hazardous in rural districts away from federal military posts. Most victims of persecution were natives of the South who had sworn fidelity to the Northern church," and "were almost invariably clergymen with established political reputations." *Northern Methodism,* 239–40.

30. Maynor, interview; *Blount County,* 99.

31. A. S. Lakin to John Jackson Brasher, 6 Nov. 1869, BP.

32. *Minutes,* Alabama Conference, 1871.

33. John Jackson Brasher to the Reverend John W. Talley, 1 July 1869, BP.

34. Brasher, "History," 15.

35. Stories of the persecution and courage of his family and its friends during and immediately after the war formed a large portion of John Lakin Brasher's narrative repertoire. For instance, he could quote the exact words his father spoke when he took his gun into the pulpit—an event that occurred before John Lakin was born: "I'm here to preach the gospel. My life has been threatened. If I have to sell my life, I'll sell it as dearly as possible." SR 11.

36. SR 10.

37. Brasher, "Autobiography," 5.

38. Ibid., 4, 7.

39. SR 11.

40. Brasher, "Autobiography," 5.

41. SR 10.

42. John L. Brasher, *Sesqui-Centennial Address, Delivered December 6, 1934, at Oneonta, Alabama, before the Alabama Conference* (Oneonta, Ala.: Blount County Messenger, n.d.), n.p., BP.

Chapter 3: "Pre-empted for a Preacher"

1. SR 75.

2. John L. Brasher, "A Meditation Concerning Mine and Mama's Children," 27 Feb. 1966, BP. H. Richard Niebuhr summarized four traditional elements of the call to the ministry as follows: "the call to be a Christian; the secret call or inward persuasion of being summoned or invited to the work of ministry; the providential call . . . equipment with talents necessary for the task through divine guidance in all circumstances; the ecclesiastical call . . . summons by institution or community." This chapter treats only "secret" and "providential" aspects of Brasher's call. H. Richard Niebuhr, *The Purpose of the Church and Its Ministry* (New York: Harper and Brothers, 1956), 64.

3. Brasher, "Autobiography," 4.

4. See Daniel B. Shea, *Spiritual Autobiography in Early America* (Princeton: Princeton University Press, 1968), 87–110; Edmund S. Morgan, *Visible Saints: The History of a Puritan Idea* (New York: New York University Press, 1963), 64–73. For English antecedents see William Haller, *The Rise of Puritanism* (New York: Columbia University Press, 1938), 90–111. For Shaker conventions see Sarah Diane Sasson, *The Shaker Spiritual Narrative* (Knoxville: University of Tennessee Press, 1983).

5. Sasson, *Shaker Narrative,* 221.

6. Jeremiah 1:5. See also Paul's similarly worded explanation of his call in Galatians 1:15.

7. See Judges 13, I Samuel 1, Luke 1.

8. Frank Baker, *From Wesley to Asbury* (Durham, N.C.: Duke University

Press, 1976), 107; James Finley, *Autobiography of Rev. James B. Finley or Pioneer Life in the West* (Cincinnati: Jennings and Pye, 1853), 26.

9. O. P. Fitzgerald, *Sunset Views* (Nashville: Publishing House of the M. E. Church, South, 1906), 97.

10. Ibid.

11. SR 72. The story appears also in SR 25, 40, 64; and in John L. Brasher, *A Simple Statement of Christian Experience* (n.p., 1962); and Brasher, "Autobiography," 2.

12. W. B. Godbey, *Happy Nonagenarian* (Zarephath, N.J.: Pillar of Fire, 1919), 8; H. C. Morrison, *Some Chapters of My Life Story* (Louisville: Pentecostal Publishing Co., 1941), 60.

13. SR 75, 72.

14. Bruce Rosenberg, *The Art of the American Folk Preacher* (New York: Oxford University Press, 1970), 24; Godbey, *Happy Nonagenarian*, 8.

15. SR 75.

16. Godbey, *Happy Nonagenarian*, 8.

17. Brasher, "How Can They Hear?"

18. John L. Brasher, "Biography of Minnie Eunice Moore Brasher," MS, BP.

19. Brasher, "Autobiography," 12.

20. Donald E. Byrne, *No Foot of Land: Folklore of American Methodist Itinerants* (Metuchen, N.J.: Scarecrow Press, 1975), 65, 78 n. 43. Adin Ballou, an American Universalist preacher, reformer, and leader of separatist movements, also recounted a similar vocational call that occurred when he was eighteen. His deceased brother Cyrus appeared and addressed him: "Adin, God commands you to preach the Gospel of Christ to your fellow-men; obey his voice or the blood of their souls will be required at your hands." Adin Ballou, *Autobiography of Adin Ballou, 1803–1890* (Lowell, Mass.: Vox Populi Press, 1896), 62.

21. Byrne, *No Foot of Land,* 73.

22. SR 13, 72; Brasher, "Autobiography," 4.

23. Brasher, "Autobiography," 5, 4.

24. Brasher, *A Simple Statement,* n.p.

25. SR 10; Brasher, "Autobiography," 4.

26. Brasher, "How Can They Hear?"; Brasher, "Autobiography," 4.

27. SR 42.

28. Brasher, "Autobiography," 4.

29. SR 2.

30. Brasher, "Autobiography," 5.

31. John L. Brasher, "Memoir of J. L. Freeman," BP.

32. Protracted meetings were major social events as well. Brasher related, "Often all our seven beds were filled and beds made down on the floor all about, and our horse lot full of horses and mules of our visitors. Mother would buy a coop or two of chickens in addition to what she had raised, and got a lady friend to help her cook. There was no limit to hospitality." John L. Brasher, "The Old Timer Rambles On: 'Old-Time Protracted Meeting,'" *Etowah News-Journal* (Attalla, Ala.), June 1956, BP. See also SR 4.

33. Brasher, "Protracted Meeting."

34. SR 59.

35. SR 10.

36. Geoffrey Wainwright, *Doxology: The Praise of God in Worship, Doctrine, and Life* (New York: Oxford University Press, 1980), 8.

37. Brasher, "Protracted Meeting."

38. SR 10. The explanation for separate seating was Brasher's. He added, "A fellow could look at his girl more than he could if he had been beside her."

39. SR 10, 11. The physical division between saints and sinners during worship was probably widely traditional throughout the nineteenth-century South in evangelical churches. H. C. Morrison alludes to the separation in an account of his boyhood church in Kentucky: "The Christians would go out into the audience and invite sinners to the mourners' bench . . . and lead them to Christ. I would get up close to the front, hoping that someone would speak to me and that would give me a good excuse to go forward." Morrison, *Some Chapters*, 41.

40. Brasher, "How Can They Hear?" The wording of the prayer apparently was traditional in southern evangelical churches. Brasher stated in the same source, "That is a very high position . . . to take God's words and give them to the people—standing, as the old folks used to pray, between the living and the dead. They used to pray for the preachers and say, "Oh Lord, bless this man as he stands between the living and the dead to proclaim the Word of God." Raymond Browning, an evangelist born 1879 in Giles County, Tennessee, showed familiarity with the prayer when he wrote of his preaching, "Here I must stand between the living and the dead to deal with the most precious thing. . . ." "The Preaching of Raymond Browning," *The Preacher's Magazine* (Nov. 1958): 11. The origin of the image is Romans 6:23: "The wages of sin is death, but the gift of God is eternal life through Jesus Christ our Lord."

The concept of *communitas,* a collective rite of passage (in this case, conversion) in which normal social distinctions are suspended by a common religious experience was developed by Victor Turner in *The Ritual Process, Structure and Anti-Structure* (Chicago: Aldine, 1969), 94–113.

41. Brasher, "Protracted Meeting."

42. Brasher, "The Ministry of the Holy Spirit in Evangelism," BP.

43. SR 7.

44. Samuel S. Hill, *Southern Churches in Crisis* (New York: Holt, Rinehart and Winston, 1966), 84–88.

45. John L. Brasher, "The Old Timer Rambles On: 'Revival Meetings,'" *Etowah News-Journal* (Attalla, Ala.), 1956, BP.

46. Hill, *Southern Churches,* 99.

47. Brasher, "Revival Meetings."

48. Ibid.

49. SR 33.

50. SR 65, 31, 44.

51. Brasher, "The Ministry."

Chapter 4: Popular Perfectionism

1. SR 64.
2. "Minutes of Several Conversations between the Rev. Mr. Wesley and Others," *The Works of John Wesley* (Grand Rapids, Mich.: Baker Book House, 1978), 8:299.
3. Sermon 85, "On Working Out Our Own Salvation," *Works*, 6:509.
4. Albert C. Outler, ed., *John Wesley* (New York: Oxford University Press, 1964), 28–29.
5. Sermon 85, "On Working Out Our Own Salvation," *Works*, 6:509.
6. Ibid.
7. See Sermon 13, "On Sin in Believers," *Works*, 5:144–56.
8. John Leland Peters, *Christian Perfection and American Methodism* (Nashville: Abingdon Press, 1956), 90–97.
9. Peters, *Christian Perfection*, 98–101. A cogent rebuttal appears in Allan Coppedge, "Entire Sanctification in Early American Methodism: 1812–1835," *Wesleyan Theological Journal* 13 (Spring 1978): 34–50.
10. Harold E. Raser explores Palmer's motivations in *Phoebe Palmer: Her Life and Thought,* Studies in Women and Religion, vol. 22 (Lewiston, N.Y.: Edward Mellon Press, 1987).
11. Phoebe W. Palmer, *The Way of Holiness, with Notes by the Way* (New York: Lane and Scott, 1851), 75, 73.
12. Ibid., 75, 55.
13. Palmer's writings were primarily concerned with the *method* of obtaining holiness. She had little to say about the nature of entire sanctification, in effect treating the form rather than the substance of piety. This preoccupation with means was prominent in much of the subsequent holiness movement.
14. Palmer, *The Way,* 37–38. Italics are Palmer's.
15. Ibid., 63.
16. Ibid., 60–71; Raser, *Phoebe Palmer,* 6.
17. Charles Edwin Jones, *Perfectionist Persuasion: The Holiness Movement and American Methodism, 1867–1936* (Metuchen, N.J.: Scarecrow Press, 1974), 3; Emory S. Bucke, ed., *The History of American Methodism* (Nashville: Abingdon Press, 1964), 2:610; Hannah W. Smith, *The Christian's Secret of a Happy Life* (Boston: Willard Tract Repository, 1875).
18. See Charles G. Finney, *Views of Sanctification* (Oberlin, Ohio: James Steele, 1840); William E. Boardman, *The Higher Christian Life* (Boston: Henry Hoyt, 1858); William Arthur, *The Tongue of Fire: Or, the True Power of Christianity* (New York: Harper, 1856). Arthur's book was required reading in the course of study for all ministerial candidates in both the Northern and Southern Methodist churches until the end of the century.
19. Bucke, *American Methodism,* 610; Melvin E. Dieter, *The Holiness Revival of the Nineteenth Century* (Metuchen, N.J.: Scarecrow Press, 1980), 3.
20. Bucke, *American Methodism,* 610.
21. Timothy L. Smith, *Revivalism and Social Reform: American Protestantism on the Eve of the Civil War* (Nashville: Abingdon Press, 1957), 63–79; Vin-

cent Synan, *The Holiness-Pentecostal Movement* (Grand Rapids, Mich.: William B. Eerdmans, 1971), 31. Some holiness dimensions of the revival are presented in J. A. Wood, *Perfect Love, or Plain Things for Those Who Need Them* (Philadelphia: Samuel D. Burlock, 1861), 300–313.

22. Donald W. Dayton, "The Doctrine of the Baptism of the Holy Spirit: Its Emergence and Significance," *Wesleyan Theological Journal* 13 (Spring 1978): 114. Identification of entire sanctification with Pentecost or "the baptism with the Holy Spirit" was made as early as John Fletcher and Joseph Benson, English contemporaries of Wesley. It was not until the Civil War, however, that this view began to supplant Wesley's. Ibid., 116.

23. The term "holiness movement" usually refers in particular to the postwar propagation through revivals and camp meetings of entire sanctification as a distinct "second blessing."

24. Jones, *Perfectionist Persuasion*, 17 and passim; Dieter, *Holiness Revival*, 96–155.

25. George Hughes, *Days of Power in the Forest Temple: A Review of the Wonderful Work of God at Fourteen National Camp Meetings from 1867 to 1872* (Boston: John Bent, 1873), 10–17.

26. Dieter, *Holiness Revival*, 127. The bishops were Randolph S. Foster, Jesse T. Peck, Gilbert Haven, William L. Harris, Stephen Merrill, and Thomas Bowman.

27. Donald W. Dayton, *Discovering an Evangelical Heritage* (New York: Harper and Row, 1976), 112–17; Timothy L. Smith, *Called Unto Holiness, The Story of the Nazarenes: The Formative Years* (Kansas City, Mo.: Nazarene Publishing House, 1962), 47–49.

28. Synan, *Holiness Movement*, 40. The holiness movement that began in rural Texas in the 1870s was an exception to the usual urban beachheads in the South. See C. B. Jernigan, *Pioneer Days of the Holiness Movement in the Southwest* (Kansas City, Mo.: Pentecostal Nazarene Publishing House, 1919), 17–20.

29. *Journal of the General Conference of the Methodist Episcopal Church, South, 1846* (Richmond: John Early, 1851), 118.

30. *Journal of the General Conference of the Methodist Episcopal Church, South, 1870* (n.p., n.d.), 165.

31. Dieter, *Holiness Revival*, 123–24; Synan, *Holiness Movement*, 31. The predominantly northern pro-holiness Wesleyan Methodists and Free Methodists were ardent spokespersons of the antislavery cause.

32. An 1876 letter from a South Carolina layman to the *Way of Holiness* (Spartanburg, S.C.) states, "I long took and read with much interest the *Guide to Holiness*. But the war cut it off from me." *The Way of Holiness: A Journal of the Higher Life Experience* 56 (Apr. 1876): 16. The *Guide to Holiness* was the most popular journal of the midcentury holiness movement. Printed in New York, it was owned and edited by Phoebe Palmer after 1858.

33. Kenneth K. Bailey, "Southern White Protestantism at the Turn of the Century," *American Historical Review* 68 (Apr. 1963): 635 and passim; Hill, *Southern Churches*, 3–70. Flourishing postwar revivalism among Southern

Methodists is treated in Hunter D. Farish, *The Circuit Rider Dismounts: A Social History of Southern Methodism 1865–1900* (Richmond: Dietz Press, 1938), 69–71.

34. Although Phoebe Palmer and her holiness theology minimized the role of emotion in sanctification, southern common folk, recalling their heartfelt conversions, often experienced the second blessing as an emotional event. See B. F. Haynes, "The Waco, Texas, Camp Meeting," *Pentecostal Herald* 9 (11 Aug. 1897): 4; Samuel Chadwick, "Letter of Samuel Chadwick," *The Way of Faith* (20 Aug. 1914): 5, 8, 9. Chadwick describes sanctification experiences at Indian Springs Camp Meeting, Flovilla, Georgia. I am indebted to Deborah V. McCauley for the clarification that the primary northern contribution was the "articulated theological formulations."

35. Some early and important southern urban holiness missions were several Atlanta missions served by W. A. Dodge and others after 1883; the Oliver Gospel Mission established 1891 in Columbia, South Carolina; and the network of Pentecostal Missions established in 1898 by J. O. McClurkan in Nashville with branches in Memphis, Chattanooga, Atlanta, Birmingham, and other cities and towns across the South. For Dodge, see Mrs. J. W. Garbutt, *Rev. W. A. Dodge as We Knew Him* (Atlanta: Franklin Printing Co., 1906), 53–60, and Briane Turley, "A Wheel within a Wheel: Southern Methodism and the Georgia Holiness Association," *Georgia Historical Quarterly* 75, no. 2 (Summer 1991): 295–320; for Oliver Mission see Albert D. Betts, *History of South Carolina Methodism* (Columbia, S.C.: Advocate Press, 1952), 347, 438–39, and Charles Fankhauser, "The Heritage of Faith: An Historical Evaluation of the Holiness Movement in America" (M.A. thesis, Pittsburg State University, Pittsburg, Kansas, 1983), 156–58; for McClurkan see John T. Benson, Jr., *A History of the Pentecostal Mission, Inc.* (Nashville: Trevecca Press, 1977), and Mildred Bangs Wyncoop, *The Trevecca Story* (Nashville: Trevecca Press, 1976). An analysis of the appeal of urban holiness missions to rural newcomers is found in Charles E. Jones, "Disinherited or Rural? A Historical Case Study in Urban Holiness Religion," *Missouri Historical Review* 66 (Apr. 1972): 395–412.

36. Samuel S. Hill, ed., *Religion in the Southern States* (Macon, Ga.: Mercer University Press, 1983), 412. The most revered early native southern voice for holiness was that of the Reverend Doctor Lovick Pierce (1785–1879). A member of the South Georgia Conference and the father of Bishop George F. Pierce, he promoted sanctification in his ministry from 1811 until his death. His account of the decline of the doctrine of sanctification in the South, written in 1878, was published posthumously. See his *A Miscellaneous Essay on Entire Sanctification, showing how it was lost from the church and how it may and must be regained* (Nashville: Publishing House of the M. E. Church, South, 1897). Another early notable southern exponent of holiness was the Reverend Leonidas Rosser (1815–92), a member of the Virginia Conference and the author of *Experimental Religion: Embracing Justification Regeneration, Sanctification, and the Witness of the Spirit* (Richmond: By the Author, 1854).

37. Dieter, *Holiness Revival*, 123–24; Jones, *Perfectionist Persuasion*, 184–

85; "A Short Autobiography of Rev. A. J. Quattlebaum," *The Way of Faith and Neglected Themes* 41 (1 Dec. 1930): 9.

38. *Southern Christian Advocate,* 14 Feb. 1880, 4. Percival A. Wesche, in *Henry Clay Morrison: Crusader Saint* (Berne, Ind.: Herald Press, 1963), 140, mentions a revival held by Inskip at Augusta, Georgia, in 1876.

39. "Pentecost in February," *Southern Christian Advocate,* 28 Feb. 1880, 4.

40. *Southern Christian Advocate,* 13 Mar. 1880, 1.

41. The Reverend William Baker, *A Concise Description of Middle Tennessee* (McMinnville, Tenn.: William Baker, 1868).

42. Reference to the first publication of the journal appears in Baker's article "An Appeal to the Friends of Holiness," *The Free Methodist* (18 July 1887): 4. (I am indebted to Stanley Ingersol for this citation.) See also Baker's "My Own Experience," *The Way of Holiness: A Journal of the Higher Life Experience* 54 (Feb. 1876): 7. Copies of the journal are rare. Duke University holds issues for February, March, May 1876. H. C. Morrison incorrectly cited *The Way of Life,* first published in Atlanta in 1882, as "the morning star paper of the holiness movement in the South." He may have ignored Baker's much earlier paper because of its association with the North. See Garbutt, *Dodge,* 43. Baker seems to have been somewhat of an opportunist. His tract promoting settlement of Middle Tennessee (see n. 41) states, "Graveyards are few and fill up slowly." By 1879, he had moved again to Chattanooga, where he continued to publish *The Way of Holiness* until 1886 and printed a hymnal of "songs and choruses in use at camp meetings fifty years ago." William Baker, *Sacred Melodies; Being a Collection of Spiritual Songs, Adapted to Social and Revival Meetings* (Chattanooga: William Baker, 1879), n.p.

43. Wesche, *Morrison,* 140.

44. Garbutt, *Dodge,* 48. In 1885, W. Asbury Dodge, a founder of Indian Springs Camp Meeting, held revivals in Illinois and appealed for workers "to go to the Southern field." Ibid., 100.

45. Jernigan, *Pioneer Days,* 18–19.

46. The Reverend E. Davies, *The Boy Preacher; or the Life and Labors of Rev. Thomas Harrison* (Reading, Mass., 1881); R. L. Selle, "Notes from San Antonio, Texas," *Christian Witness and Advocate of Bible Holiness* (17 June 1897): 13; Brasher, "Autobiography," 18; Smith, *Called Unto Holiness,* 53.

47. Wyncoop, *Trevecca,* 32–33. See n. 35.

48. Synan, *Holiness Movement,* 43–50; Harold W. Mann, *Atticus Greene Haygood, Methodist Bishop, Editor, and Educator* (Athens: University of Georgia Press), 154–56.

49. Peters, *Christian Perfection,* 138. The earliest prominent southern holiness evangelist was the eccentric Kentuckian William B. Godbey, the most prolific author of the nineteenth- and early twentieth-century holiness movement. He began preaching holiness in local Southern Methodist revivals about 1870 but was officially "put in the field" by Bishop McTieyre in 1884. William B. Godbey, *Autobiography* (Cincinnati: God's Revivalist Office, 1909), 103–5. Some other popular holiness evangelists of the Methodist Episcopal Church, South, who began traveling evangelism before 1900 were (with states of birth):

W. Asbury Dodge (Georgia); Beverly Carradine (Mississippi); Leander L. Pickett, evangelist and songbook compiler (Kentucky); Henry Clay Morrison (Kentucky); Reuben "Bud" Robinson (Tennessee); Charlie D. Tillman, song-leader and songbook compiler (Alabama).

50. "Bishops' Address," *Journal of the General Conference of the Methodist Episcopal Church, South, 1894,* 24. For the controversy over appointment of evangelists in the Southern Methodist Church, see Harold Ivan Smith, "An Analysis and Evaluation of the Evangelistic Work of Samuel Porter Jones in Nashville 1885–1906" (M.A. thesis, Scarritt College for Christian Workers, Nashville, 1971), 129–32.

51. The evangelist B. H. Irwin promoted a third blessing of fire. Other radical ideas in Texas included salvation from death, interest in demonology, marital purity, abstinence from pork and coffee, denial of the need for doctors or medicine. Jernigan, *Pioneer Days,* 151–57.

52. Jones, in *Perfectionist Persuasion,* 159 n. 32, notes that most national association evangelists were postmillennialists, most regional leaders premillennialists. B. F. Haynes, in *Tempest-tossed on Methodist Seas; or a Sketch of My Life* (Louisville: Pentecostal Publishing Co., 1921), 78–79, presents the standard postmillennial teaching of the Methodist Episcopal Church, South.

53. Jones, *Perfectionist Persuasion,* 58.

54. Smith, "Sam Jones," 129–30. The bishops had no legal way through the rules of the Methodist *Discipline* to appoint a preacher as "evangelist." Some evangelists, such as Godbey and Jones, had been appointed to other nominal offices in order to free them for touring evangelism.

55. Atticus G. Haygood, "A Thousand Souls Won Today," *Christian Advocate,* 2 June 1892, 3.

56. Synan, *Holiness Movement,* 48. Tillett accused holiness teachings of implying that salvation could be obtained through willing it.

57. J. M. Boland, *The Problem of Methodism* (Nashville: Publishing House of the M. E. Church, South, 1888). Boland attacked the motives of holiness evangelists and partisans in "A Psychological View of Sin and Holiness," *Quarterly Review of the M. E. Church, South* 12 (1892): 339–54.

58. Clement C. Cary, *The Second Coming of Christ, Showing Pre-Millenarianism to Be Unscriptural and Unreasonable* (Atlanta: Doctor Blosser Co., 1902), 6. Cary was a ministerial member of the North Georgia Conference, a holiness stronghold. In this Southern Methodist polemic against premillennialism, with an introduction by Bishop Warren A. Candler, Cary cited the doctrine as "an important plank in the holiness platform" and criticized the southern evangelists L. L. Pickett and W. B. Godbey as leading exponents. See 3, 83, 85. Early influential premillennialist southern holiness leaders included Pickett and Godbey, as well as B. F. Haynes, H. C. Morrison, Bud Robinson, Charlie Tillman, and J. O. McClurkan. The noted evangelist Beverly Carradine may have been an exception.

59. See, for instance, Smith, *Called Unto Holiness,* 151–52.

60. See Haynes, *Tempest-tossed*, 73–74; L. L. Pickett, *Why I Am a Premillennialist* (Louisville: Pentecostal Publishing Co., 1927), 5–11, 75–86.

61. Premillennialism was taught at Dwight L. Moody's Northfield, Massachusetts, Bible conferences in the 1880s and in his nationally distributed literature. Southern evangelists cited their reading of the Californian W. E. Blackstone's *Jesus Is Coming* (1878) as instrumental in their acceptance of the doctrine. See Haynes, *Tempest-tossed*, 72–73; Raymond Browning, *My Christian Experience* (Louisville: Pentecostal Publishing Co., n.d.), 23. J. O. McClurkan appropriated the premillennialism of A. B. Simpson, the founder in New York of the Christian and Missionary Alliance.

62. For a discussion of nineteenth-century American folk belief in remarkable providences, see Byrne, *No Foot of Land*, 42–54. Indicative of southern holiness-folk fascination with supernaturalism is W. B. Godbey's *Demonology . . . to Which Is Added Chapters on the Devil and Demons by Evangelist L. L. Pickett, Demon Possession in Russia by Rev. F. B. Meyer, the Devil by Rev. Andrew Johnson, an Angel Visit by Rev. J. M. Dustman* (Greenville, Tex.: Pickett Publishing Co., 1902). Godbey, Pickett, and Johnson were leading southern holiness evangelists. In 1922, Brasher observed, "The common people believe in His coming." John L. Brasher to the *Methodist Advocate Journal*, 22 Apr. 1922, BP.

63. Brasher stated, "Just as He will come in His second advent when He's ready, He will come to your heart and make a little heaven down here to go to heaven in." SR 25.

64. Godbey, *Autobiography*, 430–31. Godbey here paraphrases Phoebe Palmer's famous hymn, "The Cleansing Wave." The favorite text employed to wed sanctification and premillennialism was Hebrews 12:14: "Follow peace with all men, and holiness without which no man shall see the Lord." For precise southern holiness statements explaining the "natural companionship" of holiness and premillennialism, see Haynes, *Tempest-tossed*, 73–75; and Browning, *My Experience*, 23–24.

65. Some proof-texts for the End Time revival were: Daniel 12:10: "Many people shall be purified and made white and tried," and Acts 1:8: "But ye shall receive power after that the Holy Ghost is come upon you, and ye shall be witnesses . . . unto the uttermost part of the earth."

66. *Guide to Holiness* 102 (June 1898): 179.

67. Merle McClurkan Heath, *A Man Sent of God: The Life of J. O. McClurkan* (Kansas City, Mo.: Beacon Hill Press, 1947), 64; John L. Brasher, "The Holiness Movement," lecture delivered at God's Bible School, Cincinnati, Ohio, 31 Mar. 1950, BP.

68. "Bishops' Address," 24–25. The Methodist Episcopal Church in 1896 also issued a statement that cautioned against exclusive emphasis upon sanctification as instantaneous. The statement also denied the necessity of testifying to such an experience, but its warnings were not as pointed as those of the southern address. *Journal of the General Conference of the Methodist Episcopal Church, 1896,* Appendix 3, 497–98.

69. L. L. Pickett, *The Pickett-Smith Debate on Entire Sanctification: A Second Blessing* (Louisville: Pickett Publishing Co., 1897).

Chapter 5: *"The Seal of the Covenant"*

1. *Age-Herald*, 18 Apr. 1900, 1.
2. *Age-Herald*, 20 Apr. 1900, 1.
3. John L. Brasher, *A Simple Statement*, 9.
4. John L. Brasher to Salvation Army Lieutenant Colonel Fletcher Agnew, 28 May 1925, BP; John L. Brasher to "The Saints at Hollow Rock," June 1966, BP. Brasher's sanctification took place on Thursday, 19 Apr. 1900. See Samuel Logan Brengle to John L. Brasher, 8 Feb. 1931, BP.
5. Entry for 22 Apr. 1900 in John L. Brasher's copy of *The Ideal Pastor's Record, 1899–1901,* BP.
6. The quotation describing Birmingham in 1900 is in a letter of Robert G. Pike to John L. Brasher, 7 Apr. 1911, BP. Pike was a close friend of Brasher in Birmingham at the time of Brasher's sanctification.
7. John Wesley, *Journal* (London: Robert Hawes, 1775), part 2, 17. In his sermon "The New Birth," 12 Oct. 1924, BP, Brasher declares that the sanctified "have passed from servants and children to sonship."
8. Brasher, "Revival Meetings."
9. John L. Brasher's "Pertinent Paragraphs," n.d., BP. According to *Binney's Theological Compend,* which Brasher read as a youth, the direct witness of the Spirit was necessary "as a safeguard against distressing doubt." Amos Binney, *Binney's Theological Compend Improved* (New York: Eaton and Mains, 1875), 127.
10. John L. Brasher, "Immortality," lecture delivered at God's Bible School, Cincinnati, Ohio, 28 Mar. 1950, BP.
11. John L. Brasher to Minnie E. Moore Brasher, 14 Nov. 1926, BP.
12. John L. Brasher to Hollow Rock Camp Meeting, 1 Aug. 1955, BP.
13. John L. Brasher, "The Moods of the Spirit," lecture delivered at God's Bible School, Cincinnati, Ohio, 28 Mar. 1950.
14. SR 2.
15. John L. Brasher, "Wanted, A New Enthusiasm," 20 July 1921, BP.
16. John L. Brasher, "Sermon Notebook," 104, BP; John L. Brasher, "The Fruit of the Spirit," lecture delivered at God's Bible School, Cincinnati, Ohio, 29 Mar. 1950, BP.
17. Brasher, "Fruit."
18. Brasher, "Moods."
19. Brasher, "Enthusiasm."
20. Minnie E. Moore Brasher to John L. Brasher, June 1930, BP; SR 11.
21. John L. Brasher to "Dear Ones at Home," 26 July 1925, BP.
22. Palmer, *The Way of Holiness,* 75.
23. Brasher, "Autobiography," 8.
24. M. W. Wilson to Caroline Boatman, 20 Oct. 1949, BP.

25. SR 48.
26. SR 13.
27. Brasher, *A Simple Statement*, 4. Another account appears in SR 41.
28. Brasher, "Autobiography," 9.
29. John L. Brasher, "The Preacher as Evangelist," lecture delivered at God's Bible School, Cincinnati, Ohio, 4 Dec. 1947, BP.
30. Brasher, *A Simple Statement*, 4–5.
31. John L. Brasher to Minnie E. Moore Brasher, 20 Oct. 1952, BP.
32. Brasher does not include the experience of the night of November 1881 in his "Autobiography," written during 1932–51, but does record it in his *A Simple Statement*, written in 1962. He cites the 1881 experience as his conversion in SR 41; John L. Brasher, Birthday Letter, ca. 1935, typescript fragment, BP. He locates his conversion in the 1886 revival in his "Autobiography," 9; SR 48; SR 56; SR 54.
33. John L. Brasher, "Methodism: Its Doctrine and Spirit," 1894, BP.
34. SR 25.
35. SR 22.
36. SR 28.
37. SR 48.
38. SR 25.
39. SR 28.
40. John L. Brasher, *Glimpses: Some Personal Glimpses of Holiness Preachers Whom I Have Known* (Cincinnati: Revivalist Press, 1954), 10.
41. Brasher, *A Simple Statement*, 4.
42. See Samuel Logan Brengle, *Fifty Years Before and After, 1885–1935* (Upland, Ind.: Published by Taylor University, n.d.), BP.
43. Brasher, *A Simple Statement*, 5.
44. Palmer, *The Way of Holiness*, 37–38.
45. W. B. Godbey, *Holiness or Hell* (Louisville: Pentecostal Publishing Co., 1899), 104.
46. Rosser, *Experimental Religion*, 149.
47. Many leaders of the holiness movement after Phoebe Palmer reported an absence of strong feelings at their moment of sanctification followed considerably later by an emotional witness of the Spirit. The following selected evangelists attested to such a pattern: Samuel Logan Brengle, in Clarence W. Hall, *Samuel Logan Brengle: Portrait of a Prophet* (Atlanta: Salvation Army, 1979), 49–52; Daniel Steele, in George E. Ackerman, *Love Illumined* (New York: Eaton and Mains, 1900), 118; A. M. Hills, in A. M. Hills, *Holiness and Power* (Cincinnati: God's Revivalist, 1897), 258–79; Samuel A. Keen, in S. A. Keen, *Praise Papers* (Louisville: Pickett Publishing Company, 1894), 27; Beverly Carradine, in Beverly Carradine, *Sanctification* (Chicago: Christian Witness Co., 1909), 21; J. O. McClurkan, in Heath, *A Man Sent of God,* 34; W. A. Dodge, in Garbutt, *W. A. Dodge,* 118–19. A. M. Hills in *Holiness and Power,* 258–79, provides the most extended discussion of this type of experience.
48. SR 62.
49. SR 72. By "altar" Brasher means the mourners' bench.

50. Brasher, *A Simple Statement*, 11. A. M. Hills (1848–1935) graduated from Oberlin and Yale and was a student of Charles G. Finney. Originally Congregational, he became a leading theologian in the Church of the Nazarene.

51. SR 62.

52. Brasher, *Glimpses*, 10.

53. SR 17. See Binney, *Binney's Theological Compend*, 128–34.

54. Brasher, *A Simple Statement;* John L. Brasher, "Memoir of James P. McGee," BP.

55. *Testimony*, 1:791. Timothy L. Smith treats the Five Points Mission in *Revivalism and Social Reform*, 170–71. Lakin used language typical of the holiness movement in his letter to John Jackson Brasher, 6 Nov. 1869, BP, in which he stated that a revival at Conference "wound up in a perfect blaze of glory."

56. Brasher, *Glimpses*, 10. Brasher does not record the woman's name. The year must have been about 1885.

57. Brasher, "Autobiography," 13.

58. *Nazarene Messenger*, 23 Aug. 1900, quoted in Smith, *Called Unto Holiness*, 146.

59. *Texas Christian Advocate*, 29 Nov. 1879, quoted in Walter N. Vernon et al., *The Methodist Excitement in Texas* (Dallas: Texas United Methodist Historical Society, 1984), 204. Southern Methodist resentment in Georgia of promoters of holiness from the northern Methodist Church is documented in Turley, "A Wheel within a Wheel."

60. *Texas Holiness Banner* 1 (Dec. 1899): 7, quoted in Smith, *Called Unto Holiness*, 163.

61. See Jernigan, *Pioneer Days*, 98–100; Bud Robinson, *Sunshine and Smiles* (Chicago: Christian Witness Co., 1903), 73–75; Morrison, *Some Chapters*, 171–72. Morrison states that about twenty Southern Methodist preachers in Texas joined the northern Methodist Church.

62. During the first forty years of the conference (1867–1906), pro-holiness bishops chaired twenty-five of the annual sessions.

63. *Minutes*, Alabama Conference, 1871, 1883, 1884.

64. Boland joined the Alabama Conference in 1855, transferred to the Mobile Conference in 1869, the North Alabama Conference in 1870, the Alabama Conference in 1878, the Kentucky Conference in 1889. See ch. 4, n. 57.

65. The presiding bishops were: Isaac W. Joyce (1892), Thomas Bowman (1893), William X. Ninde (1894), J. H. Vincent (1895), John F. Hurst (1896), Cyrus D. Foss (1897), C. C. McCabe (1897), Daniel A. Goodsell (1898), Willard F. Mallalieu (1899), J. N. Fitzgerald (1900). Joyce, Bowman, Foss, Goodsell, Mallalieu, and Fitzgerald's mother, Mrs. Osee M. Fitzgerald, officially endorsed the great General Holiness Assembly held in Chicago, 1901. See S. B. Shaw, *Echoes of the General Holiness Assembly Held in Chicago, May 3–13, 1901* (Chicago: S. B. Shaw, 1901), 12–14. John F. Hurst acknowledged sanctification as a second work, sought it earnestly as a young man, but never claimed the experience. As a student at Dickinson College he was introduced to holiness theology by his teacher, Jesse T. Peck (later, bishop), author of the

holiness classic *The Central Idea of Christianity* (Boston: Henry V. Degen, 1858). See Albert Osborn, *John Fletcher Hurst: A Biography* (New York: Eaton and Mains, 1905), 33–34, 36, 120, 122–23.

66. Brasher, *Glimpses*, 9, 21. Brasher states, "It is reported that when [Joyce] was elected bishop, he dropped his head on the seat in front of him and sobbed out these words: 'Thank God, I can now preach holiness around the world.'" Fitzgerald's mother, Mrs. Osee M. Fitzgerald of Newark, New Jersey, held weekly holiness meetings in her home for over sixty years. See Shaw, *Echoes*, 14; Brasher, *Glimpses*, 20.

67. *Minutes*, Alabama Conference, 1893; Brasher, *Glimpses*, 9; SR 13.

68. Brasher, *Glimpses*, 6, 20; *Minutes*, Alabama Conference, 1898. William Xavier Ninde was sanctified (during his pastorate at Adams, New York) in the great revival of 1857–58. He and Bishop Mallalieu were classmates at Wesleyan College, Middletown, Connecticut, during the presidency of Stephen Olin, a leader of the prewar holiness revival. See Mary Ninde Gamewell, *William Xavier Ninde, A Memorial* (New York: Eaton and Mains, 1902), 58.

69. Brasher, *Glimpses*, 21; Willard F. Mallalieu, *The Fulness of the Blessing of the Gospel of Christ* (New York: Eaton and Mains, 1903).

70. *Minutes*, Alabama Conference, 1894; *The Doctrines and Discipline of the Methodist Episcopal Church, 1892*, 329. Further evidence of a strategy to attract converts in the South through the promotion of holiness was the appointment in 1904 of holiness bishops Mallalieu, McCabe, and Joyce to head the new General Conference Special Committee on Aggressive Evangelism. Especially concerned with establishing churches in the South, the General Conference Committee on Church Extension from 1892 to 1903 employed as executive secretary Dr. Manley S. Hard, a noted holiness advocate. *Journal of the General Conference of the Methodist Episcopal Church, 1904*, 101, 807; Shaw, *Echoes*, 13.

71. *Minutes*, Alabama Conference, 1899; John L. Brasher, "Brief Story of the Beginning of Hartselle Camp Meeting," BP; John L. Brasher, "Hartselle Holiness Camp Meeting," BP. Within a year, Huckabee moved to Texas. There he joined the Holiness Association of Texas and became editor in 1905 of its *Pentecostal Advocate*. *Minutes*, Alabama Conference, 1900; Smith, *Called Unto Holiness*, 165.

72. SR 20.

73. In Brasher's *Clergyman's Pocket Diary* for Wedowee, Alabama, 1892–94, BP, he recorded receiving *The Problem of Methodism* in 1893. See Brasher, *A Simple Statement*, 6. For reference to his antiholiness sermon, see SR 72. The sermon, "One Work," appears as an entry for Sunday, 21 Jan. 1900, in Brasher's copy of *The Ideal Pastor's Record*, BP. James Benton Ellis, an Alabama holiness (later, Pentecostal) preacher heard Brasher's sermon in early 1900 and reported: "I never heard a more forceful sermon against holiness in all my life. My heart was crushed as this masterly minister proceeded to denounce my experience. I cried out audibly . . . while he was preaching. I felt that the cause of holiness was ruined." James Benton Ellis, *Blazing the Gospel Trail* (Plainfield, N.J.: Logos International, 1976), 34–35.

74. Brasher, *A Simple Statement*, 6.
75. Brasher used the metaphor in SR 33.
76. John L. Brasher, "Methodism: Its Doctrine and Spirit," 1894, BP.
77. Ibid.
78. *Minutes,* Alabama Conference, 1897.
79. Gilbert E. Govan and James W. Livingood, *The University of Chatta-nooga: Sixty Years* (Chattanooga: University of Chattanooga, 1947), 10. The school of theology operated at Chattanooga 1891–1910 and served seven conferences: Holston, Blue Ridge, Alabama, Virginia, Georgia, Kentucky, Central Tennessee. In 1883, when the northern church chose Chattanooga as the site of its university, the *Christian Advocate,* a Methodist Episcopal paper for the South, began publishing there. It succeeded the church's *Methodist Advocate,* published in Atlanta, 1869–83.
80. Synan, *The Holiness-Pentecostal Movement,* 48.
81. Govan, *University of Chattanooga,* 48, 69, 251, 260. Joyce was chancellor during 1891–97; Ackerman, dean, 1890–91; Newcomb, dean, 1891–1904.
82. Ackerman, *Love Illumined,* 8; Govan, *University of Chattanooga,* 69. Ackerman graduated from Garrett in 1878 and was sanctified two years later. Gamewell, *Ninde,* 109; Ackerman, *Love Illumined,* 14. He served as secretary of the Alabama Conference 1892–1902. His major theological work was *Man, A Revelation of God* (New York: Phillips and Hunt, 1888). Brasher's two other professors were John H. Race and Richard J. Cooke. Race (Princeton, B.A., M.A.) taught Greek. Cooke, a graduate of East Tennessee Wesleyan, taught church history and doctrine, authored over a dozen scholarly books, and was elected bishop in 1912.
83. Ackerman, *Love Illumined,* 10.
84. Ibid., 71. Ackerman acknowledged the legitimacy of "other modes" of sanctification, although he did not specify them. He took care to defend the second blessing against "extreme views" (9), particularly against proponents of sinless perfection; belief in the simultaneous occurrence of justification and sanctification (Boland); and those who emphasized sanctification over justification. He drew upon the thought of Randolph S. Foster, John Miley, and Miner Raymond, and also appealed to the authority of John Fletcher, Francis Asbury, Daniel Steele, Bishop C. C. McCabe, Dwight Moody, James Brainerd Taylor, and Frances Ridley Havergal.
85. Brasher, *Glimpses,* 11.
86. John L. Brasher, "A Biography of Minnie Eunice Moore Brasher," BP.
87. Brasher, *A Simple Statement,* 7.
88. Brasher, "Autobiography," 19–20; John L. Brasher, Report to Quarterly Conference of Simpson M. E. Church, 21 Oct. 1902, BP. The "discouragement" in Simpson Church was probably related to the economic depression of the 1890s, peculiar urban problems, and its relative weakness compared to nearby Southern Methodist churches. In 1900, Simpson paid the highest salary in the Alabama Conference. The average annual salary of the fifty-four pastors in the Conference was $145. *Minutes,* Alabama Conference, 1900. Brasher's correspondence with his church members and other family

sources show that church members had such occupations as tradesmen, artisans, boardinghouse keepers, and nurses. See Brasher, "Autobiography," 19–22; Brasher, "Biography of Minnie Brasher"; Leona Brasher Copeland, "Mama," BP. Charles Edwin Jones demonstrated that typical turn-of-the-century urban holiness churches attracted rural newcomers who were middle class or who aspired to it. See his "Disinherited or Rural?" 395–412. There are over twenty thousand letters in the Brasher Papers from Brasher's colleagues and converts. Most exhibit writing ability and concerns indicative of the middle class. Some letters appear from holiness adherents who were owners of small businesses, even sizable industries. For evidence of middle-class holiness constituency in late-nineteenth-century Georgia, see Turley, "A Wheel within a Wheel."

89. SR 57.

90. Brasher, "Biography of Minnie Brasher"; Brasher, *A Simple Statement,* 7.

91. Carl L. Carmer, *Stars Fell on Alabama* (New York: Farrar and Rinehart, Inc., 1934), 79–80. Carmer's description, though written three decades later, would have been appropriate in 1900.

92. *United States Census,* 1870, 1900; *Age-Herald,* 1 Apr. 1900; Hamilton, *Alabama,* 135.

93. Leah Rawls Atkins, *The Valley and the Hills, an Illustrated History of Birmingham* (Woodland Hills, Calif.: Windsor Publications, 1981), 74, 85.

94. Ibid., 56, 75; Hamilton, *Alabama,* 135. Hamilton notes that the number of arrests per year was equivalent to one-third of the population, but the statistics also included the outlying mining districts.

95. The towns in which Brasher served were Wedowee, Randolph County, and Edwardsville, Cleburne County. While in Birmingham, both John and Minnie were directly involved in "rescue work" among prostitutes. SR 26.

96. Interview with Leona Brasher Copeland, Gallant, Alabama, July 1982.

97. Leona Brasher Copeland, "Mama."

98. SR 51; John L. Brasher, "Happy New Year," *The Way of Faith* 42 (1 Jan. 1931): 4.

99. Paul Brasher to John L. Brasher, 15 Aug. 1913, BP. A contemporary letter from R. G. Talmage, Bethel Holiness Mission, Des Moines, Iowa, to John L. Brasher, n.d., BP, laments that Des Moines "has got as near hell as any city could get and not be there."

100. Brasher, "Autobiography," 19.

101. John L. Brasher to the *Birmingham News,* 10 Dec. 1903, BP; *Methodist Advocate-Journal* 10 (3 May 1900), 4.

102. Brasher, "Autobiography," 20.

103. Brasher, *Glimpses,* 12. Pike was superintendent of the Pentecostal Mission Tabernacle, corner of First Avenue and Twenty-first Street.

104. *Methodist Advocate-Journal* 10 (8 Mar. 1900), 8–9, 12–13.

105. Ibid., 8.

106. Ibid., 12.

107. Ibid., 9.

108. Brasher, *A Simple Statement,* 7.

109. Minnie Eunice Moore Brasher, "Autobiography," BP. Other accounts of her sanctification appear in *The Aletheia* (Mar. 1924): 4, BP; Brasher, "Biography of Minnie Brasher"; SR 21. Martha Inskip, whose husband, John Inskip, was first president of the National Camp Meeting Association for the Promotion of Holiness, also was sanctified before her husband was and led him to the experience. William McDonald and John E. Searles, *The Life of the Rev. John S. Inskip* (Boston: Christian Witness Co., 1885), 150–52.

110. Brasher, *Glimpses*, 14; Brasher, *A Simple Statement*, 12. Colonel Samuel Logan Brengle (1860–1936), later commissioner, was the foremost promoter of holiness from within the Salvation Army. He was a graduate of DePauw University and Boston Theological Seminary, where he was a student of the noted holiness scholar Daniel Steele. See Hall, *Samuel Logan Brengle*. Christian W. Ruth (1865–1941), an evangelist from Indiana, was an early organizer of the Church of the Nazarene. Brasher heard him preach at revivals in Robert Pike's Birmingham mission immediately before and after his sanctification.

111. *Methodist Advocate-Journal* 10 (2 Aug. 1900), 4.

112. Brasher, *A Simple Statement*, 11; SR 34.

113. *Methodist Advocate-Journal* 10 (31 May 1900), 4; Brasher, "Autobiography"; Brasher, *A Simple Statement*, 11.

114. See four manuscript sermons (1892–95), BP; see also these addresses: "Methodism, Its Doctrine and Spirit" (1894), BP; "The Duty of the Pastor to the People" (1894), BP; "The Methodist Church and Reforms" (1896), BP; "The New Era" (189–?), BP; "Man, the Epitome of History" (Graduation Address, Ulysses S. Grant University School of Theology, May 1899), BP.

115. John L. Brasher to the *Methodist Advocate-Journal*, 26 Jan. 1910, BP. Although Brasher here cites his sanctification as occurring on 16 April 1900, later correspondence with Samuel Logan Brengle indicated that the date was 19 April. See n. 4.

116. Brasher, "A New Enthusiasm." In 1910, Brasher itemized "the old fashioned faith of our fathers" as belief in "the fall of man, the trinity, the deity of Jesus Christ, the personality and deity of the Holy Ghost, the inspiration of the sacred canon, regenerating and sanctifying grace, the witness of the spirit, the supernaturalness of the Christian religion, the future and eternal punishment of the wicked, and the eternal reward of the righteous." John L. Brasher to the *Methodist Advocate-Journal*, 26 Jan. 1910, BP.

117. SR 26.

118. John L. Brasher, "Report to Quarterly Conference of Simpson M. E. Church," 21 Oct. 1902, BP.

119. John L. Brasher to R. J. Cooke, 4 Nov. 1902, BP.

120. Brasher, "Report."

121. *Methodist Advocate-Journal* 10 (2 Aug. 1900), 4; Brasher, *A Simple Statement*, 11; Brasher, "Autobiography," 23.

122. John L. Brasher to R. J. Cooke, 4 Nov. 1902, BP.

123. John L. Brasher, "Memo to Dr. Cooke," 23 Oct. 1902, BP.

124. John L. and Minnie E. Brasher, "A Heart Talk with Our Children, near Christmas Season, 1958," BP. The evaluation of ministry according to the number of conversions effected is a central theme of A. M. Hills's *Holiness and*

Power, which Brasher read at the time of his sanctification. Hills wrote, "An annual average of 140 Congregational Churches in Massachusetts did not report a conversion in a year. It took thirty church members to make one convert in a year" (27). Brasher wrote, "In three years there has been an average for our membership of one profession for every two members each year, which [makes us] one of the leading churches in effectiveness in the world today." "Report."

125. *Methodist Advocate-Journal* 10 (8 Mar. 1900), 13.

126. John L. Brasher to R. J. Cooke, 4 Nov. 1902, BP.

127. *Methodist Advocate-Journal,* 10 (2 Aug. 1900), 4.

128. John L. Brasher to the *Methodist Advocate-Journal,* 29 Apr. 1905, BP.

129. John L. Brasher, "The Old-Timer Rambles On: 'Circuit Riders,'" *Etowah News-Journal* (Attalla, Ala.), 1956, BP; SR 59.

130. SR 72.

131. Ibid.; Brasher, "The New Era."

132. John L. Brasher, "And the People Rose up to Play," 1914, BP.

133. Brasher, "The Holiness Movement"; SR 42.

134. SR 42; Minnie Moore Brasher to John L. Brasher, 30 July 1926, BP. In this letter of encouragement to John, Minnie wrote, "Now is the time for evangelism. The time is short when they will hear sound doctrine."

135. Brasher's personal copy was William E. Blackstone, *Jesus Is Coming* (New York: Fleming H. Revell, 1898). Blackstone, born in Adams, New York, was a Methodist and an associate of Dwight L. Moody in the 1880s. See Timothy P. Weber, *Living in the Shadow of the Second Coming: American Premillennialism 1875–1925* (New York: Oxford University Press, 1979), 137–41.

136. Brasher, *Glimpses,* 14; SR 25.

137. SR 72.

138. John L. Brasher, "Founders' Day Message," Trevecca Nazarene College, Nashville, Tenn., 13 Nov. 1963, BP.

139. Wyncoop, *Trevecca,* 33; see also Frederick Leonard Chapell, *The Eleventh-Hour Laborers* (Nyack, N.Y.: Christian Alliance Publishing Co., 1898).

140. John L. Brasher, Record Book, 1903–4, BP; Brasher, "Founders' Day"; Benson, *Pentecostal Mission,* 86–87; Wyncoop, *Trevecca,* 91. Brasher used the image of "eleventh-hour laborers" in the same sense as Chapell in SR 42.

141. John L. Brasher to H. C. Morrison, 11 Dec. 1920, BP.

142. Tillman (1861–1943), the preeminent southern holiness songleader and composer, was "licensed" as an evangelist by McClurkan's Pentecostal Mission in 1902. One of his many songbooks was entitled *Eleventh-Hour Songs for the Eleventh-Hour Laborers* (Atlanta: Charlie D. Tillman, 1902). Benson, *Pentecostal Mission,* 234.

143. SR 72.

144. Brasher, *A Simple Statement,* 12.

145. SR 42.

146. John L. Brasher to A. H. Glascock, 3 Sept. 1909, BP.

147. SR 56.

148. SR 72.

149. Ibid.; SR 42.

150. John L. Brasher to the *Methodist Advocate-Journal*, 29 Apr. 1905, BP.
151. Brasher, *A Simple Statement*, 11, 12.
152. See n. 115.
153. *Methodist Advocate-Journal* 10 (2 Aug. 1900), 4.
154. Minnie Eunice Moore Brasher, "Autobiography." Minnie states that John became convinced of his call at Hartselle Camp Meeting, 1900.
155. Brasher, "Autobiography," 22.
156. John and Minnie Brasher, "A Heart Talk."

Chapter 6: "Their Hands on My Head"

1. Bruce A. Rosenberg, *The Art of the American Folk Preacher* (New York: Oxford University Press, 1970), 25, 28.
2. Hill, *Southern Churches*, 101.
3. Brasher, *A Simple Statement*.
4. Brasher, "Autobiography." These were circuit riders of Brasher's childhood.
5. Brasher, "J. L. Freeman." Freeman was also a circuit rider of Brasher's childhood and youth.
6. Fitzgerald, *Sunset Views*, 48.
7. Morrison, *Some Chapters*, 77, 184. Morrison attended theological school at Vanderbilt.
8. Beverly Carradine, *Pastoral Sketches* (Chicago: Christian Witness Co., 1896), 7–22. Carradine attended the University of Mississippi and subsequently studied medicine and law. See his *Graphic Scenes* (Cincinnati: God's Revivalist Office, 1911), 80–81.
9. Heath, *A Man Sent of God*, 20. McClurkan attended Tucuna College, Tucuna, Texas. His father, John McClurkan, was an itinerant preacher in the Cumberland Presbyterian Church in central Tennessee. See Wyncoop, *Trevecca*, 41–42.
10. John L. Brasher, "Memoir of Tarpley Redwine Parker," BP.
11. Andrews Institute, named for Bishop E. G. Andrews, was the first of several "seminaries of learning" founded by the reorganized Alabama M. E. Conference for the education of white children. Promoted by Bishop Gilbert Haven, the school opened in 1873 and closed its doors in 1903. John Jackson Brasher moved his family to the institute in DeKalb County in 1873 for the education of his two older sons and daughter. There was no school at the time in their home community. *Minutes*, Alabama Conference (1873, 1874, 1903); SR 10.
12. The quotation from Lakin is a paraphrase of Shakespeare, *Henry IV*, part 1, act 1, scene 3. Brasher was not aware of and Lakin may not have given credit to the original source. See Brasher, "Arad S. Lakin" and SR 2.
13. John L. Brasher, "'Elijah and Elisha,' as sung by Arad S. Lakin," BP. The other five stanzas are here.
14. Reuben Davis, *Recollections of Mississippi and Mississippians* (Boston: Houghton, Mifflin, 1891), 69.
15. Cash, *Mind of the South*, 51.

16. Waldo W. Braden, *The Oral Tradition in the South* (Baton Rouge: Louisiana State University Press, 1983), ix.

17. Ibid., 42.

18. *Golden Hours, A Magazine for Boys and Girls* 8–10 (1876–78) (Cincinnati: Methodist Book Concern); SR 17.

19. Clement Eaton, *A History of the Old South* (New York: Macmillan, 1949), 478.

20. Braden, *Oral Tradition,* 5.

21. SR 72.

22. SR 17.

23. The writers cited are found in the 1879 edition of McGuffey's fifth and sixth readers.

24. Braden, *Oral Tradition,* 7.

25. Brasher, "Arad S. Lakin."

26. SR 72.

27. SR 72; John L. Brasher, "My Old Childhood Home," BP. By the time of his early pastorates, he had read Wesley's sermons, required by the Methodist Course of Study, and sermons and lives of other notable preachers he had not heard. In his own sermons, Brasher routinely cited northern bishop Matthew Simpson and Southern bishop Henry Bascom as "the greatest preachers the world ever saw" (see SR 56). In *Glimpses,* Brasher indicates that he had read the sermons of Charles Spurgeon, Richard Storrs, Phillips Brooks, DeWitt Talmage, and Henry Ward Beecher, as well as the addresses of William Jennings Bryan and Henry W. Grady.

28. Brasher, "Circuit Riders."

29. Davis, *Recollections,* 69; the preachers, with their states of birth, and birth and death dates, were: Lemuel Bowers (Tennessee, 1815–88), John Jackson Brasher (Alabama, 1820–87), Christopher Columbus Burson (Alabama, 1846–1925), Levi Aaron Clifton (Georgia, 1836–1924), James L. Freeman (Alabama, 1841–1926), Arad S. Lakin (New York, 1810–90), James E. McCain (Tennessee, 1830–96), James P. McGee (North Carolina, 1806–98), William P. Miller (North Carolina, 1818–91), Tarpley Redwine Parker (Georgia, 1825–87), John Potter (M. E., South, Georgia, 1817–83).

30. John L. Brasher, "The Old Timer: 'Gadsden, Some Personalities Noted,'" *Etowah News-Journal* (Attalla, Ala.), 1956, BP.

31. Ibid.

32. Braden, *Oral Tradition,* 31.

33. Brasher, "Personalities Noted."

34. SR 72.

35. Brasher, "Personalities Noted."

36. Owsley, *Plain Folk,* 140.

37. Hamilton W. Pierson, *In the Brush; or, Old-Time Social, Political, and Religious Life in the Southwest* (New York: D. Appleton, 1881), 130, 162–63, quoted by Braden, *Oral Tradition,* 35–36.

38. John L. Brasher, "The Old-Timer: 'Elections in the 70's and 80's,'" *Etowah News-Journal* (Attalla, Ala.), 1956, BP.

39. Morrison, *Some Chapters,* 77.

40. SR 13.
41. John L. Brasher, "Lecture Six," delivered at God's Bible School, Cincinnati, Ohio, 29 Mar. 1950, BP.
42. W. R. Murphy to J. L. Brasher, 13 Apr. 1920, BP.
43. SR 52.
44. Brasher, "Autobiography," 18.
45. John L. Brasher, "Sam Jones, Prophet Preacher," BP. H. C. Morrison, when a student in the theological department at Vanderbilt, also heard Jones and commented that the "young preachers and . . . students thronged his ministry, and he was the subject of discussion at the table, on the campus, in the classroom." Morrison, *Some Chapters*, 98.
46. See Davies, *The Boy Preacher.*
47. Brasher, "Autobiography," 18.
48. John L. Brasher, Editorial, *The Way of Faith* 42 (15 June 1931): 4.
49. For a summary of "muscular Christianity" in nineteenth-century Methodist biography see Byrne, *No Foot of Land*, "Giants and Heroes," 275–99. Ralph Morrow, in *Northern Methodism*, 242–43, states that the institution of the frontier circuit rider was given a new lease on life by the conditions of the reorganized church in the Deep South.
50. SR 10, 68.
51. SR 16.
52. Brasher, "Circuit Riders."
53. SR 68. On the circuit in the winter, Brasher's father reportedly arrived at his lodging after fording a river on horseback but could not dismount until someone broke the ice that bound his boots to the stirrups. The itinerant T. R. Parker, whose horse "Colfax" had "a racking walk that could knock the land out all the way fast," was celebrated for riding thirty miles between dinner and supper, usually a full day's journey. Brasher recalled that when the saddle was removed from a preacher's horse, there often would be "a skinned place as big as a hand, nearly." They "put some healing leaves on it and then put the saddle back on." Lemuel Bowers, an elderly preacher and "a very holy man," "never missed an appointment unless he was too sick to get up." Even in his last years, he was known to swim a river so as not to "disappoint a congregation." See SR 17, 2; John L. Brasher, "Memoir of Lemuel Bowers," BP.
54. SR 17.
55. Brasher, "Circuit Riders." Byrne cites four printed versions of the story in which the song is sung by Francis Asbury, the founding father of American Methodism. See *No Foot of Land*, 205–6 n. 81.
56. John L. Brasher, "Christopher Columbus Burson," BP.
57. SR 15.
58. George G. Smith, *The Life and Times of George Foster Pierce* (Sparta, Ga.: n.p., 1888), 143–49, quoted by Mann, *Atticus Haygood*, 35.
59. Brasher held some credence in the popular nineteenth-century pseudo-science of phrenology. He occasionally entertained his family by giving phrenological analyses.
60. Brasher, *Glimpses*, 8; SR 13.

61. Brasher, "Sam Jones."
62. SR 2; Brasher, "J. L. Freeman."
63. Brasher, "James P. McGee."
64. John L. Brasher, "Memoir of James E. McCain," BP.
65. Brasher, "Lemuel J. Bowers." T. R. Parker, a preacher of uncommon education, possessed a mind that "sometimes so mastered him that he did absurd things," such as going home with a man from church and forgetting his horse, or traveling to his next appointment and leaving one of his children asleep at the church. Brasher, "T. R. Parker."
66. Brasher, "How Can They Hear?"
67. Brasher, "Sam Jones."
68. SR 15.
69. Brasher, "Circuit Riders."
70. SR 54.
71. Brasher, "Lemuel J. Bowers."
72. SR 2.
73. John L. Brasher, "Memoir of Levi Aaron Clifton," BP.
74. SR 2.
75. Brasher, "J. L. Freeman."
76. Brasher, "T. R. Parker."
77. Brasher, "James P. McGee."
78. Brasher, *A Simple Statement;* SR 2. Landmarkism was a type of "high church" movement that enjoyed a resurgence among Baptists in the South after the Civil War. It proclaimed that since the time of Christ, believers baptized by immersion had passed on the true church in unbroken succession. "The local Baptist congregation, therefore, was an apostolic institution with a continuous history." See Sydney Ahlstrom, *A Religious History of the American People* (New Haven: Yale University Press, 1972), 722–25.
79. Brasher, "J. L. Freeman."
80. SR 2.
81. Brasher, "T. R. Parker"; SR 2.
82. Brasher, "Sam Jones"; Davies, *The Boy Preacher,* 30.
83. Brasher, "Levi A. Clifton."
84. SR 2.
85. Blount County Historical Society, *The Heritage of Blount County,* 99; SR 13.
86. Brasher, "J. L. Freeman."
87. Brasher, "Sam Jones."
88. Brasher, *Glimpses,* 8.
89. SR 13.
90. Brasher, "Sam Jones."
91. Brasher, "T. R. Parker."
92. SR 2.
93. Brasher, "J. L. Freeman."
94. Brasher, "Circuit Riders."
95. Brasher, "Arad S. Lakin"; SR 13. Bishop Haven reported that Lakin

was "the best stump speaker in the state," that he was "as full of tropes as Beecher or Spurgeon or Longfellow, though, like the last he sometimes gets the figures mixed in the effluence of his fancy." "A Conference in a Tent," 1.

96. Brasher, "T. R. Parker"; SR 2.

97. Brasher, "Lecture Six."

98. See Byrne, *No Foot of Land,* 244; Lorin H. Soderwall, "The Rhetoric of the Methodist Camp-Meeting Movement, 1800–1850" (Ph.D. diss., University of Southern California, 1971), 289. H. C. Morrison also named Henry Bascom as one of his models. Bascom stayed in the home of Morrison's grandfather when on the circuit in Kentucky. Morrison recalled Bascom's "marvelous eloquence, dignity, how very handsome he was, how impressive in reading the hymns, in pronouncing a benediction, how courteous and kindly to preachers and people." Morrison, *Some Chapters,* 78.

99. Brasher, "Sam Jones"; "J. L. Freeman."

100. John L. Brasher, "Great Preaching," *The Way of Faith* 40 (1 Oct. 1929): 5.

101. Ibid.

102. SR 61.

103. Ibid.

104. John L. Brasher to "The Saints at Hollow Rock," June 1966, BP.

105. Brasher, "Lecture Six"; Brasher, "T. R. Parker"; SR 10.

106. Brasher, "Autobiography," 18. Goodsell preached at the Alabama Conference in 1898.

107. Brasher, "Elections."

108. Brasher, "J. L. Freeman."

109. Ibid.

110. SR 63.

111. John L. Brasher, "Meditation at Age 97," 20 Jan. 1966, BP; Brasher, "J. L. Freeman."

112. SR 18. *Systematic Theology,* by the Methodist theologian John Miley (1813–95), was one of Brasher's texts while he was a student at U. S. Grant University School of Theology.

113. Brasher, "James E. McCain."

114. Brasher, "T. R. Parker." A printed account of the incident appears in J. L. Freeman, "Notes on the Death of Rev. T. R. Parker," *The Methodist Advocate* 3 (16 Apr. 1887). Brasher claimed that people who wanted to shoot his father wouldn't miss hearing him preach. SR 15.

115. SR 2.

116. John L. Brasher to Carolyn Boatman, 20 Apr. 1953, Boatman Papers, Duke University, Durham, N.C.

117. Brasher, *Glimpses,* 8.

118. Brasher, "T. R. Parker"; Brasher, "Circuit Riders." The quotation borrows from Romans 5:2.

119. Jon Tal Murphree, *Giant of a Century Trail: The Life and Labors of John Lakin Brasher, Great Southern Orator* (Apollo, Pa.: West Publishing Company, 1969), 17.

Chapter 7: Style with a View to Power

1. John L. Brasher, birthday letter, 20 July 1949, BP.
2. Dayton, "Baptism of the Holy Spirit," 116–18.
3. Ibid., 114, 118, 122. Dayton describes the dominant holiness position as a balance between purity and power. Reformed and Keswick interpretations of sanctification deemphasized purity in favor of power. Brasher's emphasis upon the power of the indwelling Holy Ghost probably was encouraged by his close association with J. O. McClurkan, who adopted the Keswick interpretation of sanctification as a "filling of the Holy Spirit for the enduement of power." See Wyncoop, *Trevecca*, 31–38.
4. Luke 24:49.
5. Lovick Pierce, "The Experience and Observations of Rev. L. Pierce on Sanctification for Seventy-One Years," *Way of Holiness* 56 (Apr. 1876): 15–16.
6. George W. Wilson, *Truths as I Have Seen Them* (Cincinnati: Jennings and Pye, 1897), n.p., quoted in Ackerman, *Love Illumined*, 36.
7. "Central Holiness University," *Christian Witness and Advocate of Bible Holiness*, 15 Mar. 1917, 5.
8. Brasher, "The Ministry."
9. John L. Brasher to Family at Home, 2 Dec. 1925, BP. Many southern holiness folk with premillennialist belief in the imminent Second Coming perceived the special power of their preachers as a sign of the close of the age, a special enduement marking the start of a final revival of Pentecostal dimensions. Likewise, the "expectant, victorious spirit" and "the disorderly exuberance" of the singing at holiness meetings, for many, betokened dispensational developments. See Joseph Owen to John L. Brasher, 12 Sept. 1919, BP; Chapell, *Eleventh-Hour Laborers*, 57–61; Davies, *The Boy Preacher*, 75.
10. SR 52.
11. Brasher, *A Simple Statement*, 11–12. Some other preachers who reported new power in preaching, or new desire to preach, after their sanctification were Nathan Bangs, in Abel Stevens, *Life and Times of Nathan Bangs* (New York: Carlton and Porter, 1863), 62; Charles G. Finney, in his *Memoirs* (New York: A. S. Barnes, 1876), 29; Thomas Harrison, in Davies, *The Boy Preacher*, 249–51; W. B. Godbey, in his *Autobiography*, 65, 94, 96; B. F. Haynes, in *Tempest-Tossed*, 79–80; Samuel Logan Brengle, in Hall, *Samuel Logan Brengle*, 54; C. B. Jernigan, in *Pioneer Days*, 12; Dwight L. Moody, in Asa Mahan, *Autobiography* (London: T. Wolmer, 1882), 442–44; Samuel Chadwick, in *Way of Faith* 40 (1 Oct. 1929): 4. Minnie Eunice Brasher spoke of new power in testifying. See SR 48.
12. Several of Brasher's manuscript sermons, all written before 1900, are in the Brasher Papers.
13. The best-known satirical story of a seminary-trained minister who tried to read his sermon was Peter Cartwright's account of a "fresh, green, live Yankee from down East" in *Autobiography of Peter Cartwright, The Backwoods Preacher* (New York: Carlton and Porter, 1856), 370–72. For other accounts see Byrne, *No Foot of Land*, 245–48.

222 Notes to Pages 88–91

14. Arthur, *Tongue of Fire*, 324.

15. Ibid., 322.

16. SR 31.

17. SR 61.

18. Ibid.

19. SR 48. Brasher believed that printed bulletins and a fixed order of worship hindered the Spirit. With a bulletin, Brasher said, "The devil could fall asleep on the back pew, if he could find one empty." John L. Brasher to Caroline Boatman, 17 Mar. 1969, Boatman Family Papers, Duke University, Durham, N.C.

20. SR 61.

21. Beverly Carradine, *Revival Incidents* (Chicago: Christian Witness Co., 1913), 101.

22. Arthur, *Tongue of Fire*, 322–23.

23. Ibid., 322.

24. Ibid., 320.

25. By "rhetoric" is meant "a persuasive strategy which includes anything framed for its effect on an audience as inducement to action or attitude." See George A. Von Glahn, "Natural Eloquence and the Democratic Gospel: The Idea of an American Rhetoric from the Second Great Awakening to Cooper's *Natty Bumppo*" (Ph.D. diss., University of North Carolina, 1969), 29.

26. Brasher, "A New Enthusiasm"; John L. Brasher to "The Saints at Hollow Rock," June 1966, BP; John L. Brasher, lecture delivered at God's Bible School, Cincinnati, Ohio, 29 Mar. 1950, BP. Brasher told a group of young preachers, "Even the Spirit himself cannot bring to your remembrance that which you have not learned." "Lecture Six."

27. Paul S. Rees to J. Lawrence Brasher, 18 Dec. 1983, BP.

28. Samuel S. Hill, Jr., "The Shape and Shapes of Popular Southern Piety," in *Varieties of Southern Evangelicalism*, ed. David E. Harrell, Jr. (Macon, Ga.: Mercer University Press, 1981), 95. Italics mine.

29. Bruce A. Rosenberg, *The Art of the American Folk Preacher* (New York: Oxford University Press, 1970). The revised edition, *Can These Bones Live? The Art of the American Folk Preacher* (Urbana: University of Illinois Press, 1988), treats only African-American chanted preaching. Subsequent references are to the 1970 edition.

30. Milman Parry, "Studies in the Epic Technique of Oral Verse-making. I: Homer and Homeric Style," *Harvard Studies in Classical Philology* 41 (1930); Alfred B. Lord, *The Singer of Tales* (Cambridge, Mass.: Harvard University Press, 1960). The "guslars" studied by Parry and Lord were supposedly the last remaining singers of oral epics in the West, who accompanied themselves on the single-stringed "gusle."

31. Rosenberg, *Folk Preacher*, 4.

32. Parry, "Epic Technique," 80, quoted by Rosenberg, *Folk Preacher*, 44.

33. Rosenberg, *Folk Preacher*, 5.

34. Ibid., 11–12.

35. Ibid., 10.

36. Ibid.
37. Ibid., 76.
38. Ibid., 10.
39. Ibid., 53, 51.
40. Ibid., 51.
41. Ibid., 123–24.
42. Ibid., 116.
43. Ibid., 62. Gerald L. Davis, in *I Got the Word in Me and I Can Sing It, You Know: A Study of the Performed African-American Sermon* (Philadelphia: University of Pennsylvania Press, 1985), analyzes the structure of African-American chanted sermons and concludes that Parry and Lord's concept of formula and theme will not work for them. Instead, he defines themes as "formula sets" that embrace "a single thought, purpose, or function," and which consist of a "group of hemistitch phrases shaped into an irrhythmic metrical unit when performed" (53). Parry and Lord's definitions, as modified by Rosenberg, are more helpful in analyzing Brasher's style.
44. Jeff Todd Titon, *Powerhouse for God: Sacred Speech, Chant, and Song in an Appalachian Baptist Church*, booklet for sound recording (Chapel Hill: University of North Carolina Press, 1982), 13. Titon has given fuller treatment of this tradition in his book *Powerhouse for God: Speech, Chant, and Song in an Appalachian Baptist Church* (Austin: University of Texas Press, 1988).
45. Rosenberg, *Folk Preacher,* 73, 85.
46. Ibid., 73.
47. Ibid., 17.
48. Titon, *Powerhouse,* 13.
49. Rosenberg, *Folk Preacher,* 38.
50. Ibid., 14, 15.
51. C. C. Goen, *Revivalism and Separatism in New England, 1740–1800: Strict Congregationalists and Separate Baptists in the Great Awakening* (New Haven: Yale University Press, 1962), 180.
52. Robert Semple, *A History of the Rise and Progress of the Baptists in Virginia* (Richmond: John O'Lynch, 1810), 4; G. W. Paschal, ed., "Morgan Edwards' Materials Towards a History of the Baptists in the Province of North Carolina," *North Carolina Historical Review* 7 (1930): 383, 386. In 1874, John A. Broadus (1827–95), who had been born into a family of Baptist preachers in the Blue Ridge country of western Virginia and was later professor of preaching at Southern Baptist Theological Seminary, described the preaching of the early southern Separate Baptists (some of which Broadus could remember). He noted that their preaching was characterized by "a rising and falling singsong tone regarded as the appropriate expression of excited feelings, a musical accompaniment which gratified and impressed its hearers like a tune we remember from childhood." J. A. Broadus, "The American Baptist Ministry of One Hundred Years Ago," *Baptist Quarterly* 9 (1875): 19. Morgan Edwards also stated that among the southern Separates, as in the North, both ministers and laity were highly subject to "impulses, visions, and revelations" (Paschal, ed., "Morgan Edwards' Materials," 383).

53. Winthrop S. Hudson, "The American Context as an Area for Research in Black Church Studies," *Church History* 52 (June 1983): 164–65. In determining the origins of black chanted preaching, significance must be given to the fact that prior to 1800 in the South, both Separate Baptists and Methodists (who shared the emotional worship forms of the Baptists) admitted blacks to full communion.

54. Teague, "Sketches," 26. Reference to the use of rhythmic themes among Methodists appears in a memoir of the Ohio Methodist circuit rider William B. Christie (1803–45): "About his countenance there was a . . . seraphic sweetness, especially when with . . . measured cadence he would labor to win his rapt audiences to the cross or bear them away on imagination's wing to heaven." James B. Finley, *Autobiography* (Cincinnati: Jennings and Pye, 1853), 431.

55. Brasher, transcript, "Funeral Service of the Rev. W. A. Murphree"; John L. Brasher to the Reverend J. E. Johnson, 9 Jan. 1922, BP; John L. Brasher to Hollow Rock Camp Meeting, 6 July 1964, BP.

56. Jones, *Perfectionist Persuasion,* 20.

57. SR 49.

58. John L. Brasher to Hollow Rock Camp Meeting, June 1966, BP.

59. John L. Brasher, "The Mountain Top Experience," sermon delivered at John Fletcher College Chapel, Oskaloosa, Iowa, 12 Oct. 1924, BP.

60. Robert G. Pike to John L. Brasher, 15 Oct. 1920, BP.

61. Brasher, "The Holiness Movement."

62. Joseph Owen to John L. Brasher, 15 Mar. 1919, BP; Joseph Owen to John L. Brasher, 24 May 1919, BP.

63. John L. Brasher, "The Evangelist: His Place in the Economy of the Church," 1913, BP.

64. SR 51.

65. SR 41.

66. SR 39.

67. SR 1.

68. Albert Outler, *Theology in the Wesleyan Spirit* (Nashville: Tidings, 1975), 72; SR 31.

69. Brasher quoted Robinson in SR 53.

70. SR 52.

71. SR 64.

72. John L. Brasher to Hollow Rock Camp Meeting, July 1968.

73. Pierce, "Experience and Observations," 13. The words are from Romans 6:11.

74. SR 64.

75. Brasher, "Mountain Top," 2.

76. SR 64.

77. Rob L. Staples has argued that the change from Christocentric to Pneumatocentric terminology in the nineteenth-century holiness movement necessitated special evidence (such as visions) to demonstrate that one was sanctified. "'Christlike' is its own evidence. 'Spirit-filled' required evidence." Rob

L. Staples, "The Current Wesleyan Debate on the Baptism with the Holy Spirit," privately circulated paper (Mar. 1979), 27, quoted by Thomas A. Langford, *Practical Divinity: Theology in the Wesleyan Tradition* (Nashville: Abingdon Press, 1983), 142.

78. Brasher, "Mountain Top," 2.
79. John L. Brasher to Will H. Huff, 11 Dec. 1920, BP.
80. SR 27.
81. Brasher, "Mountain Top," 5.
82. SR 41.
83. Brasher, "Mountain Top," 2–3. Images drawn from Bunyan's *Pilgrim's Progress* appear frequently in holiness literature. See SR 27; see also James Blaine Chapman, *The Terminology of Holiness* (Kansas City, Mo.: Beacon Hill Press, 1947), 87–89, 91.
84. SR 27.
85. Brasher, "Mountain Top," 7.
86. SR 30.
87. Brasher, "Mountain Top," 5.
88. Brasher, "Circuit Riders."
89. Perry Miller, *The Life of the Mind in America from the Revolution to the Civil War* (New York: Harcourt, Brace, World, 1965), 61.
90. SR 36.
91. John L. Brasher to the Reverend Wiley Stephenson, 16 Oct. 1959, BP.
92. Carradine, *Revival Incidents,* 236.
93. John L. Brasher to the Reverend J. Thomas Price, 19 Apr. 1922, BP; John L. Brasher to Hollow Rock Camp Meeting, July 1969, BP.
94. John L. Brasher to the Reverend J. H. Beadle, 26 Dec. 1922, BP.
95. SR 42.
96. John L. Brasher to Minnie Eunice Brasher, 30 July 1928, BP.
97. George W. Meredith to John L. Brasher, 16 Apr. 1920, BP.
98. Anna Laura Brasher to Home Folks, 9 June 1928.
99. Henry Howard to John L. Brasher, 11 Jan. 1922, BP.
100. Wallace A. Murphree to John L. Brasher, 17 May 1924, BP.
101. SR 56. The Scripture text is "that they may receive forgiveness and inheritance among them which are sanctified by faith that is in me."
102. Braden, *Oral Tradition,* 67.
103. Bruce, *And They All Sang Hallelujah,* 5, 18–19.
104. Braden, *Oral Tradition,* 74.
105. Joseph Campbell, "The Historical Development of Mythology," in *Myth and Mythmaking,* ed. Henry A. Murray (New York: G. Braziller, 1960), 19.
106. Braden, *Oral Tradition,* 73.
107. Brasher's words immediately follow a version of the theme of the plantation that he presents in SR 54.
108. SR 25.
109. Carradine, *Graphic Scenes,* 254.
110. SR 64.

111. SR 39. Scriptural precedents for "facial glory" as a sign of sanctification are found in the account of the shining face of Moses (Exodus 34:29–35), the Transfiguration of Jesus (Matthew 17:1–8), and especially in Paul's use of the Moses account in II Corinthians 3:7–8, 18: "But if the ministration of death written and ingraven in stones was glorious, so that the children of Israel could not steadfastly behold the face of Moses for the glory of his countenance, which glory was to be done away, how shall not the ministration of the Spirit be rather glorious? . . . But we all with open face beholding as in a glass the glory of the Lord are changed into the same image from glory to glory even as by the Spirit of the Lord." The description was a favorite of Beverly Carradine. See his *Sanctification,* 12–13; *Pastoral Sketches,* 16–17; *Revival Incidents,* 164. For other references see Godbey, *Autobiography,* 92; Bud Robinson, *A Pitcher of Cream* (Louisville: Pentecostal Publishing Co., 1906), 132; *Zion's Outlook* (newspaper published by J. O. McClurkan, Nashville), 7 Mar. 1901; Chapell, *The Eleventh-Hour Laborers,* 68–73. Brasher's references to the "faraway look," beyond those quoted, are too numerous to cite.

112. Chapell, *The Eleventh-Hour Laborers,* 72.

113. Eloway Hurst to John L. Brasher, 8 Oct. 1907, BP; Ruth Upson to John L. Brasher, 28 Sept. 1924, BP.

114. Broadside for Sharon Camp Meeting, Sharon Center, Ohio, 22–31 July 1932, BP.

115. Raymond Browning, "Deeper Than the Stain Has Gone" (Lawrenceburg, Tenn.: James D. Vaughn, n.d.), BP.

116. James H. Brasher, interview held at Brasher Springs, Attalla, Ala., July 1982.

117. D. W. Haskew, "Great Crowds Attend Indian Springs Meeting," news clipping, n.p., 1933, BP.

118. John L. Brasher to Minnie E. Brasher, 3 Nov. 1927, BP.

119. Broadside for Sharon Camp Meeting, Sharon Center, Ohio, 22–31 July 1932, BP; "Sychar's Young People in March," news clipping (Sharon Center, Ohio), n.p., ca. 1930, BP; Heath, *A Man Sent of God,* 76.

120. Brasher, "Mountain Top," 5.

121. Ibid., 4. David E. Harrell, Jr., maintains that "the heart of the sectarian gospel" in the South after 1900 proclaimed "escapist and narcotic ideas." Brasher's theology of visions led to involvement in the world and either refutes this generalization or places his brand of interdenominational holiness outside the bounds of early-twentieth-century southern sectarianism as described by Harrell. See "The South: Seedbed of Sectarianism," in Harrell, *Varieties,* 54.

122. A. D. Peck, "A Day at Clear Creek," *Methodist Advocate-Journal,* 3 June 1915, 5–6; SR 75.

123. Michalson, former president of the School of Theology at Claremont, Claremont, Calif., heard Brasher preach in 1933 at Red Rock Camp Meeting, St. Paul, Minn., and in Park Avenue Methodist Church, Minneapolis. Interview with Gordon E. Michalson, Claremont, Calif., Nov. 1983.

124. Perry Miller, *The New England Mind: The Seventeenth Century* (New York: Macmillan, 1939), 331–62.

125. Samuel Chadwick (1860–1932), president of the Wesleyan Methodist Conference in England, whom Lloyd George hailed "a pulpit giant," heard Brasher preach in 1908 at Indian Springs Camp Meeting, Flovilla, Ga. Chadwick reported, "His address bore all the marks of exact scholarship and wide culture, and he expounded the Scriptures with the care of Apollos." "Letter from Samuel Chadwick," *Way of Faith* 25 (20 Aug. 1914): 5, 8, 9.

126. A clear example of Brasher's usual sermon structure is the stenographically recorded sermon, "Now Is the Accepted Time," Jamestown Camp Meeting, Jamestown, N.D., 28 June 1916, BP.

127. John L. Brasher, "Sermon Notebook," 111, BP. In this sermon, the early mention of the "cost" of a soul would indicate some variation of the frequently used theme of the Crucifixion. Themes were employed in the first half of some sermons.

128. Ibid., 91.

129. John L. Brasher to Paul Rees, 20 Feb. 1925, BP.

130. John L. Brasher, "A Tribute," *The Christian Witness* 64 (6 June 1946): 2, BP. Brasher's metaphor is engaging, but he clearly was not a seaman. The ship would have crashed. The image does, however, portray an overwhelming impact.

131. Rosenberg, *Folk Preacher,* 34, 26.

132. A. M. Baumgartner, "The Lyceum Is My Pulpit: Homiletics in Emerson's Early Lectures," *American Literature* 34 (Jan. 1963): 477–86.

133. Rosenberg, *Folk Preacher,* 54–55.

134. The versions are respectively from SR 56, 56, 57, 54, 58, 36, 18, 18, and 53. This formula appears in written form in Brasher's letter to his brother James, 29 Oct. 1902, BP: "For the sake of God who wills it, and of Christ who died for it, and of the Holy Ghost who lives to consummate it . . . do not let Satan betray you." Another written version in Robinson's *A Pitcher of Cream* (45) indicates the formula circulated among turn-of-the-century holiness evangelists: "God willed it to us . . . Christ died to sanctify us with his own blood, and . . . the Holy Ghost witnesses to it." Brasher's letter shows that he used the formula for over sixty years.

135. The two versions are respectively from SR 42, 72.

136. Selected epigrammatic formulas of Bud Robinson are printed under the heading "Flashlights," in Robinson, *Sunshine and Smiles,* 83–110.

137. J. O. McClurkan to John L. Brasher, 17 July 1914, BP; D. W. Haskew, "Great Crowds Attend Indian Springs Camp Meeting," news clipping, n.p., 1933, BP; James McGraw, "The Preaching of Sam Jones," *The Preacher's Magazine* 32 (Nov. 1957), 11; Morrison, *Some Chapters of My Life Story,* 98.

138. The first three formulas are from SR 38. The last two are from SR 55.

139. See John L. Brasher's Date Book, 1905, BP; John L. Brasher, "Nuggets from a Sermon Gold Mine," *Way of Faith* 41 (1 Sept. 1930): 11.

140. John L. Brasher, sermon at Jamestown Camp Meeting, 28 June 1916, 6, BP.

141. SR 58.

142. SR 53.
143. SR 58.
144. SR 36.
145. Brasher, "Immortality."
146. SR 49.
147. SR 59, 65, 55.
148. SR 42.
149. In the transcript of Brasher's sermon "Forgiveness of Sins and Inheritance Among Them Which Are Sanctified," Rock Methodist Church, Tarrant, Ala., 1963 (SR 54), no one theme dominates. Instead, at least ten separate themes constitute the sermon. In order of appearance they are: the devil; conversion and preparation for it; Scripture verses interspersed with glosses; an inheritance; grace as a gift; how to feel sanctified (a plantation inheritance); effects of sanctification; the immortal company; the pearl of great price; being right with God. In some sermons, primarily didactic in style, no clear themes appear. See SR 51, 62.
150. SR 13.
151. W. R. Murphy to John L. Brasher, Sept. 1921, BP.
152. John L. Brasher, "Wanted, a New Enthusiasm," 20 July 1921, BP.
153. SR 2.
154. Brasher, "Lecture Six."
155. *The Methodist Hymnal* (Nashville: Methodist Book Concern, 1939), 530, 534.
156. The Last Supper, the betrayal, Gethsemane, the trial before Pilate, and the scourging are themes that appear in SR 55. Themes of post-Resurrection appearances to Mary Magdalene, on the road to Emmaus, and to Thomas appear in SR 67.
157. SR 46.
158. SR 40.
159. SR 55.
160. SR 40.
161. SR 65.
162. Brasher's remarkable flexibility of voice ranged from sonorous tones "clothed with authority," as described by Samuel Chadwick, to a "kind, tender" pathos reported by a listener in Kansas. See "Letter from Samuel Chadwick," *Way of Faith* 25 (20 Aug. 1914): 5; Mrs. Hazel Barnhill, Wichita, Kans., to John L. Brasher, 3 Sept. 1920, BP. An example of his most powerful voice may be heard in the theme of "the rich young ruler's loss," in SR 48, 11–12 (see Appendix E); his voice of tender pathos in his reenactment of the deathbed conversation of John Fletcher, in SR 46, 16. Brasher said of his colleague H. C. Morrison, "There were tones in his voice that I would have loved to hear for an hour, whether he was saying anything or not." Brasher, *Glimpses,* 89.
163. William E. Hatcher, *John Jasper: The Unmatched Negro Philosopher and Preacher* (New York: Fleming H. Revell, 1908), 9.
164. SR 38.
165. Interview with Julius Brasher, Brasher Springs, Ala., July 1982.

166. Brasher, "T. R. Parker."

167. Brasher uses variations of the theme in SR 53, 54. The theme circulated in oral tradition; a version of it is reported in Hatcher, *Jasper*, 177–82.

168. Gaddis's account appears in his complimentary remarks before Brasher's birthday speech of SR 75.

169. Morrison's sermon is described in J. C. McPheeters, "Henry Clay Morrison, The Magnificent Preacher," *The Herald* 83 (8 Mar. 1972): 3, 13.

170. The letter from Dr. John Paul to Brasher, 22 Mar. 1922, BP, reads: "Then I must whisper to you for your own advice, our dear Brother Morrison is becoming more unbalanced in mind every year, though I would lose the friendship of thousands who blindly follow him, intoxicated by his oratory and his heroic tone, if I should come out with my own view of the fact. We can only pray that our great cause may not suffer disaster from a crack in his direction." Morrison, whom Brasher affectionately called "the General," was noted for his elegant scissor-tailed coat and long, wavy hair. When preaching, he sometimes during a dramatic pause would run his fingers through his hair—reportedly much to the fascination of women in the audience. The story still circulates of an incident in which he sought Brasher's forgiveness for his jealousy of Brasher's preaching ability. Interviews with Anna Laura Brasher Pooley and Jon Tal Murphree, Brasher Springs, Attalla, Ala., July 1984; Gordon B. Rainey, "John Lakin Brasher: A Personal Tribute to a Centenarian," *The Herald* 83 (21 Apr. 1971): 7–8.

171. Brasher, "Immortality."

172. Rainey, "Brasher," 8.

173. Brasher, "The Evangelist"; "The Moods of the Spirit."

174. Joseph Owen to John L. Brasher, 15 Mar. 1919, BP.

175. Haynes, "Waco Camp Meeting," 4. The evangelists were H. C. Morrison and J. O. McClurkan.

176. Paul S. Rees to J. Lawrence Brasher, 18 Dec. 1983, BP. The eccentric W. B. Godbey was markedly grandiloquent. See his extemporaneous prayer at John H. Snead Seminary, 160.

177. Brasher, "Lecture Six."

178. SR 1.

179. SR 64.

180. Paul S. Rees to J. Lawrence Brasher, 18 Dec. 1983, BP.

181. Paul Brasher to John L. Brasher, 10 Apr. 1920, BP.

182. SR 55.

183. SR 39.

184. SR 53.

185. John L. Brasher, manuscript essay for *Methodist Advocate-Journal*, ca. 1915, BP.

186. Carradine, *Revival Incidents*, 101. Although Brasher received some letters from holiness partisans in the South and elsewhere who were well-to-do, his overall judgment was that the "holiness people are usually from the common people, not from the poorest or from the richest of the groups of people." "We Are Able," typescript essay, ca. 1924, BP.

187. Even Brasher, who had a respectable education—more than many of his colleagues and certainly more than most members of his audiences—wrote privately: "I have always been painfully conscious of my lack of the freedom and confidence which comes from a liberal library and scientific education." "Thoughts on the Fifty-first Anniversary of My Birth," 20 July 1919, BP.

188. "Spring Term Revival," *The Aletheia,* Apr. 1919, n.p., BP.

189. Brasher, *Glimpses,* 17.

190. William Butler Yeats, *Ideas of Good and Evil* (London: A. H. Bullen, 1903), 248, quoted in Rosenberg, *Folk Preacher,* 43–44.

191. SR 40.

192. W. A. Murphree to John L. Brasher, 30 Aug. 1920, BP.

193. SR 7. For "Hardshell" stories see SR 2; Brasher, "Lecture Six."

194. SR 1. A longer printed version appears in Benjamin A. Botkin, *A Treasury of Southern Folklore* (New York: Crown, 1949), 112–14. Brasher's lengthy "Hardshell" parody of David and Goliath appears in the same transcript. Two other "Hardshell" parodies, "The Harp of a Thousand Strings" and "Brother Crafford's Farewell," appear in Arthur P. Hudson's *Humor of the Old Deep South* (New York: Macmillan, 1936), 233–38.

195. Perhaps the most famous use of anaphora in recent American oratory is the conclusion of Martin Luther King's "I Have a Dream" speech.

196. SR 40.

197. Ibid.

198. SR 79. A contemporary of Bishop Bascom (one of Brasher's models) described the bishop's homiletical use of additive language: "If he multiplied synonyms in expressing an idea, it did not appear tautology at all, but great thoughts struggling to clothe themselves in a manner suited to their importance, and if the first term employed appeared inadequate, another with a deeper shade of color or power was added." M. M. Henkle, *The Life of Henry Bidleman Bascom, D.D.* (Louisville: Morton and Griswold, 1854), 347–48.

199. SR 48.

200. Ibid.

201. John L. Brasher, sermon stenographically recorded, Jamestown Camp Meeting, Jamestown, N.D., 28 June 1916, BP.

202. Kenneth Burke, *A Rhetoric of Motives* (New York: Prentice-Hall, 1945; reprint, Cleveland: World, 1962), 582.

203. SR 56.

204. The example is indicative of what was probably a stronger, perhaps more musical, version when Brasher was in his prime. George List, in "The Boundaries of Speech and Song," *Ethnomusicology,* 7 no. 1 (1963): 1–16, refers to such passages as "heightened speech," a form intermediate to speech and song. When speech is heightened in a socially structured situation (such as a preaching service), List cites two tendencies: "a leveling out of intonation into a plateau approaching a monotone; an amplification of intonation, especially of the downward inflection that serves . . . as a phrase, sentence, or paragraph final" (3). Brasher's heightened speech exhibited the plateau effect and the final downward inflection, but some of his final inflections were upward,

as in the example in Appendix E. For other selected tonal passages see "resisting the message" (SR 53, p. 10 of transcript), "the bloodwashed" (SR 53, p. 11 of transcript), "I can only look down . . . death of a felon" (SR 38, p. 7 of transcript), "consecration and faith" (SR 51, p. 9 of transcript), and "If He has kindled His love" (SR 40, p. 10 of transcript).

205. SR 2.

206. John Witherspoon, *The Works of the Rev. John Witherspoon,* vol. 3: *Lectures on Eloquence* (Philadelphia: W. W. Woodward, 1800), 513–14. Witherspoon (1723–94) was a Presbyterian divine, president of Princeton University, signer of the Declaration of Independence, and member of Congress.

207. The quotation is from the hymn "Blessed Assurance." The words were written by Fanny Crosby (1820–1915), the music by Mrs. Joseph F. Knapp (1839–1908), publisher of the *Guide to Holiness* and daughter of Phoebe Palmer.

208. *Memoirs of Life and Writings of Benjamin Franklin,* 1:87, quoted in Luke Tyerman, *The Life of the Rev. George Whitefield* (New York: A. D. F. Randolph, 1877), 1:375–76.

209. SR 63.

210. See Brasher's Sermon Notebook and Sermon Notes, BP.

211. Jacob Moses Harris to John L. Brasher, 23 Aug. 1921, BP.

212. Hatcher, *Jasper,* 104.

213. These sermons, highly acclaimed by holiness people, appear in print, considerably edited, in Brasher's book *Reckoning with the Eternals* (Apollo, Pa.: West Publishing Co., 1950). There were other favorites, of course.

214. Two of Morrison's most popular sermons were "Abraham and Isaac" and "The Rich Young Ruler"; McClurkan's, "Sin Crouched at the Door"; Chapman's "Christ and the Bible." See J. C. McPheeters, "Henry Clay Morrison, the Magnificent Preacher," *The Herald* 83 (8 Mar. 1972): 3, 13; Heath, *A Man Sent from God,* 38; George Chapman Moore, "An Analytical Study of Invention and Style in Selected Sermons of J. B. Chapman" (M.A. thesis, University of Oklahoma, 1948), 60–83.

215. John L. Brasher to the Reverend J. W. H. Beale, 24 Oct. 1922, BP.

216. SR 42.

217. See, for instance, his theme on his wife's blindness, in SR 59; and his exemplum of nuclear rockets, which "curse rather than bless," in SR 44.

218. SR 21.

219. One of Brasher's favorite formulas, which he used in the 1960s, is found in a letter of 1902 (see n. 134). The genesis of the themes in his sermon "The Glorious Church" appears in his address "The New Era," ca. 1896, BP. He preached "The Glorious Church" as the climactic sermon at the first Hartselle Camp Meeting in 1900. He preached it regularly afterward—notably at Indian Springs Camp Meeting in 1933, at Hartselle again in 1966, and as the Alabama Conference Memorial Address in 1969 (a full seventy-four years after the record of its incipient form). See his "History of Hartselle Holiness Camp Meeting," BP; J. P. Gilbreath to John L. Brasher, 11 Oct. 1933, BP; transcripts of sermons, "The Glorious Church," Hartselle Camp Meeting, Hartselle, Ala., 7 Aug. 1966 (SR 59), and "Memorial Address of the North Al-

abama United Methodist Conference," Birmingham, 1969 (SR 65). The transcript of the sermon "Dispensational Truth," preached at Hartselle Camp Meeting, Aug. 1950 (SR 42), contains themes, specific references, and imagery that date its composition ca. 1903–5.

220. Paul Rees to J. Lawrence Brasher, 18 Dec. 1983, BP. An acute memory was a necessity in effective spiritual preaching—especially in that which employed formulas and themes. Brasher spoke of his fellow evangelist Andrew Johnson as having a memory "like a wax plate, never forgetting any matter he wished to use." "Memoir of Andrew Johnson, D.D.," ca. 1960, BP. Bud Robinson, like Brasher, employed some themes that were long series of Bible verses. Probably to facilitate their delivery in sermons, he reportedly "upon awakening early in the morning (would) lie in bed and quote scriptures for as long as thirty minutes or an hour." James McGraw, "The Preaching of Bud Robinson," *The Preacher's Magazine* (Jan. 1954): 10.

221. John L. Brasher to the Reverend J. W. H. Beale, 24 Oct. 1922, BP.

222. SR 21.

223. Brasher, "Immortality."

224. SR 57.

225. Paul S. Rees to John L. Brasher, 21 Aug. 1938, BP.

226. Brasher, "Mountain Top," 3, 4, 7.

227. The Reverend J. P. Gilbreath to John L. Brasher, 11 Oct. 1933, BP; Jacob Moses Harris to John L. Brasher, 23 Aug. 1921, BP.

228. Hatcher, *Jasper*, 104.

Chapter 8: Sanctification and the "Foolishness of Folks"

1. SR 13.

2. Brasher, "Autobiography," 3.

3. Humor of the Old Southwest (the antebellum Deep South) derived from conflicts ensuing from the juxtaposition of settled areas and frontier; it often focused on traditional masculine adventures such as hunting, tests of strength, and fighting.

4. Linda Dégh emphasizes a correlation between skilled narrators and itinerant professions. As a narrator travels, he gains colorful experience and also develops objectivity toward his original community. *Folktales and Society* (Bloomington, Ind.: Indiana University Press, 1969), 170.

5. John L. Brasher, "The Old Timer Rambles on: 'Church Customs,'" manuscript copy for *Etowah News-Journal* (Attalla, Ala.), 1956, BP.

6. SR 46.

7. The posthumous collection was published by Joseph Gurney of London immediately after Whitefield's death. See Tyerman, *Whitefield*, 565–68.

8. Brasher, "J. L. Freeman."

9. Tyerman, *Whitefield*, 568.

10. Haynes, "Waco Camp Meeting," 4.

11. Brasher, sermon, Jamestown Camp Meeting, typescript, BP.

12. Byrne, *No Foot of Land*, 43. For the general description of remarkable providences, I am indebted to Byrne, 43–50.

13. Ibid.

14. Advertisements for the books appear in the end pages of S. B. Shaw, *Echoes of the General Holiness Assembly: Touching Incidents and Remarkable Answers to Prayer* (Grand Rapids, Mich.: S. B. Shaw, 1895); *The Dying Testimonies of Saved and Unsaved, Gathered from Authentic Sources* (Chicago: S. B. Shaw, 1898); *Children's Edition of Touching Incidents and Remarkable Answers to Prayer* (Grand Rapids, Mich.: S. B. Shaw, 1895). A fine southern holiness collection of remarkable providences is Beverly Carradine's *Revival Incidents*.

15. James H. Moorhead, "The Erosion of Postmillennialism in American Religious Thought, 1865–1925," unpublished manuscript, privately circulated.

16. Arthur, *The Tongue of Fire*, 331.

17. Standard points of fundamentalist and holiness orthodoxy included inerrancy of Scripture, the virgin birth, substitutionary atonement, bodily resurrection, authenticity of biblical miracles.

18. Statement of the General Holiness Convention, Cadle Tabernacle, Indianapolis, Ind., 11–16 Sept. 1923, BP. Paul M. Bassett discusses the differences between fundamentalist and holiness theology in "The Fundamentalist Leavening of the Holiness Movement, 1914–1940, the Church of the Nazarene: A Case Study," *Wesleyan Theological Journal* 13 (Spring 1978): 65–91.

19. John L. Brasher to Hobart Murphree, 28 Apr. 1922, BP.

20. For reference to stories of remarkable providences in southern religion, see Kenneth K. Bailey, "Southern White Protestantism at the Turn of the Century," *American Historical Review* 68 (Apr. 1963): 618–35.

21. Sanctified readers of Scripture claimed the *testimonium Spiritus sancti*—an ancient Christian doctrine that held that the Holy Spirit interprets or illuminates the Scriptures for the believer. For holiness statements on receiving "new light," a "new Bible," or a "second Bible," see Brasher, *A Simple Statement*, 11; Godbey, *Autobiography*, 96; Haynes, *Tempest-tossed*, 78–82; Heath, *A Man Sent of God*, 84.

22. The "sunburst" was the second blessing. See SR 52; Godbey, *Autobiography*, 96; H. C. Morrison, *Life Sketches and Sermons* (Louisville: Pentecostal Publishing Co., 1903), 39.

23. SR 50.

24. Henry Clay Morrison to John L. Brasher, 10 May 1932, BP.

25. SR 31, 26.

26. SR 10.

27. SR 26.

28. SR 61.

29. SR 61, 46, 56, 51.

30. SR 30.

31. Brasher SR 51, 56; Robinson SR 61, 46, 47, 53.

32. SR 51.

33. SR 48. Minnie Brasher's sanctification also came in the form of a test. See Appendix B.

34. SR 52.
35. Byrne, *No Foot of Land*, 55–57.
36. See, for instance, Godbey's *Demonology* and Shaw's *Touching Incidents*.
37. SR 13.
38. SR 10.
39. Brasher, "Biography of Minnie Brasher."
40. SR 39. Brasher's "three-fold method" of determining the origins of "impressions" was "the leadings of the Spirit which are gentle, and sweet, and reasonable; then the illumination of the holy Scriptures that agrees with the leading; and then the Providential opening."
41. SR 66.
42. SR 38.
43. SR 67.
44. SR 33, 28, 46.
45. SR 39.
46. SR 19, 61.
47. SR 46.
48. Brasher, *Glimpses*, 12–13.
49. SR 21.
50. Pentecostals cited I Corinthians 12 for spiritual gifts. Holiness folk cited James 5:15 for the efficacious prayers of the faithful.
51. SR 57.
52. For Brasher, healing was an accepted part of the holiness gospel but never a major emphasis in his own ministry.
53. SR 55.
54. Godbey, *Happy Nonagenarian*, 181. See also Jernigan, *Pioneer Days*.
55. SR 72.
56. SR 61. For the same story, see SR 57. For a similar account of a "Grandma Bradley" at Hartselle, Ala., see SR 55, 59.
57. SR 9.
58. SR 15.
59. SR 7.
60. SR 6.
61. SR 5.
62. See also SR 50, 58 for other versions of the same narrative.
63. SR 37.
64. Ibid.
65. SR 38.
66. SR 62.
67. SR 37.
68. SR 39.
69. SR 42. Brasher's canon of models included many saints who predated him or whom he did not know personally. He made frequent reference in sermons to the following early Methodists: John and Charles Wesley, John Fletcher, Joseph Benson, Adam Clarke, Richard Watson, Francis Asbury, Philip Embury, Joseph Pilmore, Barbara Heck, and Hester Ann Rogers. He also of-

ten referred to several nineteenth-century Methodist bishops: Henry Bascom, Randolph S. Foster, Leonidas Hamline, John Keener, and Matthew Simpson. Other frequent references were to Francis Fenelon, Madam Guyon, Lovick Pierce, John Inskip, Phoebe Palmer, "Mother" (Mrs. Osee M.) Fitzgerald, William Judson, William Booth, and William Boardman.

70. See Galatians 5:22–23.

71. SR 42, 44.

72. SR 44.

73. SR 50. For the same narrative, see SR 39.

74. SR 47.

75. SR 46.

76. SR 47.

77. SR 25. Ira D. Sankey (1840–1908) was the song leader of preeminent late-nineteenth-century evangelist Dwight L. Moody. For accounts of prayer saving a man from being struck by a bullet and prayer causing the unanimous selection of Brasher for the presidency of Central Holiness University, see Brasher, "Moods of the Spirit," and SR 72.

78. SR 38.

79. SR 38.

80. SR 47. For accounts with the same contrasting formula regarding the ministry of Brasher and Bishop Arthur Moore, see SR 52, 47.

81. SR 25.

82. SR 38. A doxology is a liturgical formula (in this case a song) of praise to God.

83. SR 72, 38.

84. SR 39.

85. SR 51. The same tale is in SR 52.

86. SR 26.

87. SR 31.

88. SR 52. See also SR 57, 54.

89. Brasher and his wife considered their own lives to be testimonies to the promise of Psalm 91: "He who dwells in the shelter of the most high . . . with long life shall I satisfy him and show him my salvation." SR 51, 52, 56.

90. See A. Gregory Schneider, "The Ritual of Happy Dying Among Early American Methodists," *Church History* (Sept. 1987): 348–63.

91. W. B. Godbey in 1909 lamented the passing of the tradition of happy dying and blamed its demise on the modern use of mind-altering drugs to relieve pain. In his youth, he stated, "People all died in their senses, either shouting the triumphs of faith, or wailing in the depths of despair, both of which are the most potent influences . . . to arouse conviction on the unconverted." Godbey, *Autobiography*, 52. In 1898, the Chicago holiness publisher S. B. Shaw issued another bestseller that helped keep the tradition alive: *The Dying Testimonies of Saved and Unsaved.*

92. Accounts of his father's death are in SR 13, 15, 74; his mother's death in SR 13, 15, 25, 72, 74.

93. SR 46, 63. Fletcher (1729–85) was an English Methodist associate of John Wesley.

94. SR 42.

95. Brasher used the term referring to the death of the holiness evangelist Joseph H. Smith in SR 41. The term was used of Enoch, the Old Testament figure so holy that he was taken to heaven without having to experience the pains of death. See Genesis 5:24, Hebrews 11:5.

96. SR 64.

97. Smith, *George Foster Pierce,* 13.

98. John A. Broadus, "American Baptist Preaching of One Hundred Years Ago," *Baptist Quarterly* 9 (1875): 18.

99. SR 63, 19, 75.

100. SR 64.

101. SR 56. A variation of the same formulaic account appears in SR 54. An interesting comparison can be made with Brasher's written account of the event, which appears in Chapter 5.

102. Chanted (tonal) exhortation and hymn: "Have you had that? If you haven't, you're lost. If your spirit doesn't tell you that that's so, then you're outside the Kingdom. Anything short of that inward knowledge that your sins are forgiven and that you're born of God is a station outside the depot of salvation. I do not wonder that that great hymn reads like this:

> O Sacred Hour, O hallowed spot,
> Where love divine first found me,
> Wherever falls my distant lot,
> My heart shall linger 'round thee.
> When from earth I rise to soar
> Up to my home in heaven,
> Down will I cast my eyes once more
> Where I was first forgiven.

103. Brasher believed that one could consecrate one's will fully to God only with the assistance of the Holy Spirit (SR 36). However, the overriding emphasis in his preaching was that the Spirit came when the human struggle to consecrate was complete: "When you go all the way with him in your will, he goes all the way with you in his blessing. He can't do it until you do" (SR 48).

104. I Peter 1:16.

105. Timothy Smith correctly asserts that in attacking worldliness in dress and behavior, holiness preachers were simply maintaining the codes of nineteenth-century evangelicalism. Holiness sects "did not create new . . . standards. They simply reemphasized the old ones when the drift of society was in the opposite direction." *Called Unto Holiness,* 37–38.

106. SR 36.

107. SR 38. Brasher's story takes on further meaning in the context of the plain-folk tradition in which he was raised. It was customary for floors in homes to be bare or sprinkled with fine sand. Only "quality folks" and owners of plantations had the wherewithal to walk on rugs.

108. For instance, a reader of *The Christian Witness and Advocate of Bible Holiness* [(15 Mar. 1917): 6] questioned the evangelist Joseph H. Smith: "Is it profitable unto God to secure the comforts of life, such as parlors with curtains, etc., when there is so much need around us?" Smith replied, "Whatever we can eat or wear or furnish with *to His Glory*, without pride, and for others' pleasing, pleases Him."

109. Brasher, "Moods of the Spirit."

110. John L. Brasher to Jessie E. Shaver, Branson, Colo., Sept. 1924, BP.

111. SR 55. Brasher exhibited some other negative stereotypes of women in several sermons: vanity (SR 49, 63), gossip and incessant talking (SR 51, 56), nagging (SR 62, 64).

112. SR 25.

113. Two excellent studies of women's roles in the holiness movement are Letha Dawson Scanzoni and Susan Setta, "Women in Evangelical, Holiness, and Pentecostal Traditions," introductory essay to section 6 of Rosemary Radford Reuther and Rosemary Skinner Keller, *Women and Religion in America*, vol. 3: 1900–1968 (San Francisco: Harper and Row, 1986), 223–34; and Robert Stanley Ingersol, "The Burden of Dissent: Mary Lee Cagle and the Southern Holiness Movement" (Ph.D. diss., Duke University, 1989).

114. SR 48.

115. SR 42. Susanna Wesley (1669–1742), mother of John Wesley, preached in her husband's parish in his absence. Catherine Booth (1829–90), cofounder with husband, William Booth, of the Salvation Army, was a public preacher.

116. SR 66.

117. SR 1.

118. SR 25. For other exempla featuring blacks, see the story cited above of "Aunt Mandy," the cook who interpreted Scripture (SR 39, 62), and the account of Charlie Jones, the Mississippi preacher and songwriter (SR 25).

119. There are no references in any of Brasher's papers or sound recordings to his having preached to integrated congregations. Early-twentieth-century holiness meetings, unlike some contemporary pentecostal assemblies, appear to have been segregated. Brasher once related to the author that while holding a meeting in Dothan, Alabama, a black church asked him to preach to them. He agreed to preach on condition that they sing for him. A letter from the holiness evangelist C. M. Dunaway (June 1922, BP), who was holding a meeting in Dalton, Georgia, mentions a separate "service for the Negroes." See also "Rev. W. A. Dodge's Work Among the Colored People," *The Pentecostal Advocate* (24 Feb. 1904): 4–5. Possible exceptions were the holiness revivals of A. J. Quattlebaum in the "milltowns of upper South Carolina and Georgia," in which "negroes were always invited." "A Short Autobiography of Rev. A. J. Quattlebaum," *Way of Faith* (1 Dec. 1930): 9.

120. SR 48.

121. SR 59.

122. SR 61. In his "A Church-going People Are a Dress-loving People: Clothes, Communication, and Religious Culture in Early America," *Church*

History (Mar. 1989): 49–50, Leigh Schmidt cites a long tradition in American spiritual autobiography of renunciation of extravagant dress at the time of repentance and spiritual awakening.

123. SR 38.

124. SR 66. Brasher in 1924 described his holiness audiences as having been "usually the common people . . . not the poorest or richest classes." (See Chapter 7, n. 186.) His ministry was to a predominantly middle-class holiness constituency. Wayne Flynt, in *Dixie's Forgotten People: The South's Poor Whites* (Bloomington: Indiana University Press, 1979), 38, correctly states that holiness and Baptist sects in the South after 1900 appealed to the distinct group of poor whites. Nonetheless, Brasher, who remained loyal to the Methodist Church, held revivals primarily in middle-class (mostly Methodist) churches (or tent meetings sponsored by them) in towns and cities and in middle-class camp meetings. He occasionally, especially in his early evangelism, did hold meetings in rural areas with relatively primitive conditions, but his audiences there were self-sufficient, rural farm folk. Holiness people were upwardly mobile. By 1920, as president of Central Holiness University in Iowa, Brasher complained that "thousands of holiness folk have plenty of money to invest in copper mines and oil stock, but not much to help us pay our grocery bills and coal and teachers." John L. Brasher to Will Huff, 11 Dec. 1920, BP.

125. John L. Brasher to Joseph H. Smith, 11 May 1922, BP.

126. Brasher, "Thoughts on the 51st Anniversary."

127. For examples, see stories of the black cook who interpreted Scripture (SR 39, 50); the illiterate Chattanooga teamster (SR 46); Bud Robinson's attempt at college (SR 61); the Irish woman in Birmingham (SR 51); Mrs. Morris, the farm wife (SR 47); Mary McAfee, the tollgate keeper (SR 61); the woman with holes in her shoes (SR 49).

128. SR 39.

129. SR 61.

130. SR 50.

131. SR 39. Brasher's emphasis on native intelligence also reflected his and premillennialist belief that immediately prior to the Second Coming the common, uneducated folk would be given unusually clear insight into the Scriptures. See SR 42, 44.

132. SR 51.

133. SR 57.

134. SR 44.

135. SR 63.

136. SR 64.

137. SR 61.

138. SR 52.

139. See Jan H. Brunvand, *The Study of American Folklore* (New York: W. W. Norton, 1968), 94–110; Joyce Joines Newman, "Humorous Local Character Stories from Wilkes County, North Carolina: An Individual Storytelling Tradition" (M.A. thesis, University of North Carolina, 1978).

140. SR 52.

141. SR 46.
142. SR 51.
143. SR 62.
144. SR 64. The same anecdote appears in SR 50.
145. SR 66.
146. For a discussion of Peter Cartwright's use of comic tales, see Robert Bray, "Beating the Devil: Life and Art in Peter Cartwright's *Autobiography*," *Illinois Historical Journal* 78 (Autumn 1985): 179–94.
147. SR 72.
148. The Aunt Catherine Bynum account follows the accusations of Mormonism in SR 57. The "Mormon" incident also appears in SR 64, 65, 66.
149. SR 62.
150. SR 47.
151. SR 42.
152. SR 46.
153. SR 21. Thomas (1763–1854) and Alexander Campbell (1788–1866) emigrated from northern Ireland in 1807 and 1809, respectively. Their movement experienced its greatest growth and influence in the upland South and Midwest.
154. SR 21.
155. SR 27.
156. SR 61.
157. SR 17.
158. SR 20.
159. SR 47.
160. Brasher, "Andrew Johnson."
161. Andrew Johnson to John L. Brasher, 30 Jan. 1943, BP.
162. Rainey, "Brasher," 8.
163. William Henry Milburn, *Ten Years of Preacher Life* (New York: Derby and Jackson, 1859), 42.
164. SR 63.
165. SR 56.
166. SR 46.
167. SR 36.
168. SR 48.
169. SR 42.
170. SR 55.
171. SR 57.
172. SR 18.
173. SR 29.
174. SR 54.
175. SR 61.
176. SR 39.
177. SR 62.
178. SR 62.
179. SR 51.

180. SR 39.
181. SR 20.
182. SR 38.
183. Haynes, "Waco Camp Meeting," 4.
184. Peter Cartwright's *Autobiography* is subtitled "the backwoods preacher."
185. SR 7, 1.
186. In order: SR 1, 7, 1, 13. The story of attempted seduction is preserved in family lore only, not on a recording. Some historians assume that most of the anecdotes in Cartwright's *Autobiography* were tales he told in his sermons. Even the crusty Cartwright probably did not use all of them in preaching. See Sidney E. Mead, "The Rise of the Evangelical Conception of the Ministry in America, 1607–1850," in *The Ministry in Historical Perspective,* ed. H. R. Niebuhr and Daniel D. Williams (New York: Harper and Row, 1956), 246.
187. Cotton Mather, *Magnalia Christi Americana: or, the Ecclesiastical History of New England, From Its First Planting, in the Year 1620, Unto the Year of Our Lord 1698,* 2 vols. (Hartford, Conn.: Silas Andrus and Son, 1852), 2:341.
188. *Methodist Advocate-Journal* 10 (8 Mar. 1900): 8.
189. SR 17.
190. SR 64.

Afterword

1. See Chapter 7, n. 125.
2. John L. Brasher to the Reverend G. R. Pease, 11 May 1922, BP.

Sound Recordings of John
Lakin Brasher, 1949–70

1. Storytelling and recitations at home with family, Brasher Springs, Gallant, Ala., 1949; birthday letter, 1949; storytelling at home by John L. Brasher, the Reverend Wallace A. Murphree, the Reverend W. Hamby, and the Reverend James H. Brasher, 1949.
2. Storytelling at home with family, 1950.
3. Storytelling and songs at the home of Mr. and Mrs. Malton Murphree, Tarrant, Ala., 1950.
4. Storytelling at home with family, 1952.
5. Conversation at home among John L. Brasher, the Reverend Doctor John Paul, and Paul Eubanks, Apr. 1952.
6. Storytelling at home, 26 Nov. 1965. Interviewed by Elizabeth Brasher Pinnell and Robert Pinnell.
7. Storytelling at home with family, 27 July 1965.
8. Storytelling at home with family, July 1966.
9. Storytelling at home with family, 1967.
10. Storytelling at home with family, 29 Jan. 1967.
11. Storytelling at home with family, 2 Sept. 1967.
12. Storytelling at home with family, 2 Sept. 1967.
13. Storytelling at home, 27 Nov. 1967. Interviewed by Elizabeth Brasher Pinnell and Robert Pinnell.
14. Storytelling at home at the dinner table, July 1968.
15. Storytelling at home with family, 24 July 1968.
16. Storytelling at home with family, Jan. 1969.
17. Storytelling at home with family, 23 Aug. 1969.
18. Bible study, I Thessalonians 5:19, "Quench Not the Spirit," Brasher Springs Camp Meeting, 1960.
19. Bible study, "Ninety-first Psalm," North Alabama United Methodist Annual Conference (?), Birmingham, Ala., 1961.
20. Bible study, "Objections to Holiness Refuted," Brasher Springs Camp Meeting, 21 July 1961.
21. Bible study, "Five Theories of Sanctification," Brasher Springs Camp Meeting, July 1961.

22. Bible study, "The Highway That Isaiah Saw," Brasher Springs Camp Meeting, July 1962.

23. Bible study, I Peter 5:6ff, "After You Have Suffered Awhile"; includes "Sufferings of Job," Brasher Springs Camp Meeting, 17 July 1962.

24. Bible study, "Two-fold Nature of Sin and Two-fold Cure," Brasher Springs Camp Meeting, 20 July 1965; fragment, birthday greeting of Bishop W. Kenneth Goodson; singing at Brasher Springs Camp Meeting.

25. Bible study, "What Manner of Love Is This, That We Should Be Called Sons of God," Brasher Springs Camp Meeting, 1966.

26. Bible study, "Ye Shall Be Witnesses Unto Me," Brasher Springs Camp Meeting, 20 July 1967.

27. Bible study, "Let Us Go On to Perfection," Brasher Springs Camp Meeting, 1967.

28. Bible study, "Sanctification," Brasher Springs Camp Meeting, 23 July 1968.

29. Bible study, Psalm 103, "Bless the Lord O My Soul," Brasher Springs Camp Meeting, 24 July 1968.

30. Bible study, "Keeping the Blessing," Brasher Springs Camp Meeting, 26 July 1968.

31. Bible study, "Fruits of the Spirit," Brasher Springs Camp Meeting, n.d.

32. Bible study, "Fruits of the Spirit," Brasher Springs Camp Meeting, n.d. Sequel to tape 31 and delivered the following day.

33. Bible study, "The Works of the Spirit," Brasher Springs Camp Meeting, n.d.

34. Bible study, Acts 1, "Ye Shall be Baptized with the Holy Ghost," Brasher Springs Camp Meeting, n.d.

35. Sermon, "Christian Perfection," Brasher Springs Camp Meeting, 1949. Recited to Eunice Brasher Eubanks and Paul Eubanks, alone.

36. Sermon, "Quench Not the Spirit," Rock Methodist Church, Tarrant, Ala., 1949.

37. Sermon, II Thessalonians, Brasher Springs Camp Meeting, 1950. Fragment.

38. Sermon, "The Mind of Christ," Brasher Springs Camp Meeting, July 1950.

39. Sermon, Romans 8:11, Brasher Springs Camp Meeting, 1950.

40. Sermon, I Corinthians 16:22, "If Any Man Love Not the Lord Jesus Christ, Let Him be Accursed," Brasher Springs Camp Meeting, 1950. Includes the Reverend Dr. Turbeyville offering closing exhortations and James H. Brasher leading in prayer.

41. Sermon, "In the Beginning, God," Hartselle Camp Meeting, Hartselle, Ala., 1950.

42. Sermon, Romans 9:32, "Dispensational Truth," Hartselle Camp Meeting, Hartselle, Ala., 1950, fragment; reading of the names of deceased camp-meeting members.

43. Sermon, "Two Works of Grace," Brasher Springs Camp Meeting, 1952, fragment.

44. Sermon, Daniel 12:10, "Many Shall be Purified, Made White, and Tried," Antioch Methodist Church, Blount County, Ala., Decoration Day, 1952.

45. Sermon, Rock Methodist Church, Tarrant, Ala., 1952.

46. Sermon, Romans 5:1–5, Brasher Springs Camp Meeting, 1956.

47. Sermon, "Be Ye Holy," Weaver Methodist Church, Weaver, Ala., 25 Nov. 1956.

48. Sermon, Matthew 19:20, "What Lack I Yet?" Clear Creek Methodist Church, Brasher Springs, Ala., 30 Sept. 1957. Includes comments by Malton Murphree.

49. Sermon, Romans 6:22, Brasher Springs Camp Meeting, 19 July 1959.

50. Sermon, "A Pure Heart," Brasher Springs Camp Meeting, 20 July 1961.

51. Sermon, "Pentecost," Lake Highland Church, Blount County, Ala., 21 May 1961.

52. Sermon, "Pentecost," Albertville Methodist Church, Albertville, Ala., 10 June 1962.

53. Sermon, I Peter 1:16, "Be Ye Holy," Brasher Springs Camp Meeting, afternoon service, 15 July 1962.

54. Sermon, Acts 26:18, "That They May Receive Forgiveness of Sins and Inheritance Among Them Which Are Sanctified," Rock Methodist Church, Tarrant, Ala., 1963.

55. Sermon, "The Sufferings of Christ," "New" Rock Church, Tarrant, Ala., 1963.

56. Sermon, Acts 26:18, "That They May Receive Forgiveness of Sins and Inheritance Among Them Which Are Sanctified," Methodist Church (name unknown), Ala. (exact location unknown), 1963.

57. Sermon, Genesis 1:26, "Let Us Make Man in Our Own Image," Antioch United Methodist Church, Blount County, Ala., Decoration Day, 1965.

58. Sermon, "Let Us Make Man in Our Own Image," Brasher Springs Camp Meeting, morning service, 25 July 1965.

59. Sermon, "The Glorious Church," Hartselle Camp Meeting, Hartselle, Ala., 7 Aug. 1966.

60. Sermon, "Now Is the Accepted Time," Bellevue United Methodist Church, Ala. (exact location unknown), 1966.

61. Sermon, Acts 1:8, Centre Methodist Church, Centre, Ala., ca. 1966.

62. Sermon, Matthew 19:20, "What Lack I Yet?" Brasher Springs Camp Meeting, 1967.

63. Sermon, II Corinthians 6:2, "Behold Now Is the Day of Salvation," Hartselle Camp Meeting, Hartselle, Ala., 6 Aug. 1967.

64. Sermon, "Blessed Are the Pure in Heart," Brasher Springs Camp Meeting, 20 July 1968.

65. Sermon, "The Glorious Church," Memorial Address of the North Alabama United Methodist Conference, Birmingham, Ala., 1969.

66. Sermon, "What Does It Profit a Man?" Brasher Springs Camp Meeting, 20 July 1969.

67. Sermon, "The Resurrection of Christ," Jasper Methodist Church, Jasper, Ala., n.d.

68. Tape letter to his children, recorded at home, spring, 1950.
69. Tape letter to his children, recorded at home, Feb. 1952.
70. Tape letter to his children, recorded at home, 1952.
71. Letter to Hollow Rock Camp Meeting, 1953; meditation, "The Second Coming of Christ"; singing by John L. and Minnie Eunice Moore Brasher; prayer at home.
72. Account of early ministry, Hollow Rock Camp Meeting, Toronto, Ohio, Aug. 1954.
73. Prayer at the funeral of the Reverend Marshall Murphree, Oneonta, Ala., 196_.
74. Greetings of Bishop W. Kenneth Goodson, John L. Brasher's birthday speech, Brasher Springs Camp Meeting, 20 July 1965; storytelling with family at home, 25 July 1965.
75. Birthday speech, Brasher Springs Camp Meeting, 20 July 1966.
76. Last prayer at the polls, Clear Creek Methodist Church, Brasher Springs, Attalla, Ala., Nov. 1970.
77. Singing, praying, and testifying, Brasher Springs Camp Meeting, July 1965.
78. Founders' Day address, the Reverend Hobart Murphree, Brasher Springs Camp Meeting, 20 July 1980.
79. Reminiscences of the Reverend Hobart Murphree, age eighty-five, at his home, Wedowee, Ala., 30 July 1982.
80. Addresses at the accessioning of the John Lakin Brasher Papers, Manuscript Department, Duke University, 13 Apr. 1983: Dr. Mattie Russell, Curator of Manuscripts; Robert L. Byrd, Assistant Librarian; Bishop W. Kenneth Goodson.

Index

220n98, 235n69; use of additive
language, 230n198
Battles, "Uncle Bob," 76
Beasley, Rev. Joseph, 13
Beatific vision, 29, 98–106, 166
Beecher, Henry Ward, 217n27
Benson, Joseph, 203n22, 234n69
Bible: holiness interpretation of, 138–39
Biblical events: in themes, 116–17
Big House, 3
Birmingham (Ala.), 60, 74, 157, 176, 180,
204n35; flood of April 1900, 41; J. L.
Brasher sanctified in, xi, 48; rescue
work in, 150–51; social conditions in,
55–57
Blacks. *See* Abolitionism; African-
Americans; Antislavery; Slavery
Blackstone, William E., 62, 215n135
Blount County (Ala.): John Jackson
Brasher represents in secession
convention, 2; lynches Reconstruction
sheriff, 13
Blount Mountain (Ala.), 140, 144–45, 168
Boardman, William E., 29, 235n69
Boaz (Ala.), 115, 160
Boland, J. M., 37, 52, 210n64; J. L.
Brasher influenced by, 52, 53; member
of Alabama conferences, Methodist
Episcopal Church, South, 51
Booth, Catherine, 157, 237n115
Booth, William, 74, 235n69, 237n115
Boston School of Theology, 179
Bowdoin College, 29
Bowers, Lemuel, 78, 217n29, 218n53
Bowman, Bishop Thomas, 51, 210n65; his
dream of daughter, 142
Brasher, Hendricks: shouted at revivals, 44
Brasher, James, Jr: his preaching, 2
Brasher, James, Sr.: migrates to Alabama,
2; Revolutionary War soldier, 1
Brasher, James (brother of John Lakin):
his dramatic conversion, 24, 44
Brasher, John Jackson, 4, 216n11, 217n29,
218n53; an abolitionist, 2, 12; appears
in dream to J. L. Brasher, 20; attends
camp meeting, 2; away on circuit, 21;
and Civil War, 198n27; as colporteur,
American Tract Society, 2; his fondness
of children, 78; his mastery of
grammar, 83; his passion for dialectic,

79; his preaching, 17, 68; his response
to persecution, 199n35; his statement
on conversion, 25; his statement on
preaching, 78; his trumpet voice, 80;
and interpretation of dreams, 142;
intimidates Ku Klux Klan, 15; leaves
home as a youth, 6; library of, 17; and
Methodist doctrine, 50; a model circuit
rider, 75; moral and educational
elevation of, 17; occupations of, 2;
organizes United Methodist Church,
13; as presiding elder, 196n27;
remarries, 7; reorganizes Methodist
Episcopal Church, 8–16; representative in Alabama secession convention,
2; as a Republican, 2, 12, 13; seeks
sheriff's appointment, 2; as storyteller,
132; strict morality of, 6; suffers
remarkable judgment, 145; threats
against, 15, 77; as Unionist, 12; wins
Baptist converts, 85
Brasher, Leona, 56
Brasher, Milly Caroline Hafley, 4; dies, 7;
her prediction of J. L. Brasher's
preaching, 19; reluctant to play fiddle,
6
Brasher, Minnie Eunice Moore, 140; her
healing, 176–77; her rescue work in
Birmingham, 56; her support of
husband, xi; sanctification of, 58–59,
157, 176–77; as street preacher, 157;
and testifying, 221n11
Brasher, Paul, 57
Brasher, Thomas, 1
Brengle, Commissioner Samuel Logan,
46, 47, 59, 178, 179, 181, 209n47,
214n110, 221n11
Bristol, Bishop: preaching of, 74
Broadus, John A., 223n52; and autobio-
graphical narratives in preaching, 153
Brooks, Phillips, 217n27
Brown, L. P. (Meridian, Miss.), 148
Browning, Raymond, 104, 201n40
Bryan, William Jennings, 217n27; at
Chattanooga, 74; J. L. Brasher
preaches with, xi
Bunyan, John, 99
Burson, Christopher Columbus, 77,
217n29
Bushwhackers, 142

humorous description of, 160–61;
warns against emotions, 47–48
Goodsell, Bishop Daniel A., 51, 54, 83,
210*n65*
Gossiping, 162
Gouthey, A. P., 123
Grace: in holiness imagery, 98
Grady, Henry W., 217*n27*
Grandiloquence, 70, 119–20
Grant, Ulysses S., 11; presidential
campaign of 1872, ix
Greasy Cove (Etowah County, Ala.), 4, 22
Great Awakening, 93
Greeley, Horace: presidential campaign of
(1872), ix
Gregory Gap (Ala.), 195*n17*
Guide to Holiness, 27
Guilford County (N.C.), 93
Guilt: and self-denial, 155
Guslars (Serbo-Croatia), 90, 222*n30*
Guyon, Madame, 235*n69*

Hafley, Cornelius, 4
Hagiography: holiness, 146–52
Hamline, Bishop Leonidas, 29, 235*n69*
Hannah, Mark, 74
Happy dying, 151–52, 235*n91*
Hard, Manley S., 211*n70*
Hardshell preaching: parody of, 124–25,
230*n194*. *See also* Chanted preaching
Harpersville (Ala.). *See under* Camp
meeting
Harris, Jacob Moses, 128, 131
Harris, John, 145
Harrison, Thomas, 35, 74, 80, 221*n11*
Hartselle (Ala.). *See under* Camp meeting
Hartselle Camp Meeting. *See under* Camp
meeting
Haskew, D. W., 104; and formulas, 112
Haven, Bishop Gilbert, 83, 216*n11*;
comments on A. S. Lakin, 8, 11;
describes Alabama Conference,
Methodist Episcopal Church, 11
Havergal, Frances Ridley, 212*n84*
Haygood, Bishop Atticus, 37
Haynes, B. F., 206*n58*
Healing, 144; of J. L. Brasher, 144; of
M. E. Brasher, 176–77, 178
Health: and sanctification, 140, 151
Heck, Barbara, 234*n69*

Heflin, Thomas, 73
Henderson, T. C., 166
Higher criticism: opposed by Bishop
Fowler, 58
Hill, Samuel, 90
Hills, A. M., 48, 180, 182, 209*n47*, 210*n50*,
214–15*n124*
Hog hotel, 3
Holiness: and biblical interpretation, 138–
39; and come-outers, 37, 39–40;
constituency, x, 30, 158, 169, 212–
13*n88*, 229*n186*, 238*n124*; controversy
in Methodist Episcopal Church, South,
37–40; hagiography, 146–52; imagery
of, 98; missions, foreign, 148–49, 155;
opposition to, 37–40, 52–54, 145–46,
162–65; and outsiders, 162–65; and
postmillennialism, 37, 206*n52*; and
power, 86–90, 165; response to urban
life, 55–57, 150, 157; and singing,
221*n9*; in South, x, 32–40, 50, 51–52,
207*n62*; and southern supernaturalism,
71, 207*n62*; stereotypes of, x, 123, 154,
162, 173–74; and urban missions, 32,
34, 35–36, 182, 204*n35*; Wesleyan, 173
Holiness movement: defined, 203*n23*; new
emphases of, 26
Hollow Rock Camp Meeting (Toronto,
Ohio). *See under* Camp meeting
Holston Conference: Methodist Episcopal
Church, 74
Holy Spirit: and consecration, 236*n103*;
and education, 222*n26*; indwelling the
saints, 147–52; interest in powerful
manifestations of, 30; in preaching, 88–
89, 92, 130–31; and remarkable
providences, 136–52; sin against, 146,
154–55; work of, 183–84
Holy whine, 93
Homeguards, 198*n27*
Hopewell Methodist Church (Greenville,
S.C.), 194*n4*
Houchins, Captain, 179
Huckabee, Benjamin W., 52, 211*n71*;
invites J. L. Brasher to Hartselle Camp
Meeting, 64–65
Huff, Will, 149
Hughes, George, 30
Humor: in analogies, 164; and dramatic
oppositions in anecdotes, 163; as

254   *Index*

Preacher tales: of J. L. Brasher, range of, 169

Preachers: inexperienced, 166

Preaching: anaphora in, 125; anecdotes in, 80, 132–71, 240*n186;* antithesis in, 127; and audience, 153; audience determines eloquence, 100–101; autobiographical narratives in, 152–54; of bishops, 73–74; Brasher's ideals of, 78–85; call narratives, 17–20, 199*n2;* chanted, 90–94, 124–25, 230*n204;* chiasmus in, 126–27; childhood training for, 67; of circuit riders, 68–85 *passim;* delivery, 80; doctrine in, 79–80; doctrine in anecdotes, 135; dreams, visions, voices in, 141–43; early Baptist style, 93–94; early Methodist style, 93–94; affects visions, 131; and eloquence, 81–85; epigrams in, 104; exempla, poorly chosen, 166; extemporaneous, 88; formulaic, 90–131 *passim;* formulas in 108–12; gestures in, 80–81; grandiloquence in, 119–20; and heightened speech, 230*n204;* holiness, changes in, 118; Holy Spirit in, 88–89, 130–31; humor about, 166–67; humor in, 80, 159–69; imagery and visions in, 80, 100–106; intoned, 189–90, 230*n204;* J. L. Brasher's, acclaimed in South, ix; J. L. Brasher's call to, 15, 17, 19, 20; J. L. Brasher's described, 89; J. L. Brasher's repertoire, 43; J. L. Brasher's homiletical conversion, 63–65; J. L. Brasher's parodies of Hardshell Baptists, 124–25, 230*n194;* J. L. Brasher's dramatics in, 116–18; J. L. Brasher's at Hartselle Camp Meeting, 52, 64–65; of James Brasher, Jr., 2; language, florid, 114; language, metrical, 114; length of sermons of J. L. Brasher, 106; logic in, 78–79; logic in preaching of J. L. Brasher, 106–7; from manuscript, 87–88, 221*n13;* memory an aid in, 130; models for J. L. Brasher, 67–85 *passim;* oral tradition and J. L. Brasher's preaching, 69–74; periodic sentences in, 125–26; plain-folk prayer describing, ix; power in, 221*n11;* power of, 86–90; practical,

79–80; and premillennialism, 221*n9;* presence in, 81; remarkable conversions and sanctifications in, 139–41; remarkable deliverances in, 143–45; remarkable judgments in 145–46; remarkable providences in, 136–52; remarkable saints in, 146–52; repertoire and the Spirit, 130; repertoire of J. L. Brasher, 128–31; reverting to early models, 67–68; rhetorical questions in, 127; rhythm in 90–94, 123–28; role of in holiness religion, xii; rustic imagery in, 166–69; and Separate Baptists, 93, 223*n52;* sermon structure of J. L. Brasher, 106–8; singing in, 147–48; and "special sermons," 128–29; theme, anaphoric, 183–84; themes used by J. L. Brasher, list of, 185–88; themes of J. L. Brasher, 112–31; themes in, 92–131 *passim;* tonal delivery, 128, 230*n204;* traditional metaphors, used by J. L. Brasher, 167–69; traditional similes, used by J. L. Brasher, 167–68; vernacular, J. L. Brasher's use of, 166–69; visions, voices, omens in, 141–43; and voice of J. L. Brasher, 117–18, 228*n168;* women preachers, 156–57

Prejudices: of holiness folk, 155

Premillennialism, 206*nn52,58,* 207*n61;* adopted by Brasher, 62–63; and education, 238*n131;* as impetus for evangelism, 62; and plain-folk revivalism, 62; and preaching, 221*n9;* and remarkable providences, 138; and sanctification, 207*nn64,65;* in southern holiness, 37–39, 40, 138

Premonitions, 142

Presbyterians, 79

Preventing grace (prevenient grace): Wesley's doctrine of, 27–28

Pride: and remarkable judgments, 145

Protracted meetings, 200*n32;* conversions in, 23–25; devout corners, 23; early candlelight service, 22; grove meetings, 22; mourners' bench, 22–23; rituals of, 22–24; stiff-knee corners, 23, 25

Purgatory, 164

Puritans, 147; and spiritual autobiography, 18, 136

holiness religion, x, 123, 154, 162, 173–74
Stimulant formulas, 109–10. *See also* Refrain formulas
Storrs, Richard, 217*n27*
Storytelling: influences on J. L. Brasher's, 171; of J. L. Brasher, 132–36; and plain folk, 171
Stratton, Leila Owen, 157
Stump speakers, 118
Sunday, Billy, 95
Supernaturalism: and premillennialists, 138; in southern holiness, 207*n62;* waning of, 138
Systemic formulas, 91, 109

Tales. *See* Anecdotes; Storytelling
Talley, Rev. John W., 14
Talmage, DeWitt, 217*n27*
Talmage, R. G., 213*n99*
Taylor, Bishop William: his vocational call in a dream, 20
Taylor, James Brainerd, 212*n84*
Temperance, 150
Testimonium Spiritus Sancti, 233*n21*
Testimony meeting, 153
Texas, 32, 35, 37, 40, 203*n28;* radical holiness in, 206*n51*
Texas Holiness Association, 35
Text-context format, 107
Themes: anaphoric, 183–84; of biblical events, 116–17; embellished, 118–23; at end of sermons, 108; essential and ornamental, 108; of holiness in the scriptures, 139; intoned, 189–90; J. L. Brasher's, content and style of, 112–16; J. L. Brasher's creation of, 115–16, 129; J. L. Brasher's repertoire of, 115–16, 185–88; J. L. Brasher's selection of, 116; in preaching, 92–131 *passim;* and rhythm, 224*n54;* rhythm in, 123–28; as sacraments, 116–17; "set pieces," 129–30
Thoreau, Henry David, 29
Tillett, Wilbur F., 37, 54
Tillman, Charlie D., 63, 206*nn49,58,* 215*n142*
Titon, Jeff, 92
Tonal delivery: in J. L. Brasher's conversion account, 154; in preaching, 128

Toronto (Ohio), 33
Trammel, Rev. Americus: murdered by Ku Klux Klan, 14
Tyerman, Luke, 135

U. S. Grant University School of Theology, 212*n79;* agency of Methodist Episcopal Church, 54–55; books read by J. L. Brasher in, 175; J. L. Brasher as valedictorian of, xi
Unionism, 58, 163; of Brasher family, xi, 4, 12–16; and Methodist Episcopal Church, 11–12
United Methodist Church (1866): founded by John Jackson Brasher, 13
University of Alabama: in Reconstruction, 11
Upham, Thomas C., 29
Urbanization: Bud Robinson's response to, 150; as spoiling religious sensibilities, 157

Vanderbilt, Cornelius, 54
Vanderbilt University: opposes holiness, 37, 54
Vernacular: in preaching, J. L. Brasher's use of, 123, 166–69, 173
Vices, 150, 162. *See also* Ethics
Victoria, Queen, 157
Vincent, Bishop J. H., 210*n65*
Vineland (N.J.), 30
Violence: of Old Southwest, 6
Virginia, 136
Visions, 141–43, 224*n74;* and dreams, 142; and ecstasy, 100; and faraway look, 103; function of 98–106; and imagery, 100–106; J. L. Brasher's theology of, 106, 226*n121;* and joy, 104; in preaching, 131; of the sanctified, 98–106; and theme of the Crucifixion, 116–17, 120–21
Voice: of J. L. Brasher, 117–18, 228*n162*
Voices, 141–43
von Steuben, Baron, 1

Waco (Tex.), 118
Waco Camp Meeting (Tex.). *See under* Camp meeting
Walden, Bishop, 51
Wallace, Hardin, 35

Note on the Recording

A two-hour cassette recording containing examples of John Lakin Brasher's extemporaneous storytelling and preaching is available as an accompaniment to this book. The original recordings were made by amateurs during the period 1949–70. Although in great old age at that time, Brasher still possessed a remarkable memory and unusually strong rhetorical gifts. The audio quality of the examples on the present tape varies widely. While most of this is attributable to the recording technology of the time, the extraneous noise on side 2, selection 2, came from night katydids. This tape represents a small fraction of Brasher's stories and sermons contained in the full set of original recordings. Many of his best stories and sermons in those recordings do not appear on the tape because of their poor audio quality. The excerpts on this recording have been chosen because they are easily audible, relatively lengthy, and contain stories and rhetoric of quality. The list of sound recordings in this volume gives complete citations of the recordings.

Side 1: Storytelling

Subject		Time	Recording Date	Text Pages
1. SR 2	Storytelling		1950	
	Excerpt A	14:34		pp. 2, 8–16, 21–22, 42–43, 68–69, 77–81, 84–85, 128, 133, 143, 169, 218n53
	Excerpt B	2:00		p. 139
2. SR 1	Storytelling	2:12	1949	p. 169
3. SR 13	Storytelling		11/27/1967	
	Excerpt A	24:03		pp. 4, 8–15, 133, 142,

Excerpt B	12:37		143, 169, 195*n17*, 198*n27* pp. 8–10, 22, 44–45, 71, 81, 115, 132–33, 151, 162–63, 200*n32*
4. SR 6	Storytelling	5:55	11/26/1965	p. 157

Side 2: Excerpts of Preaching

	Subject	Time	Recording Date	Text Pages
1. SR 42	"Dispensational Truth"	13:36	1950	pp. 52, 62–63, 110, 111–12, 147, 156–57, 231–32*n219*
2. SR 40	"If Any Man Love Not the Lord"	15:09	1950	pp. 117, 124–26
3. SR 56	"That They May Receive Forgiveness of Sins"	4:13	1963	pp. 127–28, 153–54, 236*n102*
4. SR 54	"That They May Receive Forgiveness of Sins"	5:42	1963	pp. 101–3, 110, 158, 225*n107*, 228*n145*
5. SR 55	"The Sufferings of Christ"	2:04	1963	p. 187
6. SR 48	"What Lack I Yet?"	13:35	9/30/1957	pp. 128, 140–41, 189–90
7. SR 64	"Blessed Are the Pure in Heart"		7/20/1968	
	Excerpt A	3:42		pp. 98–99, 120, 162
	Excerpt B	4:24		p. 171